GUITAR: BLUES SONGBOOK

MICHAEL WILLIAMS

BERKLEE BLUES GUITAR SONGBOOK

EDITED BY JONATHAN FEIST

Berklee Press

Vice President: David Kusek
Dean of Continuing Education: Debbie Cavalier
Chief Operating Officer: Robert F. Green
Managing Editor: Jonathan Feist
Editorial Assistants: Mina Cho, Yousun Choi, Emily Goldstein, Martin Fowler
Cover Designer: Kathy Kikkert
Cover Photo: Wolfie (www.coronium.co.uk)

CD Credits

Guitar: Michael Williams
Keyboards: Bruce Bears
Acoustic and Electric Bass: Jesse Williams
Drums: Mark Teixeira
Tenor Sax: Paul Ahlstrand
Trumpet: Walter Platt
Engineered/Recorded by Craig Hlady at Tower Productions in Dedham, MA

ISBN 978-0-87639-100-6

DISTRIBUTED BY

HAL•LEONARD®
CORPORATION
7777 W. BLUEMOUND RD. P.O. BOX 13819
MILWAUKEE, WISCONSIN 53213

1140 Boylston Street
Boston, MA 02215-3693 USA
(617) 747-2146

Visit Berklee Press Online at
www.berkleepress.com

Visit Hal Leonard Online at
www.halleonard.com

Copyright © 2010 Berklee Press
All Rights Reserved

No part of this publication may be reproduced in any form or by
any means without the prior written permission of the Publisher.

CONTENTS

CD TRACKS		iv
ACKNOWLEDGMENTS		v
PREFACE		vi
CHAPTER 1	**"Frosty"** Albert Collins	1
CHAPTER 2	**"I Need You So Bad"** Magic Sam	12
CHAPTER 3	**"The Last Time (I Get Burned Like This)"** Robert Cray	23
CHAPTER 4	**"Okie Dokie Stomp"** Clarence "Gatemouth" Brown	33
CHAPTER 5	**"Papa Ain't Salty"** T-Bone Walker	44
CHAPTER 6	**"The Sad Nite Owl"** Freddy King	51
CHAPTER 7	**"San-Ho-Zay"** Freddy King	56
CHAPTER 8	**"Wait on Time"** Jimmie Vaughan	65
CHAPTER 9	**"The Woman I Love"** B.B. King	76
CHAPTER 10	**"Worried Life Blues"** Robert Lockwood Jr.	85
APPENDIX A.	**Original Recordings**	105
APPENDIX B.	**Blues Guitar Glossary and Articulation Key**	106
ABOUT THE AUTHOR		109

CD TRACKS

NAME	TRACK
"Frosty" Albert Collins: Full Band	1
"Frosty" Albert Collins: No Guitar	2
"I Need You So Bad" Magic Sam: Full Band	3
"I Need You So Bad" Magic Sam: No Guitar	4
"The Last Time" Robert Cray: Full Band	5
"The Last Time" Robert Cray: No Guitar	6
"Okie Dokie Stomp" Clarence "Gatemouth" Brown: Full Band	7
"Okie Dokie Stomp" Clarence "Gatemouth" Brown: No Guitar	8
"Papa Ain't Salty" T-Bone Walker: Intro Solo Full Band	9
"Papa Ain't Salty" T-Bone Walker: Intro Solo No Guitar	10
"Papa Ain't Salty" T-Bone Walker: 2nd Solo Full Band	11
"Papa Ain't Salty" T-Bone Walker: 2nd Solo No Guitar	12
"The Sad Nite Owl" Freddy King: Full Band	13
"The Sad Nite Owl" Freddy King: No Guitar	14
"The Sad Nite Owl" Freddy King: No Guitar; extended to five choruses	15
"San-Ho-Zay" Freddy King: Full Band	16
"San-Ho-Zay" Freddy King: No Guitar	17
"Wait on Time" Jimmie Vaughan: Full Band	18
"Wait on Time" Jimmie Vaughan: No Guitar	19
"The Woman I Love" B.B. King: Full Band	20
"The Woman I Love" B.B. King: No Guitar	21
"Worried Life Blues" Robert Lockwood Jr.: Full Band	22
"Worried Life Blues" Robert Lockwood Jr.: No Guitar	23

ACKNOWLEDGMENTS

Thanks to B.B. King and the other artists featured in this book, for providing inspiration, and for laying the groundwork for the music to move forward.

Thanks to my wife Anna and son Calvin for their support, and for putting up with my extended working hours, along with the sheet music and musical equipment spread throughout the house! Thanks also to my parents and family for their encouragement over the years.

Thanks to my friends and associates at Berklee: to Larry Baione and Rick Peckham from Berklee's Guitar Department, for their continued support and commitment to excellence in teaching, and to Dan Bowden and Martin Fowler for lending their ears and proofreading skills to the project.

I'd also like to extend my gratitude to Debbie Cavalier and the first-rate staff at Berkleemusic, along with Jonathan Feist at Berklee Press, for his editing skills, patience, and expertise to see this book through to completion.

Thanks to Starr Ackerman and the folks at IK Multimedia, for providing killer guitar sounds through their AmpliTube Fender software. Their product's huge range of tones–from the '50s classic tweed "growl," to their '60s blackface models such as the '65 Twin Reverb and '64 Vibroverb—sounded right at home on this recording project.

Finally, thanks to Bruce Bears, Jesse Williams, and Mark Teixeira, for laying down the great (live) rhythm section tracks, and to Paul Ahlstrand for tenor sax and horn arrangements, along with Walter Platt on trumpet. Thanks also to Craig Hlady at Tower Productions in Dedham, MA for his first-rate work in recording and engineering this project.

PREFACE

Arriving at this collection of songs was a natural process, since they're ten of my favorite electric blues solos. Writing and recording the solos in this book was both extremely challenging and hugely rewarding, at the same time. I've played several of these tunes during live performances (for years), and although I may have "quoted" parts from the original artist's solos on gigs, my solos are generally improvised.

I have to admit that recording solos by ten of my musical mentors for this book felt a little strange at times. It was like heading out on a 120-day hike retracing someone else's "musical footprints."

It's been an adventure, and a great learning experience.

Transcribing and recording these solos took me "back to school" to learn more about phrasing and the nuances of rhythms and note choices from the masters themselves—more about the subtle variations in sound and feel from articulations such as slides, hammer-ons, pull-offs, and vibrato, and about the vast variations in pitch during string bends. In their solos, Robert Lockwood Jr., B.B. King, Freddy King, and the others demonstrate that there are so many (other) notes and pitches to tap into—the "deep blues" notes, that fall *way* between the cracks of the 6-note blues scale.

There's an ongoing debate as to just how useful it is (or isn't) to learn solos note-for-note, as opposed to simply learning/playing our own solos. Here's my two cents on the subject.

Learning solos note-for-note is a musical means, not an end. It's a valuable part of the learning process, but not the whole process. I agree about the importance of playing our own solos. That's essential. However, our long-term practice emphasis shouldn't come down to one or the other method of practice. For the purpose of expanding soloing vocabulary, it's very helpful to spend hours and hours doing both.

Once you've learned the transcription, the *real* hard work begins. I encourage students to spend at least four times as many hours figuring out how to reuse the phrases in their own way, as they did learning the transcription. Once you learn the solo, tear it apart, kick the tires—get "under the hood," so to speak. Analyze the solo, then figure out what you can reuse from the solo. Change the phrases around. Rework them into other keys, tempos, and contexts, to internalize them and eventually make them a part of your own soloing vocabulary. To summarize, spend more time improvising, rather than learning solos note-for-note, but do both.

While living, breathing, eating, and sleeping these solos over the past few months, I've developed an even deeper appreciation and respect for the ten guitarists that are featured in this book. These tracks represent a small piece of each artist's unique perspective, vocabulary, and language of the blues, but there's much to learn from them.

I've taken my best shot at recreating the guitar parts from the ten songs in the book. A full band version of each song is included on the CD, along with rhythm section tracks (minus guitar), for practice. However, my renditions are not intended as a substitute for the originals. In order to reap the maximum benefits from the pages that follow, it's essential to learn the language of the blues from the masters themselves. I urge you to purchase the original recordings of the songs that are featured here. (A discography of original recordings is included in the appendix.) So listen, sing, and play along with the original artists for months—and years!

CHAPTER 1

"Frosty" Albert Collins

Albert Collins (1932 to 1993) was born in Leona, Texas, and that's where the roots of his easily recognizable sound originated. Along with other early inspirations such as B.B. King and Robert Lockwood Jr., Collin's playing style was influenced by fellow Texans T-Bone Walker and Clarence "Gatemouth" Brown. Brown's use of a capo had a direct impact on shaping Collins' playing technique and sound; Collins also played with a capo, which he referred to as a "choker," tuned to an open F minor chord (strings tuned bottom to top, F C F A♭ C F).

Albert Collins was a consummate electric blues guitarist. Also known as "the Master of the Telecaster" and the "Ice Man," he could light up the room with incendiary solos on his Telecaster, plugged into a Fender Quad Reverb amp. Onstage, Collins was a master showman. With his "mile-long" guitar chord, he would "take a walk" during performances, wooing crowds inside—even outside, on streets and sidewalks in front of the club—with his funky, stinging, and extended solos.

Collins was also a master storyteller. He was great at delivering a catchy lyric or story line, and was as good as it gets at continuing the story, from the lyrics to his guitar. With his finger-style (sans pick) technique, he was capable of conjuring up a huge range of sounds and textures on his Telecaster. Collins could mimic (to an uncanny degree) humorous sounds from everyday life, such as the frigid "crunch" of his boots trudging through the snow and ice, to get to his truck during the blizzard of '78. He could recreate the "chugging" sound of the truck's engine turning over but not quite starting, as the battery gradually wears down, in the biting cold of a Chicago winter's night. Or the seductive sound of his wife, mischievously cooing in his ear, after she arrived home late from a night on the town with her girlfriends. Then, at precisely the right moment, Collins would launch into a blistering electric blues solo, to wrap the story up with searing "take-no-prisoners" volume, intensity, and impact.

Throughout his career, Albert Collins influenced many well-known blues and rock guitarists, including Robert Cray, Stevie Ray Vaughan, Anson Funderburgh, Gary Moore, Coco Montoya, Sue Tedeschi, and John Mayer. Collin's career was unfortunately cut short when he succumbed to lung cancer in 1993.

"Frosty" was a huge hit for Collins, selling a million copies when it was released as a single in 1962. It was also included in *The Cool Sounds of Albert Collins* by TCF Hall Records in 1965, and re-released as *Truckin' with Albert Collins*, by Blue Thumb records in 1969.

PERFORMANCE TIPS

Collins wrote songs that featured unique musical "hooks" (motifs) and catchy titles, such as "Don't Lose Your Cool," "Freeze," and "Frost Bite." Collins performed "Frosty" with a capo on the 9th fret, so for this track, his (open) strings sounded an open D minor chord. However, several of his popular instrumentals, such as "Don't Lose Your Cool," "Backstroke," and "Frosty," have become standards in the blues repertoire, and they're often performed in standard tuning. With that in mind, I transcribed the music and the tab fingerings to "Frosty" in standard tuning.

Despite its name, this instrumental is nine choruses of a funky, steaming gumbo, cooked up from the D blues and D pentatonic scales, and it features several of Collin's "signature" phrases. The example below, from chorus 9 of "Frosty," demonstrates Collins' unique approach of combining notes from the D blues and D pentatonic scales.

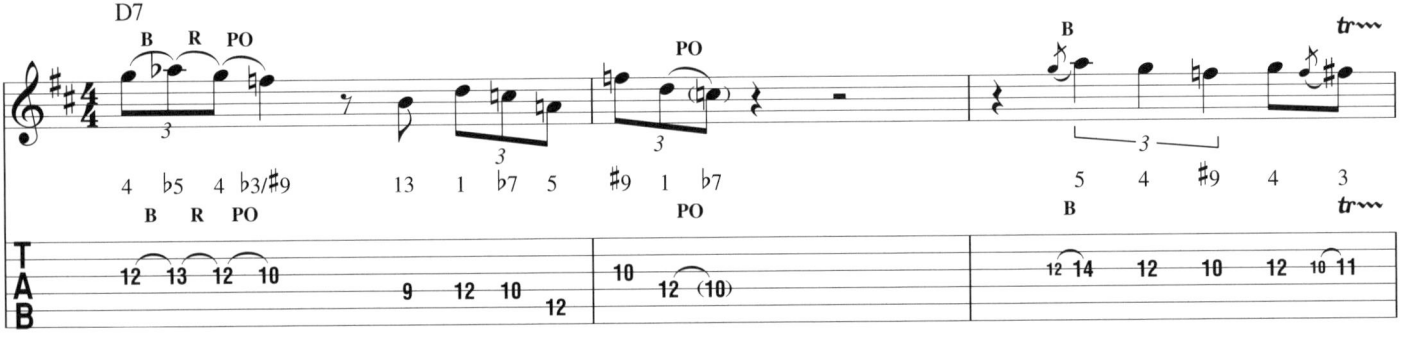

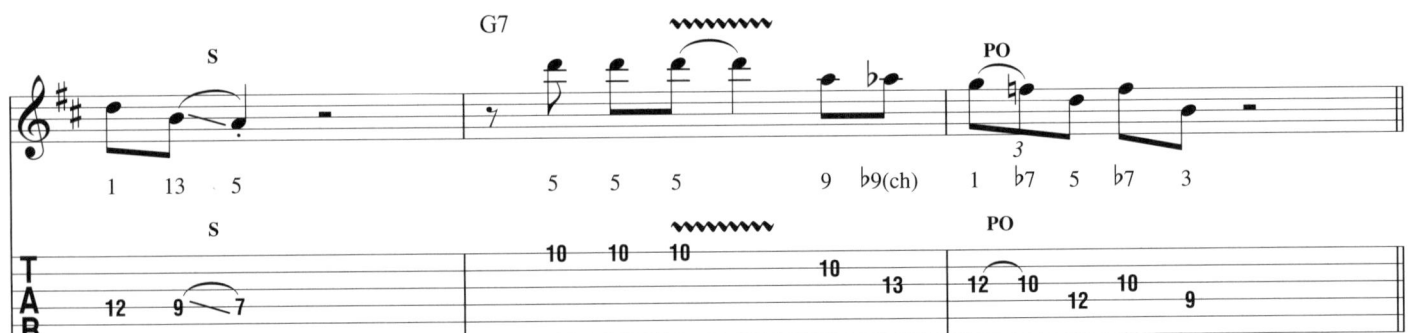

Fig. 1.1. "Frosty" Chorus 9, Bars 1–6

The notes 1, ♭3 (or ♯9), 4 (or 11), ♭5, 5, and ♭7, are in the D blues scale, and the 3rd (F♯) and the colorful 6th or 13th (B) is from the D pentatonic scale. The analysis (1 3 5 ♭7, etc.) included in figure 1.2 illustrates the phrases' relationships to the D7 (I7) and G7 (IV7) chords and to the D blues, and pentatonic scales, which are also written below.

CHAPTER 1 "Frosty" Albert Collins

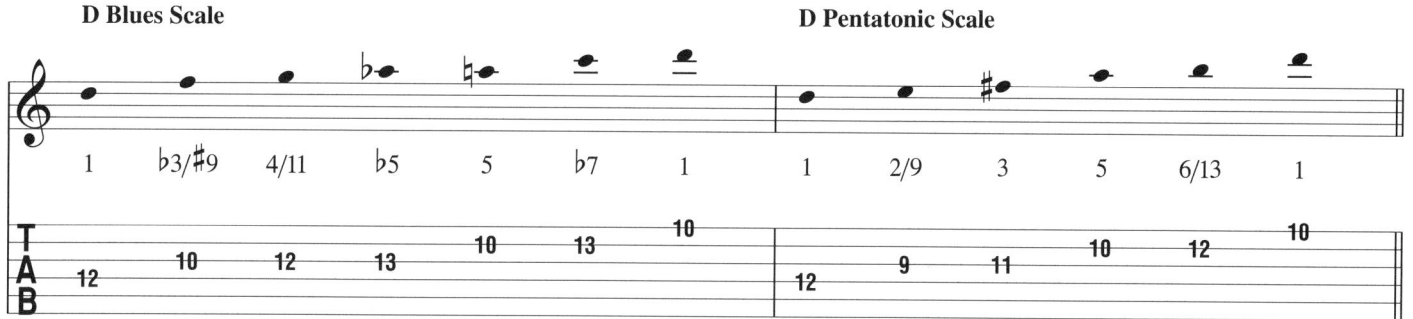

Fig. 1.2. D Blues Scale and D Pentatonic Scale. As used in "Frosty."

Because of his open minor-chord tuning, Albert Collins' phrases are a little unique. In standard tuning, they're fingered a little differently from "standard" blues licks on the neck, so his phrases are challenging to work up to tempo. Collins' frequent use of the 13th (on the D string, 9th fret) plays a big part in his unique melodic approach and soloing vocabulary. These frequent first-finger stretches to the 13th require a little getting used to, but they open up a great range of sounds!

PLAYING THE HIGH NOTES

Collins' scorching high D notes in bars 29 to 30 are challenging, particularly if your guitar's highest note is a C♯ on the 21st fret, like a Fender Telecaster or Stratocaster. As previously noted, Collins' high E string was tuned up one half step, as part of his open F minor tuning that was capoed at the 9th fret. So those repeated high D notes in bars 29 to 30 sounded on Collins' highest note, on the 21st fret.

If that high D note lays beyond your top fret, you'll need to bend up one half step, from C♯ (on the highest fret) into D on the "and" of beat 2. That's how I played the high Ds on the full band track for "Frosty," on track 1.

PLAYING THE TRILLS

Collins' (ferocious) trills throughout bars 91 to 94 and 105 to 106 were *impossible* to notate exactly, because he varied the amount of notes slightly from bar to bar. (So the notation and tab is as close as I could get it…) To play those extended trills, hammer on and pull off as fast—and with as much intensity—as possible. Keep track of where you are in the bar, so that you can nail the phrase that follows the trill, such as the ending lick in bar 107!

"Frosty" showcases Collins' stinging finger-style picking attack, along with his fiery, intense rhythmic feel. Combined with his unique mix of blues and pentatonic phrases, this solo conveys tons of attitude and Collins' bigger-than-life stage personality, so play these phrases with a punchy, aggressive picking attack, and with as much conviction as you can tap into. Have fun with "Frosty!"

ABOUT THE CD

 "Frosty" Full Band

 "Frosty" No Guitar

Tracks 1 and 2 for "Frosty" are based on Albert Collins' original recording, which is nine choruses in length.

Frosty
As played by Albert Collins

By Albert Collins

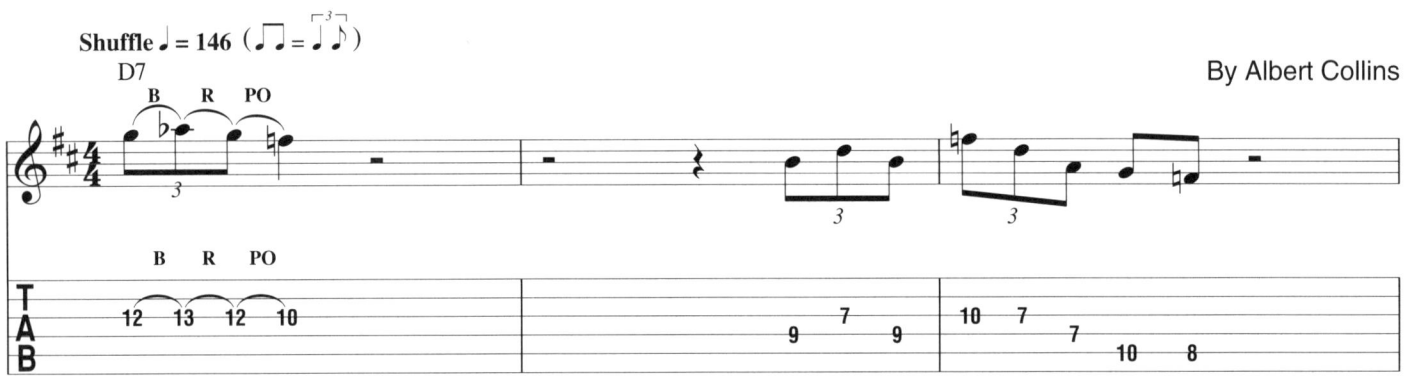

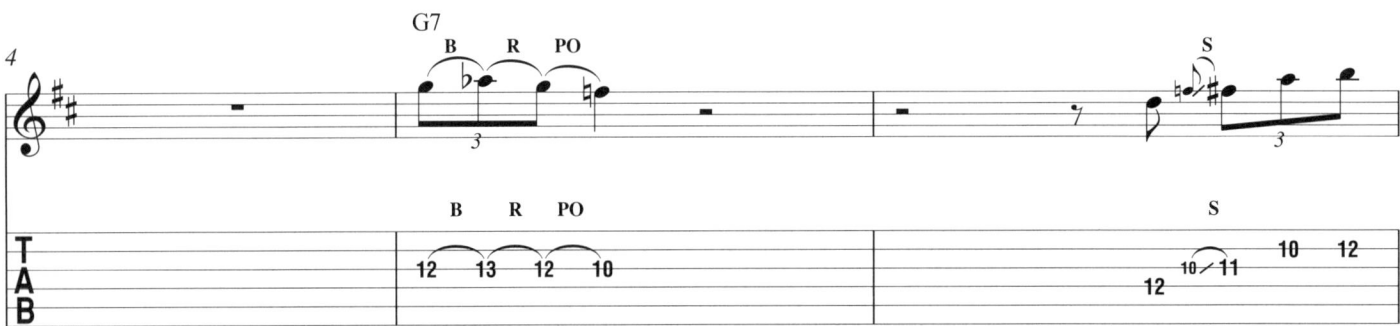

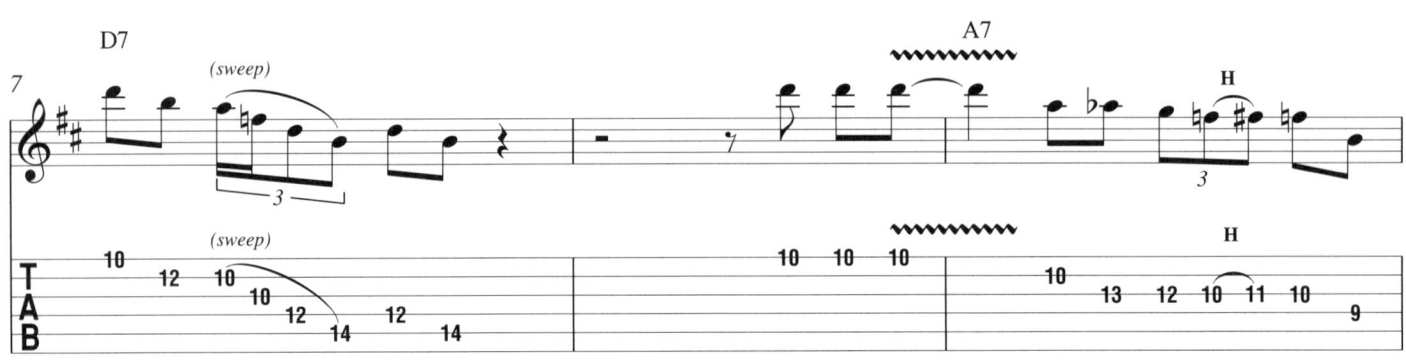

Copyright © 1965 UNIVERSAL - SONGS OF POLYGRAM INTERNATIONAL, INC.
Copyright Renewed
All Rights Reserved   Used by Permission

CHAPTER 1 "Frosty" Albert Collins

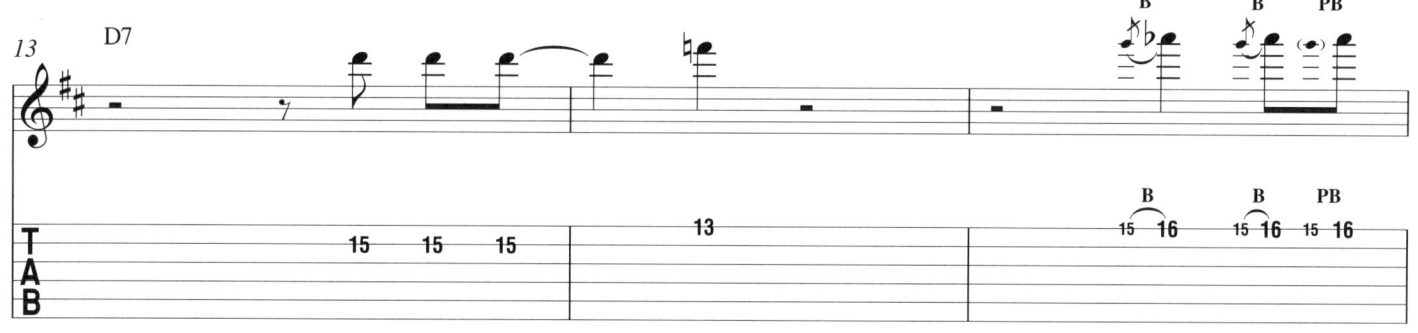
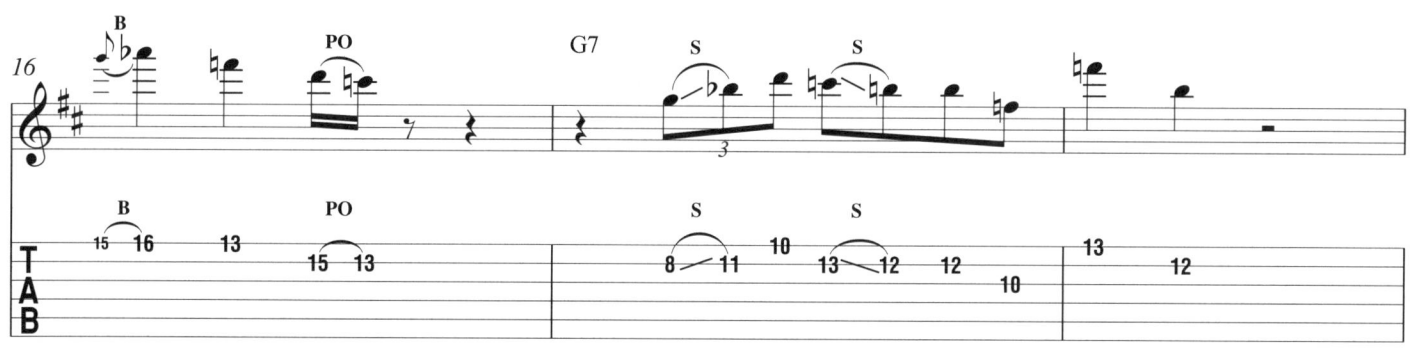

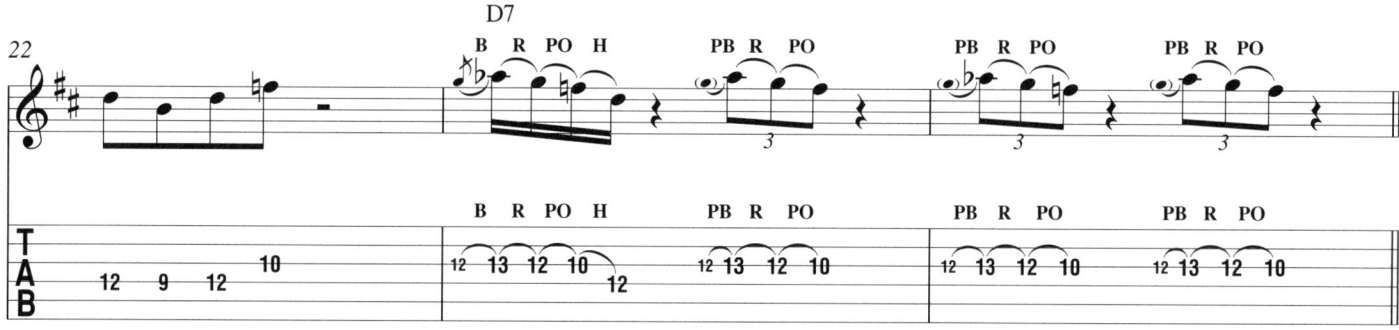

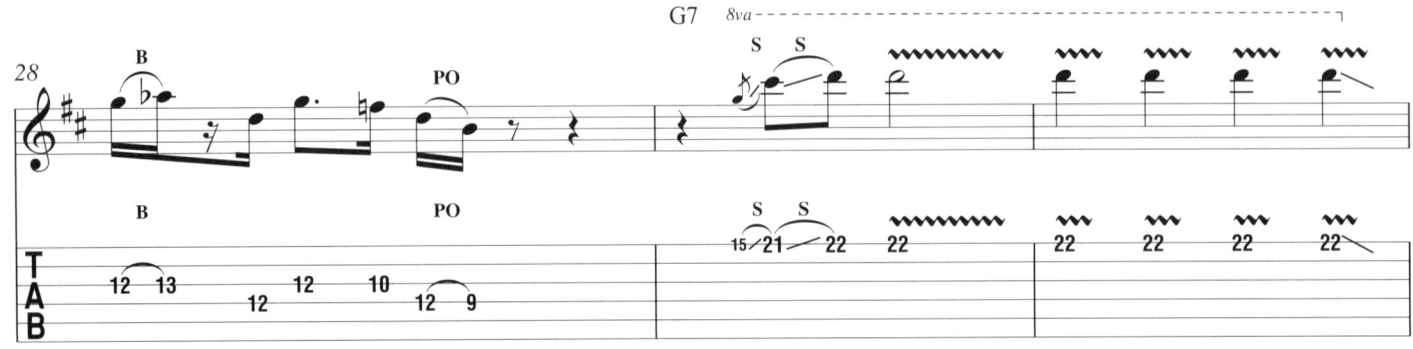
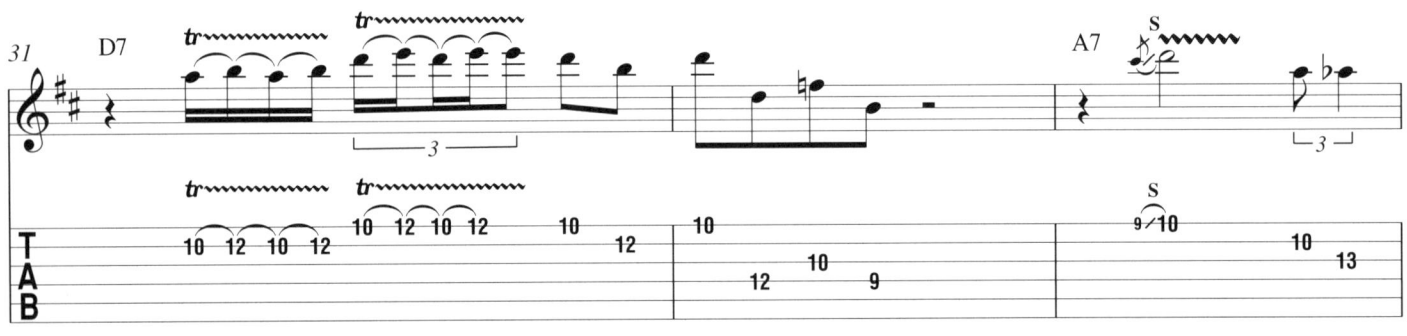
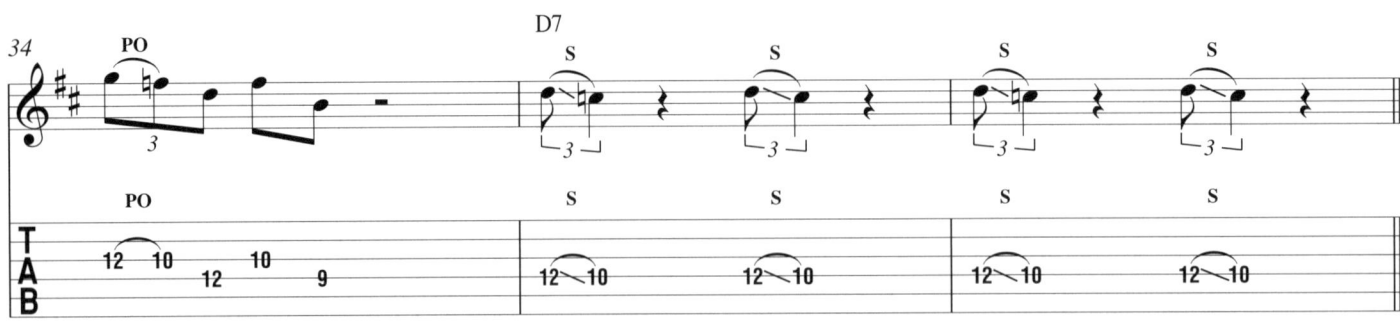
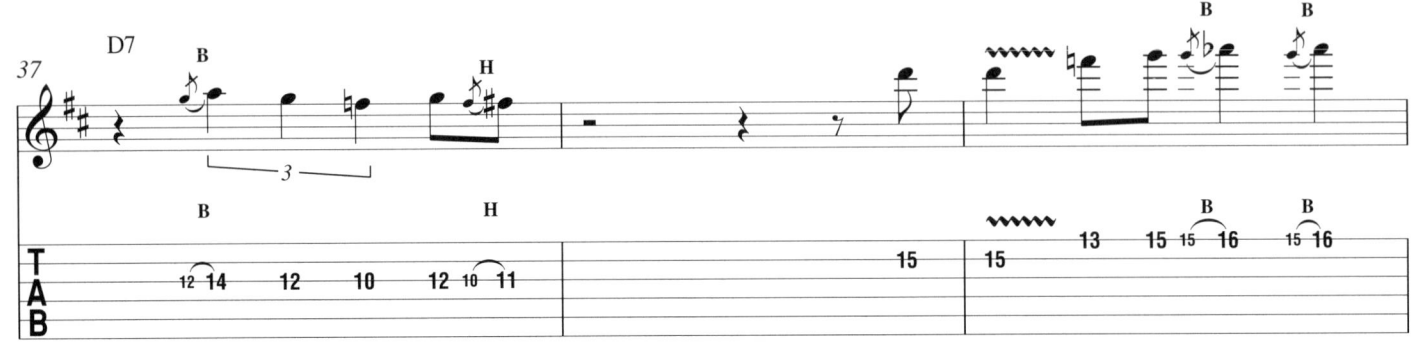

CHAPTER 1 "Frosty" Albert Collins

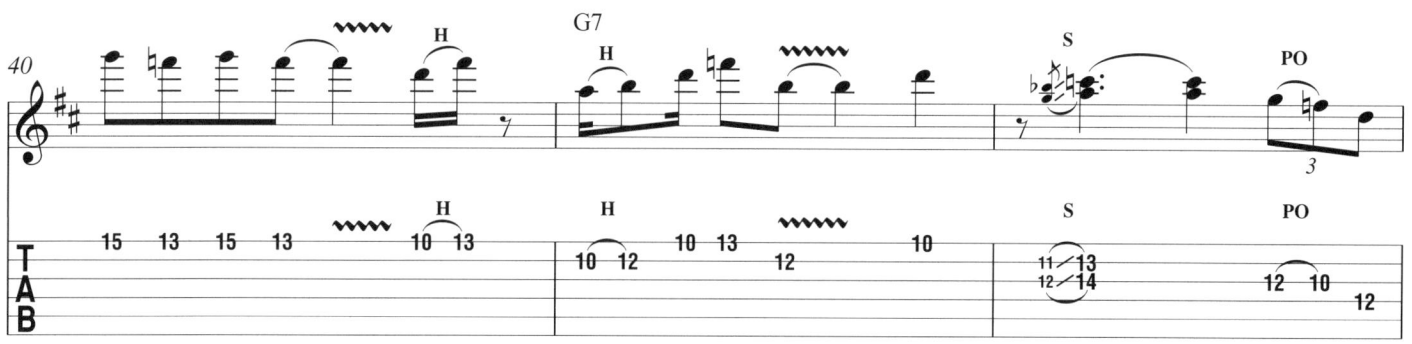

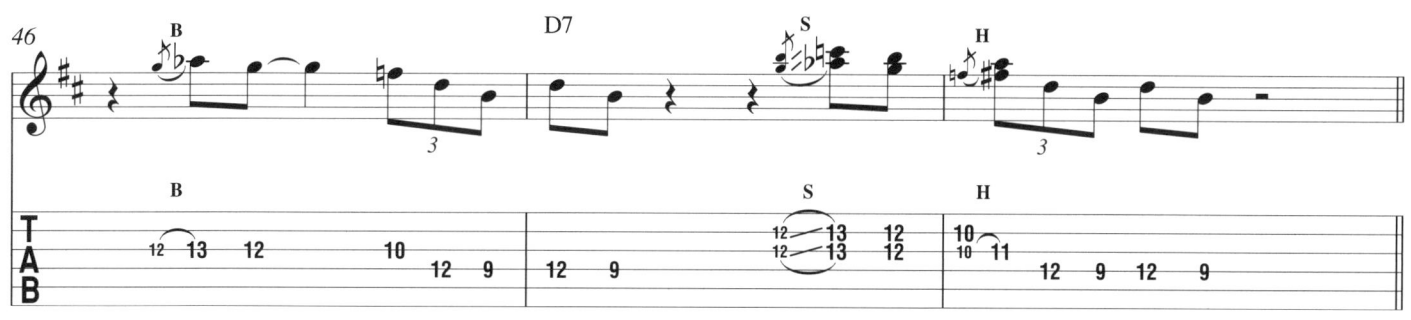

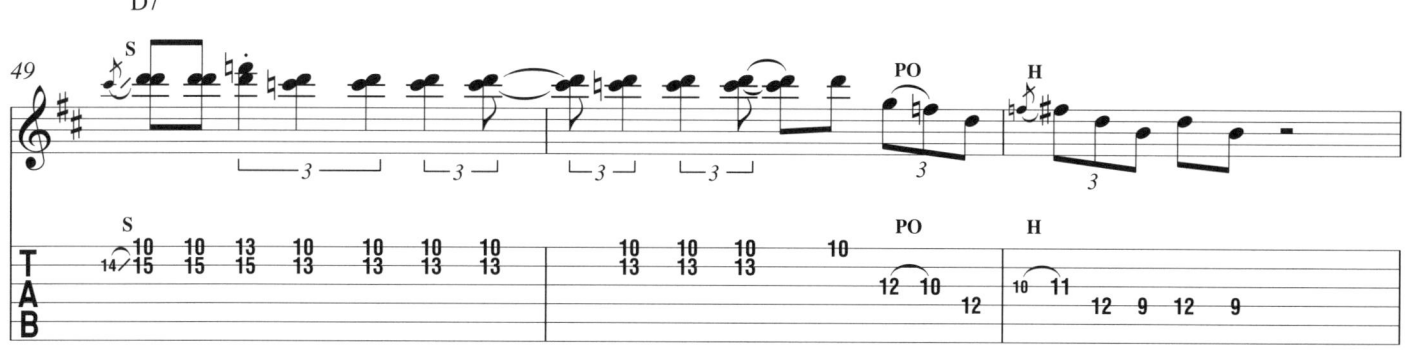

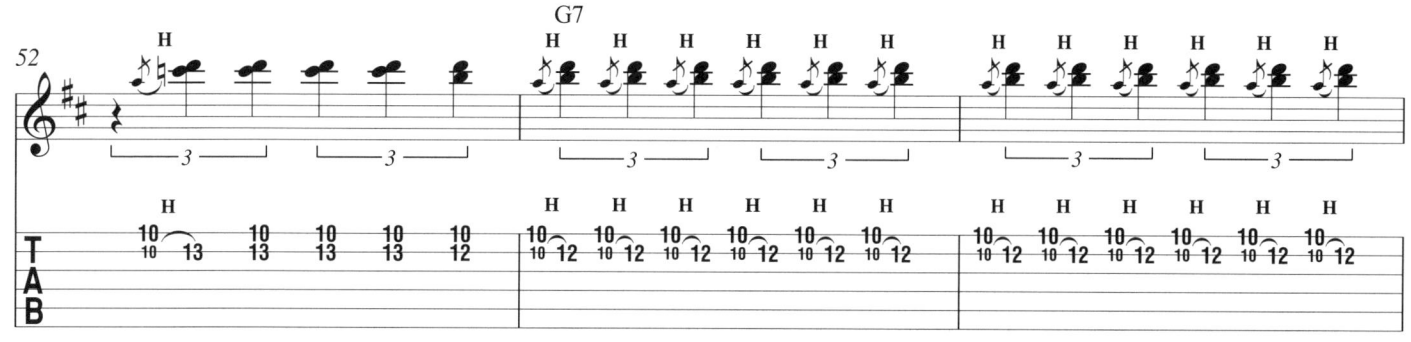

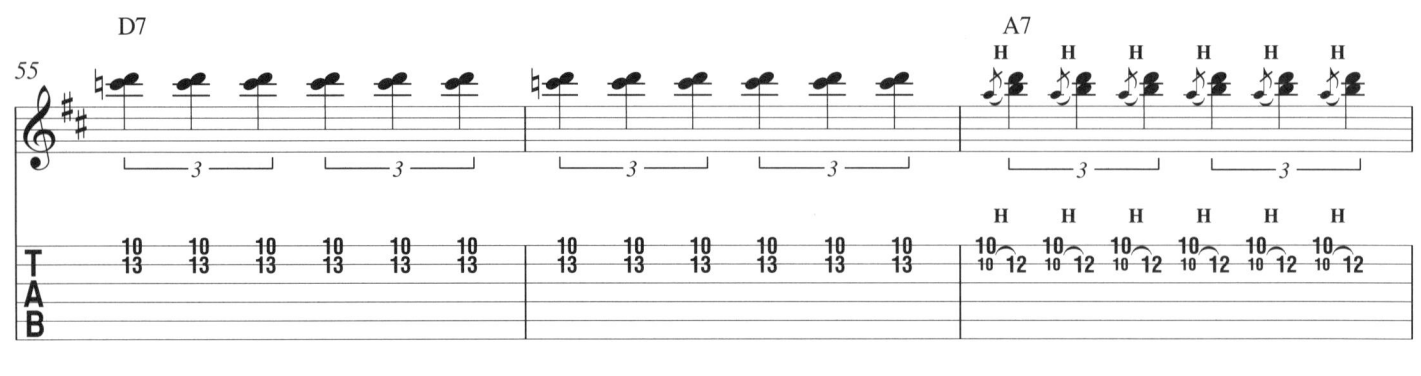
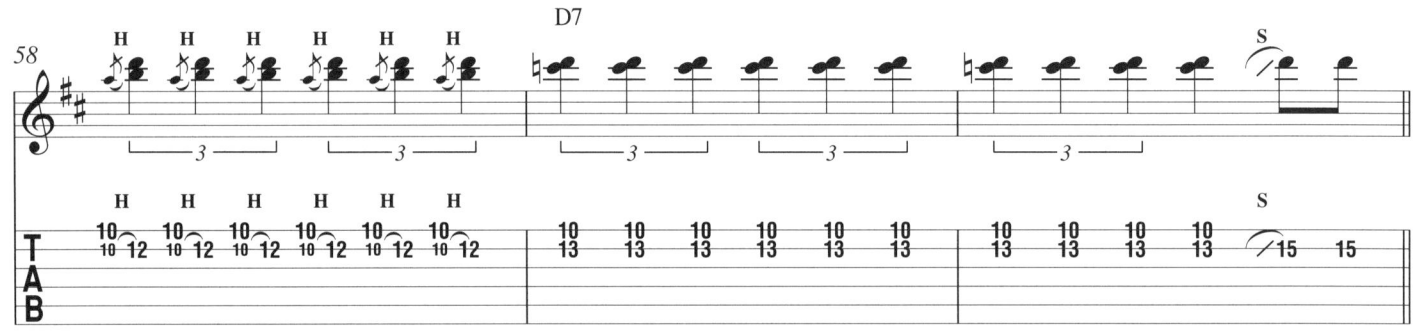
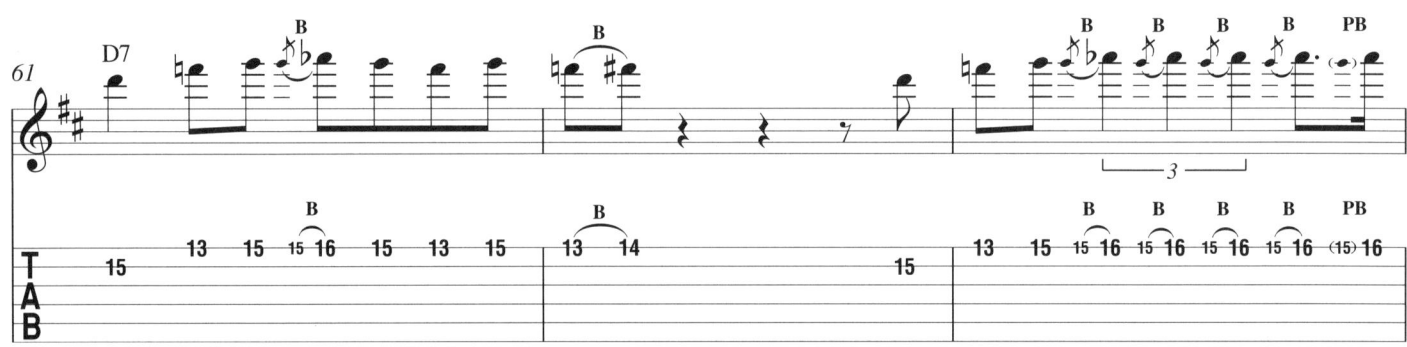
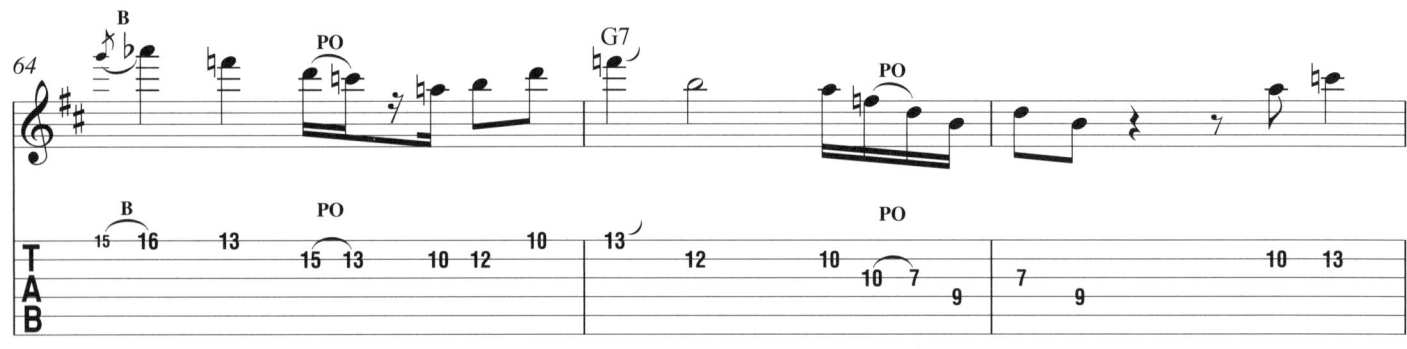
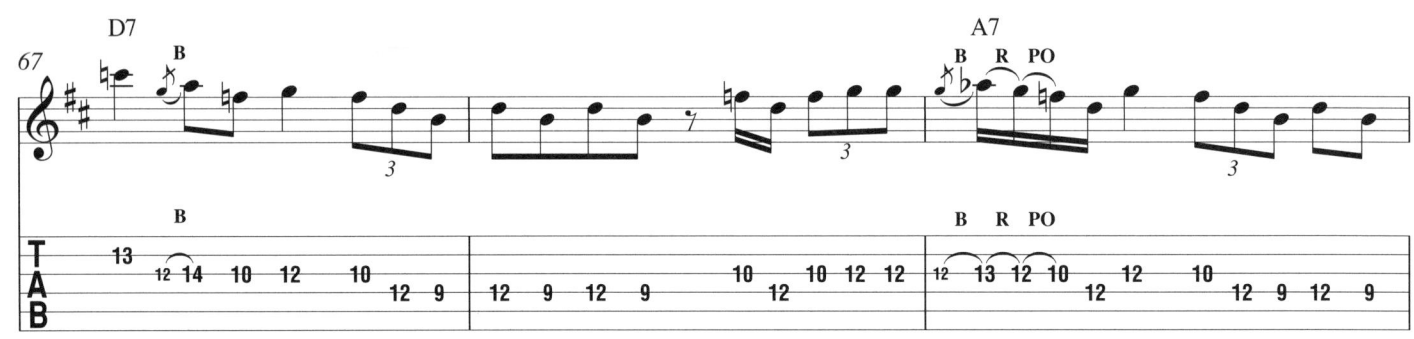

CHAPTER 1 "Frosty" Albert Collins

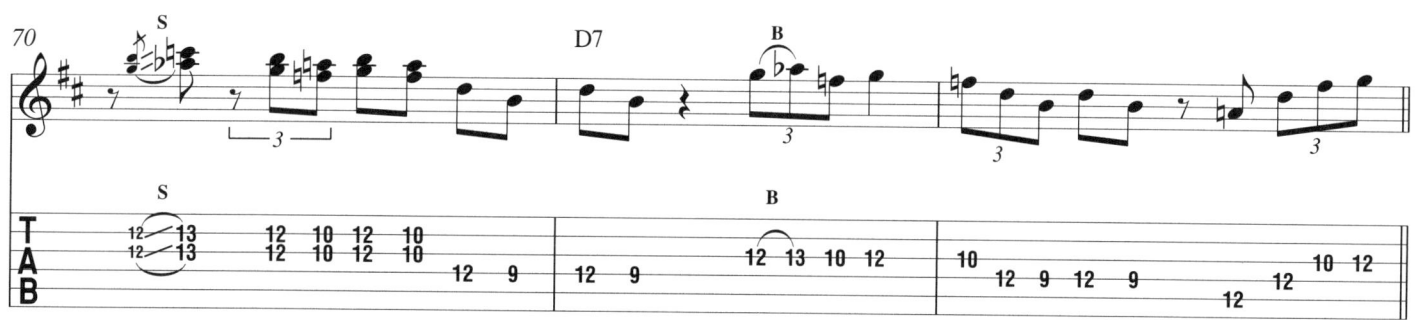
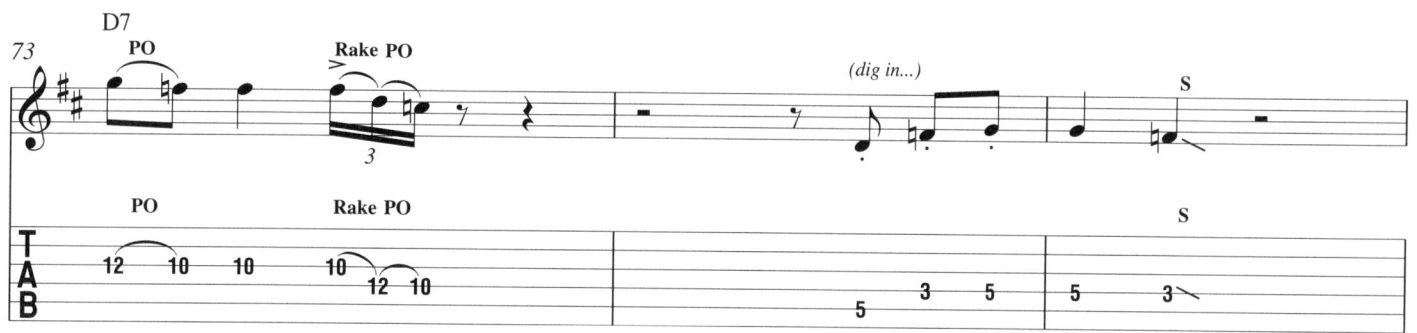
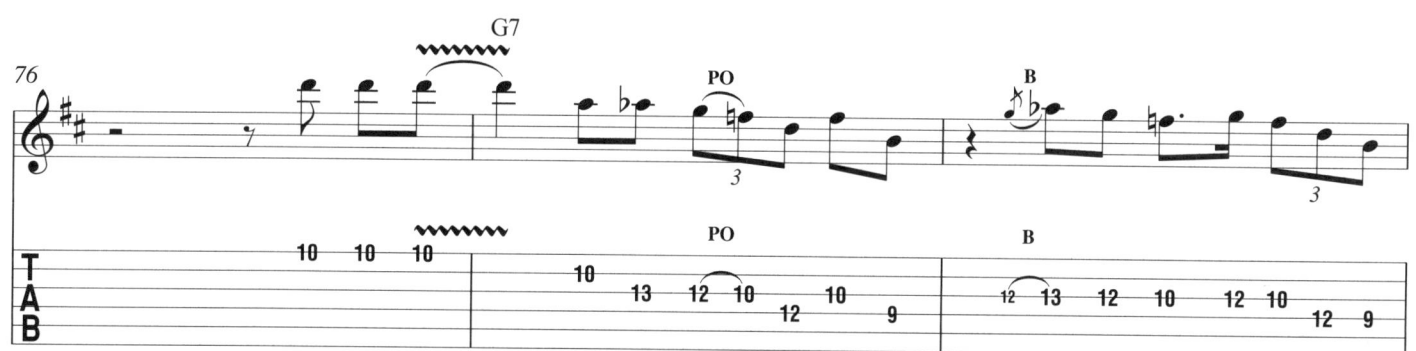

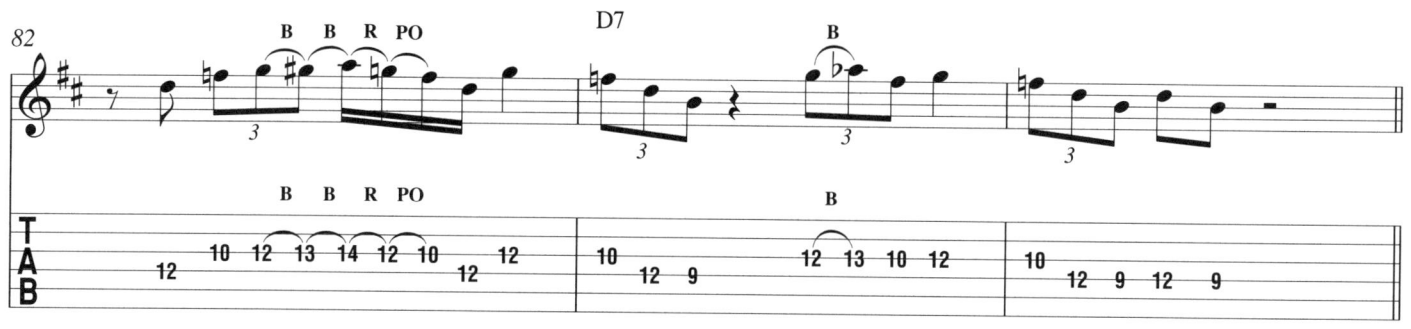

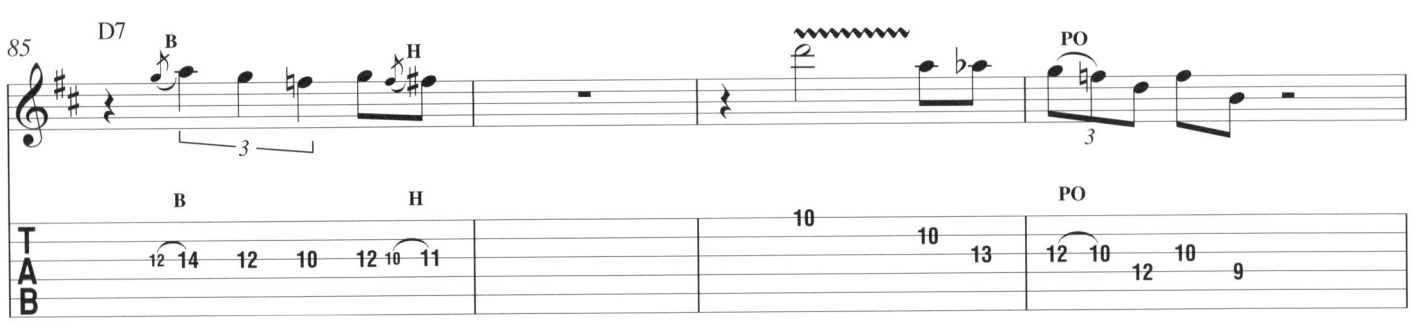
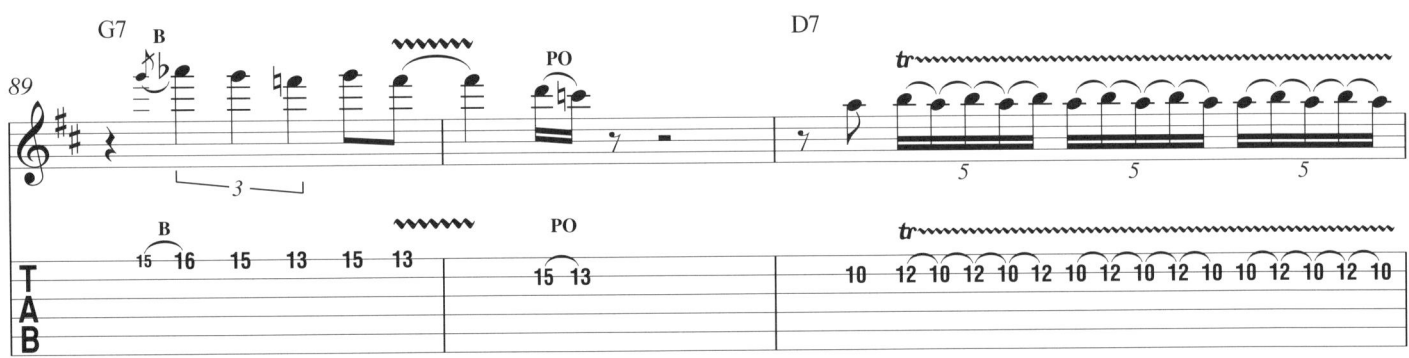
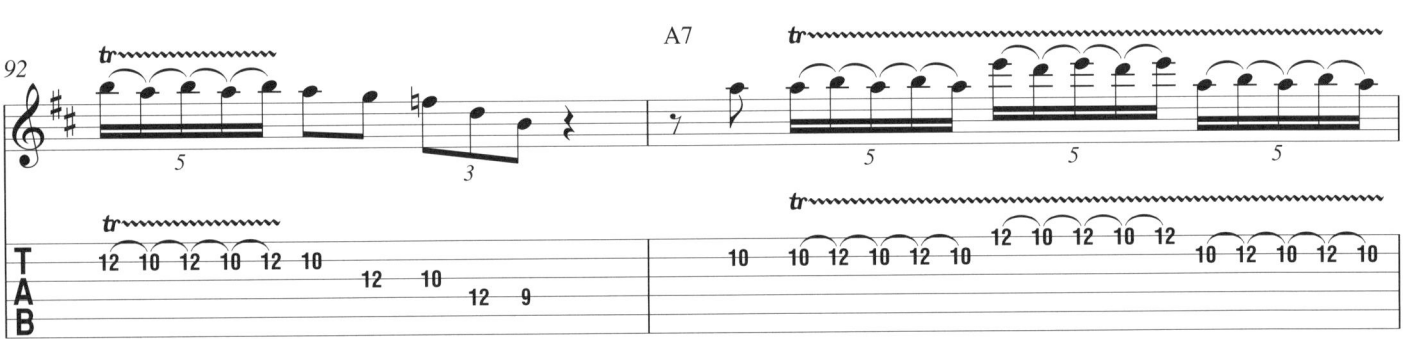
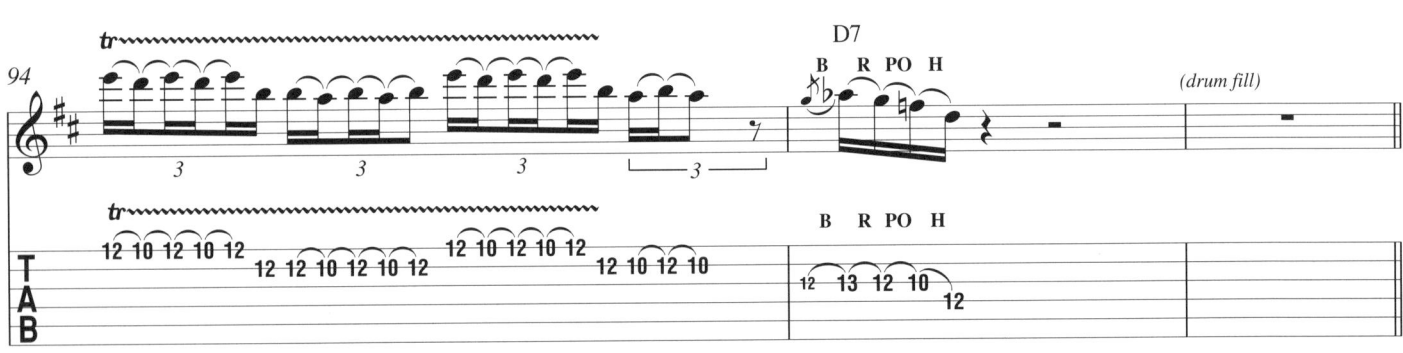
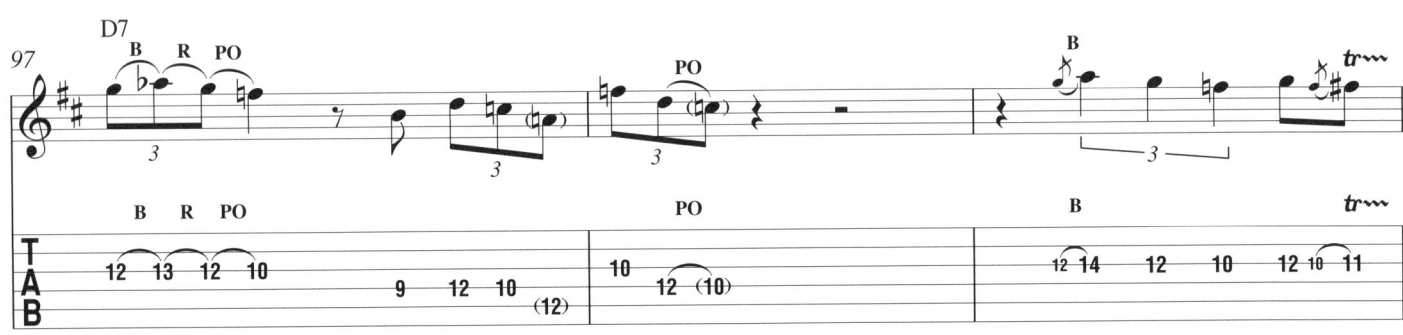

CHAPTER 1 "Frosty" Albert Collins

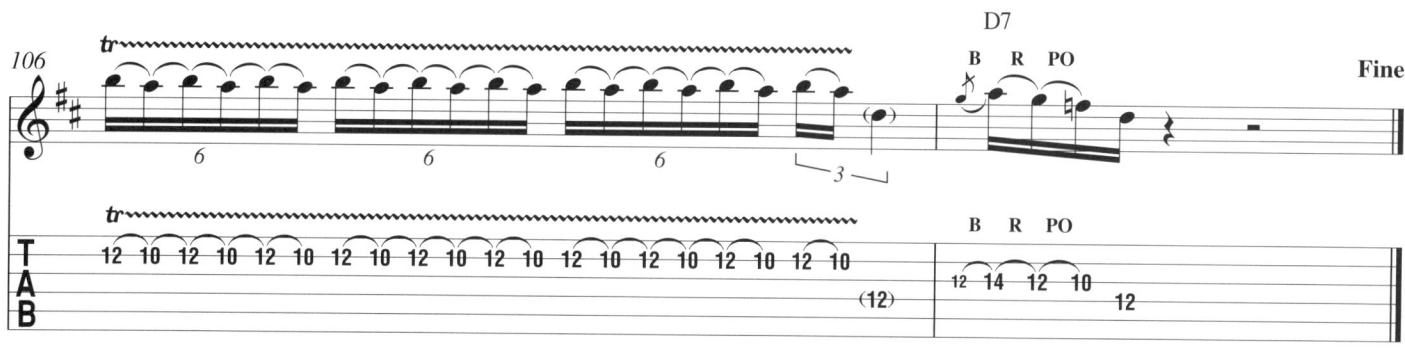

CHAPTER 2

"I Need You So Bad"
Magic Sam

Samuel Gene Maghett, aka Magic Sam (1937 to 1969), was born in Mississippi and moved to Chicago when he was in his early teens. During his brief career, Magic Sam made a huge mark on Chicago blues as one of the originators of the West Side style, along with Buddy Guy, Freddy King, and Otis Rush.

"I Need You So Bad" (by B.B. King) was released in 1965 on Delmark's *West Side Soul*, which is considered by many blues aficionados (and critics) to be one of the *very best* LPs in electric blues.

One of the first things you'll notice when you listen to Magic Sam's original recording of "I Need You So Bad" is his razor-sharp (finger-style) picking attack and intense, penetrating tone. His brittle bridge-pickup sound and sharp attack from his seemingly effortless finger-style technique, combined with a ferocious rhythmic drive (and feel), set him apart from a very crowded field of blues guitarists. Magic Sam's recordings such as *West Side Soul*, *Black Magic*, and *Magic Sam Live*, and his unique guitar and vocal style have heavily influenced latter-generation blues guitarists, such as Jimmie Vaughan, Stevie Ray Vaughan, Robert Cray, Duke Robillard, Ronnie Earl, and too many others to mention. Tragically, Magic Sam's career was cut short when he died from a heart attack at the age of 32.

For this book, I transcribed Magic Sam's entire track, including four inspired solo choruses, along with six vocal choruses, since his chords, fills, and turnarounds are intertwined with the lyrics to provide essential support for his vocals. Magic Sam's 12-bar intro solo on "I Need You So Bad" is a great window into his soloing style. It introduces several phrases and techniques that recur throughout the track, so it's the perfect place to begin.

PERFORMANCE TIPS

Magic Sam's intro solo is very heavily rooted in the A blues scale; in fact, with the exception of a few Bs, C♯s, and F♯s from the A pentatonic scale, every note of this intro is from the A blues scale. For this first chorus, Magic Sam works off two fingerings of the A blues scale. Most of this chorus is played in position 5. In bars 4, 5, and 11, he slides up into position 8 (as described in detail below).

B.B. King wrote and previously recorded this song (*RPM Hits 1951–57*, on Ace Records), and there's no mistaking his influences in Magic Sam's phrases throughout the track. Magic Sam mirrored the timing, pacing, and notes of several of King's phrases. At the same time, he changed the phrases enough to put his own personal and powerful stamp and sound on each.

In bar 4, Magic Sam launches into one of King's signature phrases on beat 1, as he outlines an A triad (C♯ E A; chord tones 3, 5, and 1) as a triplet on the top three strings. He follows the last note of the triplet (the A on the high E string, 5th fret) by quickly sliding up the B string to the 10th fret to strike A (root) three more times in a triplet on beat 2.

Note: To play the phrase, Magic Sam quickly moves up the fretboard from position 5 (perhaps the world's favorite pentatonic and blues scale fingering) into the 8th position, which is the very next pentatonic "box" up the neck. Magic Sam plays a very similar phrase in bar 11 also, as he strikes and repeats the note A on the 1st and 2nd strings (on beats 1 and 2). He repeats that phrase in bar 107 of chorus 9, and for his ending phrase in bar 120 of chorus 10.

Bar 5 showcases the vocal quality and intensity of Magic Sam's string bends. After bending up a whole step from D to E on the high E string, he colorizes the note with his brand of fast vibrato, to make it sing out with even more intensity. Magic Sam added vibrato to several sustained notes and string bends throughout the solo, and that's one of the nuances that makes his phrasing and sound unique. Be advised, it's difficult to even come close to matching Magic Sam's intensity, and I found this seemingly simple sustained whole-step bend as difficult to play as any other phrase in the intro!

In bar 6, Magic Sam repeats that whole-step bend as part of a triplet in beat 2, and he again sustains the note. Next, on beat 4 (after releasing the bend), he strikes the note D (first string, 10th fret) and quickly pulls off to the note C, then picks an A (second string, 10th fret) to complete a sixteenth-note triplet, followed by the note C on the "and" of 4 to set up a slide back down the B string in bar 7. Magic Sam again pays tribute to B.B. King, by playing this classic phrase exactly as B.B. played it in his (earlier) recording. With another sixteenth-note triplet on beat 1 of bar 7, he strikes the note A (B string, 10th fret), then pulls off to the note G (8th fret) with the third and first fingers, and then immediately slides down, sounding an E on the 5th fret, to end the phrase.

Bars 8 and 9 (figure 2.1) feature a couple of Magic Sam's "signature" phrases. These quick and dense flurries of notes are a powerful mix of A blues and A pentatonic scales in the 5th position, and they kick the intensity level up a few notches.

Note: The analysis (3 5 1 etc.) included below Magic Sam's phrases in bars 8 and 9 illustrate each note's relationship to the A blues and A pentatonic scales, which are also written below. Bar 9 includes analysis against the E7 chord, but every note of this 2-bar phrase is in the A blues or A pentatonic scale.

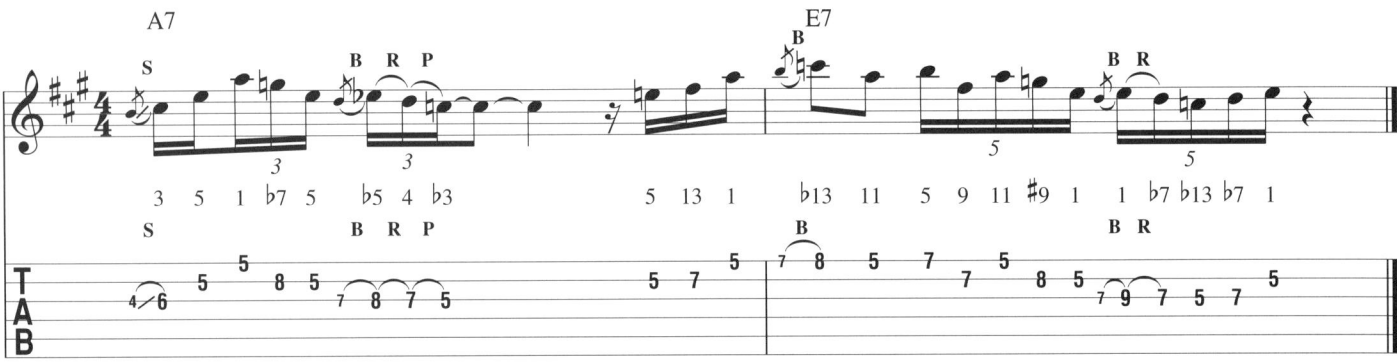

Fig. 2.1. "I Need You So Bad" Intro Chorus, Bars 8 and 9

These are the scales used as pitch sources for this solo.

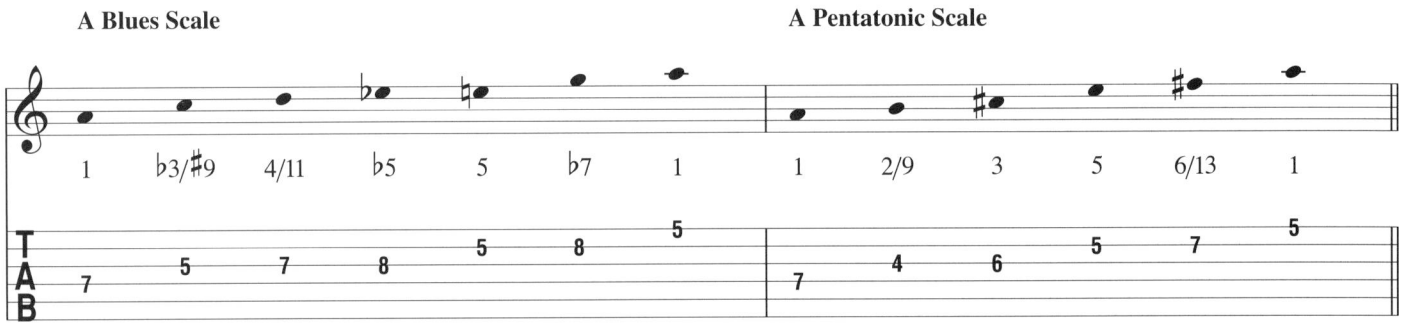

Fig. 2.2. A Blues and Major Pentatonic Scales

Magic Sam starts bar 8 with a quick (grace note) slide on the 3rd string into an arpeggio up the A triad (notes C♯, E, and A) on the top three strings. (This is similar to beat 1 of bar 4, but here, it's played as sixteenth notes.) Next, he pulls off from G to E (8th to 5th frets, on the B string), and as a sixteenth note triplet on beat 2 (on the G string), he bends a half step up to E♭, releases the bend down to D, and pulls off to C. Continuing with more sixteenth notes just before bar 9, he plays the notes E, F♯, and A. In bar 9, he starts with two eighth notes by bending a half step up into C (on the high E string) followed by A (on the 5th fret). To finish the phrase, beats 2 and 3 are played as quintuplets—five notes per beat. (Once again, these two beats are a very cool mix of A blues and A minor pentatonic!) It can be a little tricky to get these denser phrases under your fingers, but they're a classic element of Magic Sam's soloing vocabulary and style. They're also great for adapting for your own solos, so they're definitely worth the extra effort.

CHAPTER 2 "I Need You So Bad" Magic Sam   15

Again, as you practice through this, you'll notice that several phrases from Magic Sam's intro solo re-occur throughout the track. Most of chorus 5 features the same phrases (note-for-note), and so do the last five bars of choruses 6 and 9.

A few of Magic Sam's chords in bar 47 of chorus 4, and bars 80, 82, and 83 of chorus 7, are buried in the mix behind his vocal part, so they're a little difficult to hear. Like the notation for grace notes, they're outlined with parenthesis ( ).

Choruses 8 and 10 feature powerful chord hits around the vocals, which reflect another connection to B.B. King's original track. Magic Sam adapted the chord hits from the (big band style) horns in King's original recording. The riff-based chord hits create tons of rhythmic drive and intensity, and Magic Sam rides that momentum through chorus 10, right until the break in bar 118, as he takes the song out with the final blues fill.

As you practice Magic Sam's solo and rhythm fills on "I Need You So Bad," try to capture as much of his clarity of sound, projection, and intensity as possible. That's no easy task!

ABOUT THE CD

"I Need You So Bad" Full Band
TRACK 3

"I Need You So Bad" No Guitar
TRACK 4

Tracks 3 and 4 for "I Need You So Bad" are based on Magic Sam's original recording. They're ten choruses long.

I Need You So Bad
Intro Chorus by Magic Sam

Words and Music by Samuel Maghett

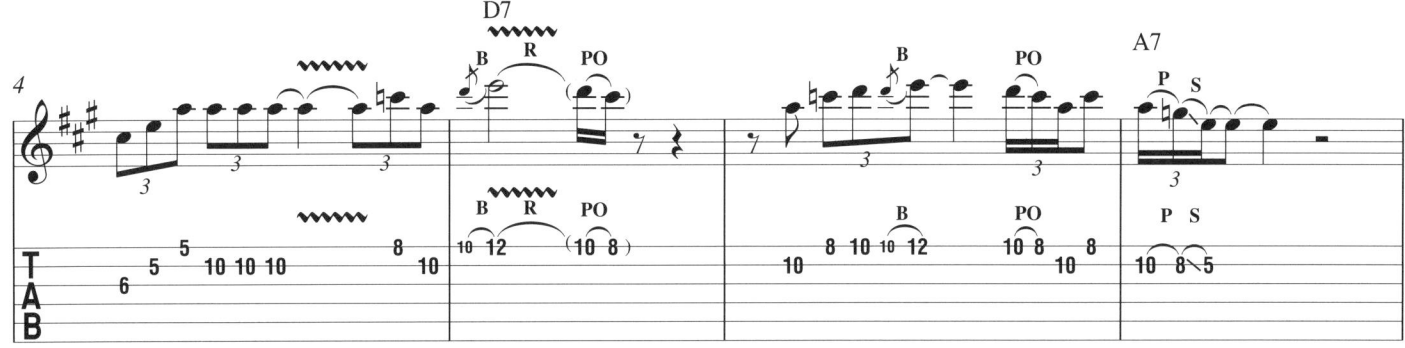

Copyright © 1999 by Arc Music Corporation (BMI) and Leric Music (BMI)/Administered by Bug Music
International Copyright Secured   All Rights Reserved
Used by Permission

16 BERKLEE BLUES GUITAR SONGBOOK

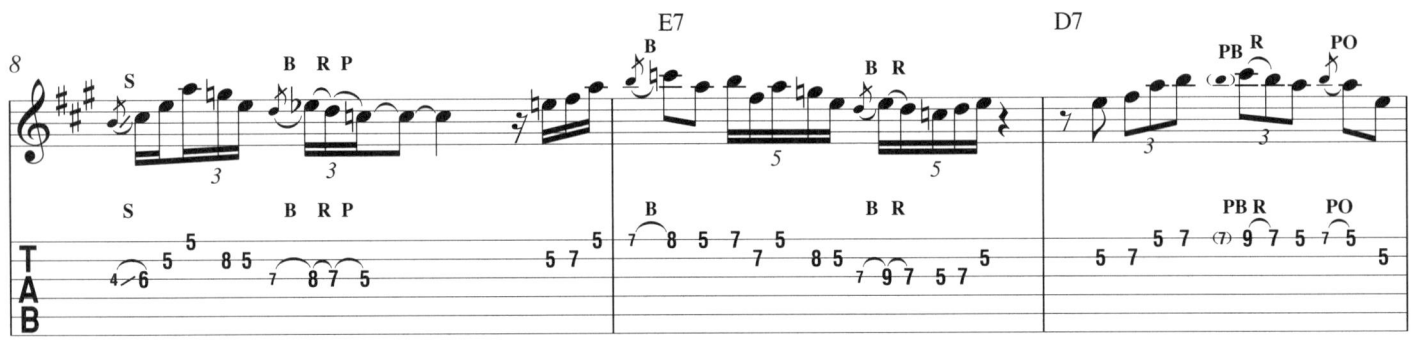

Chorus 2 - Vocals

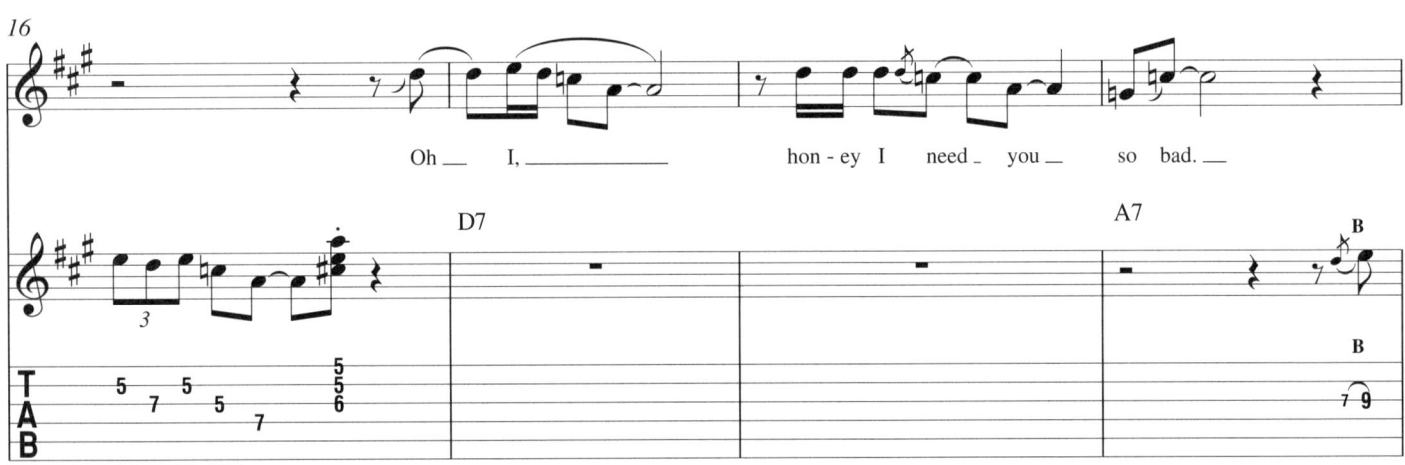

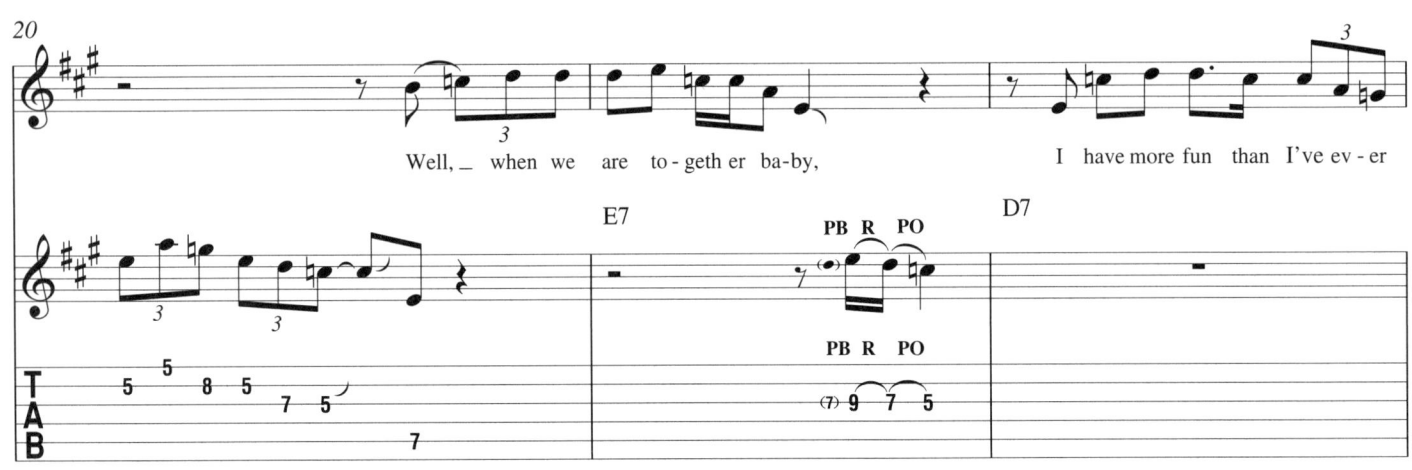

CHAPTER 2 "I Need You So Bad" Magic Sam

CHAPTER 2 "I Need You So Bad" Magic Sam 19

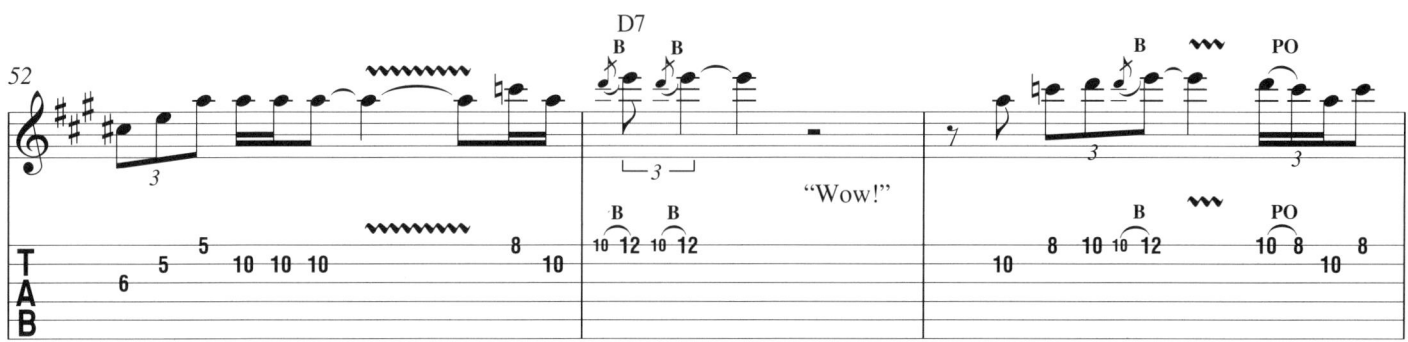

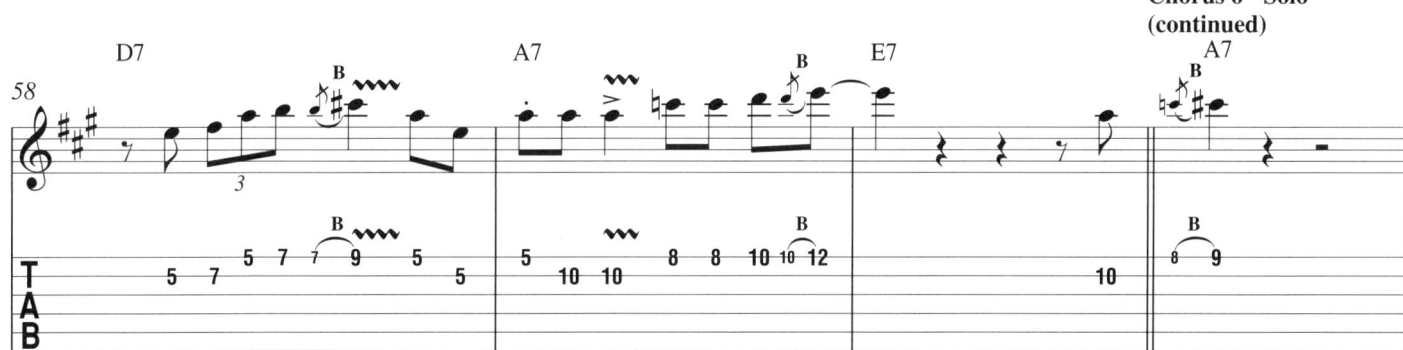
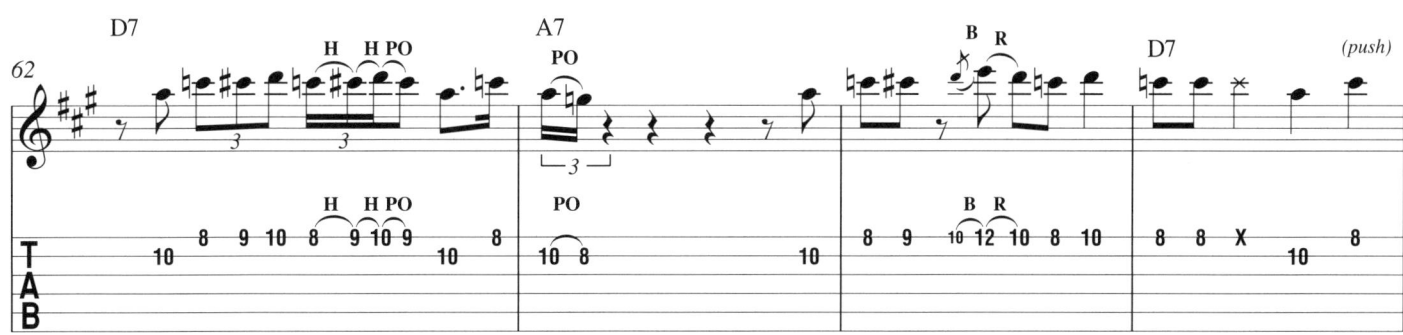
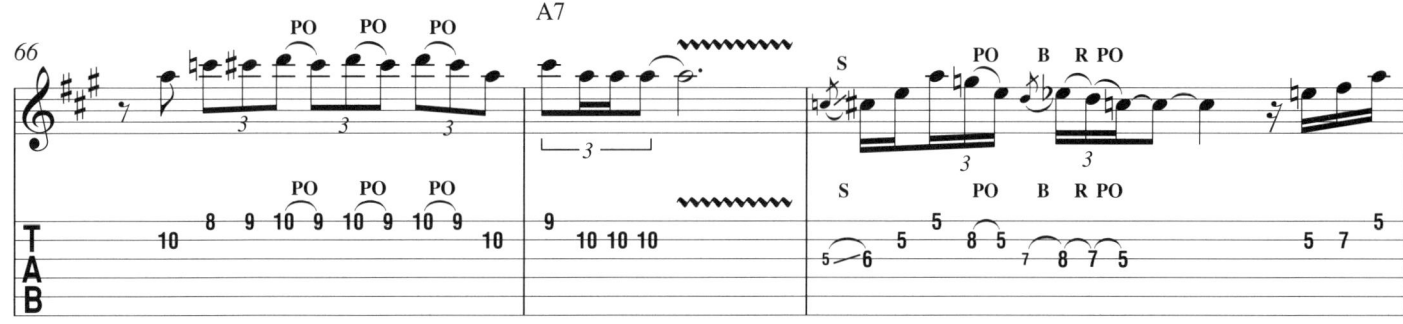

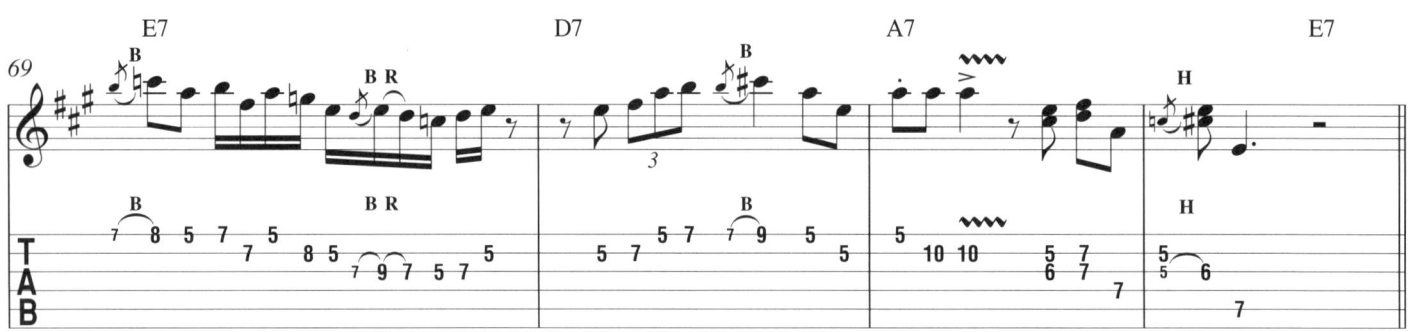

Chorus 7
(fills behind vocals - see additional lyrics)

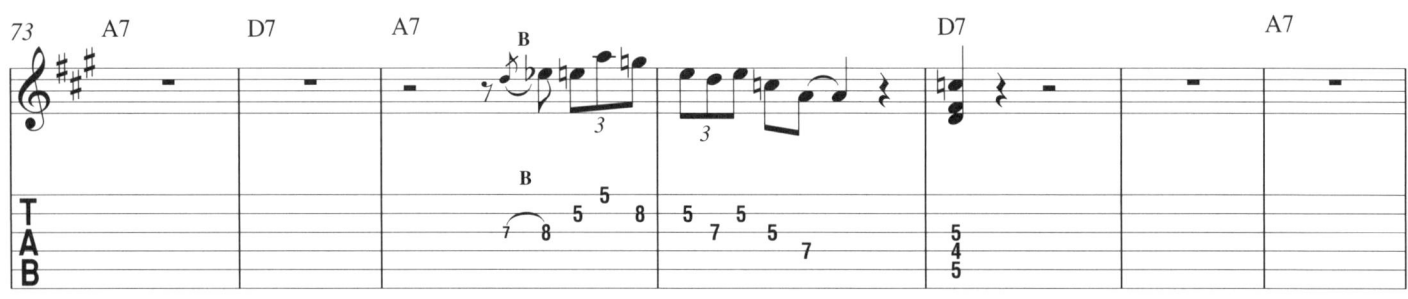

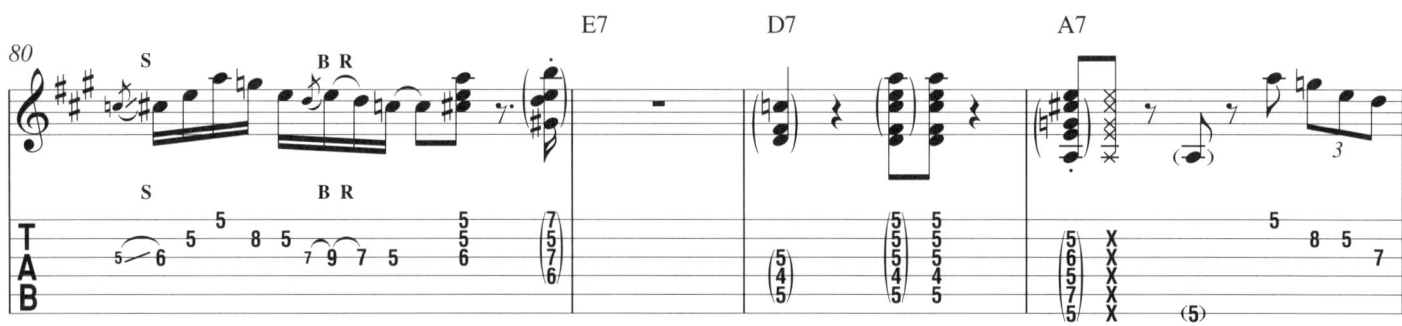

Chorus 8
(chords behind vocals - see additional lyrics)

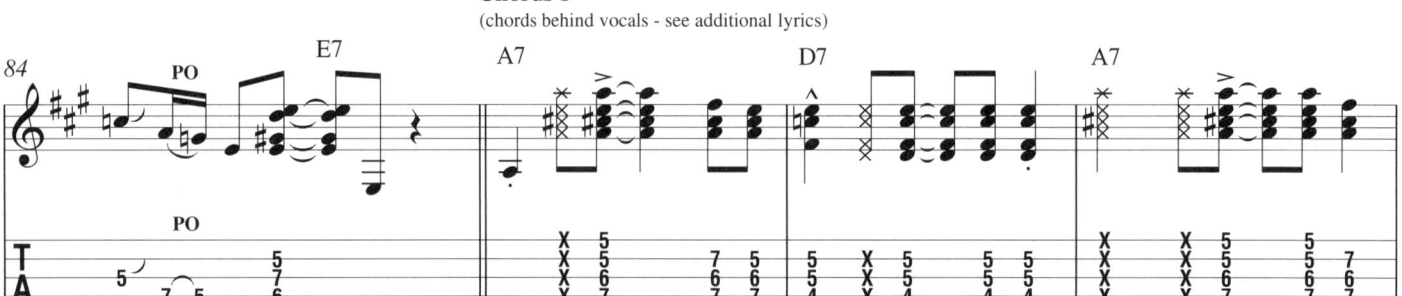

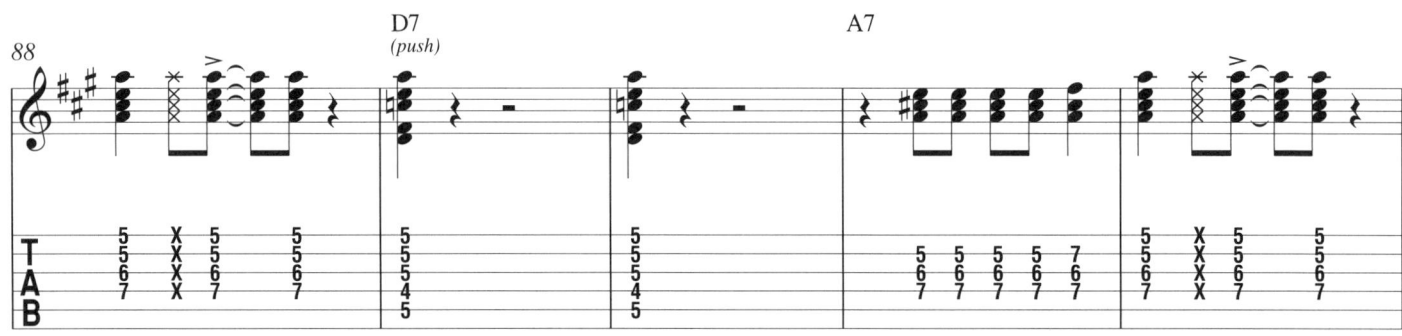

CHAPTER 2 "I Need You So Bad" Magic Sam   21

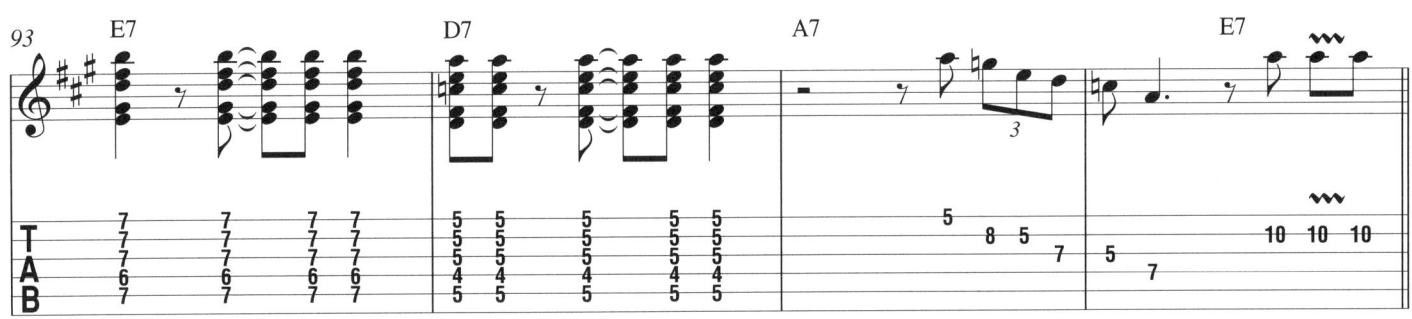

Chorus 9 - Solo

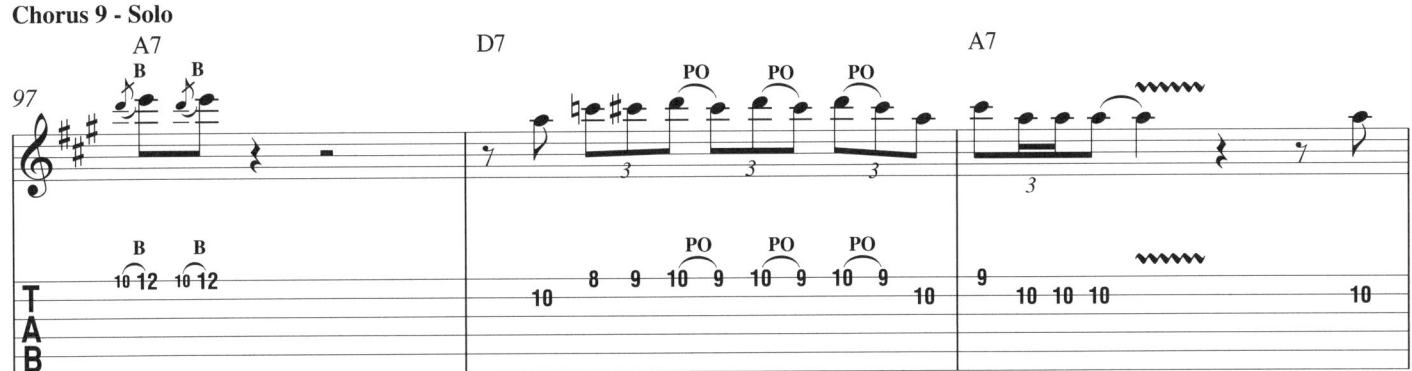

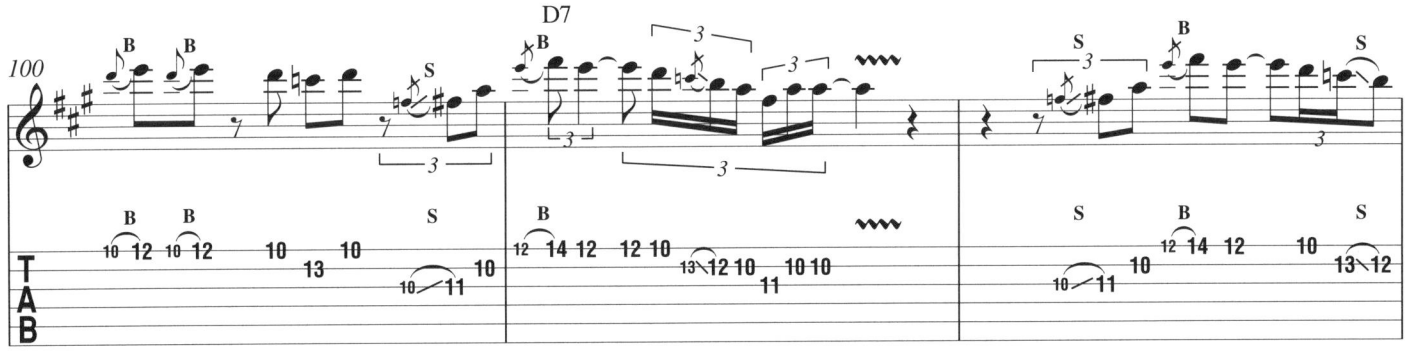

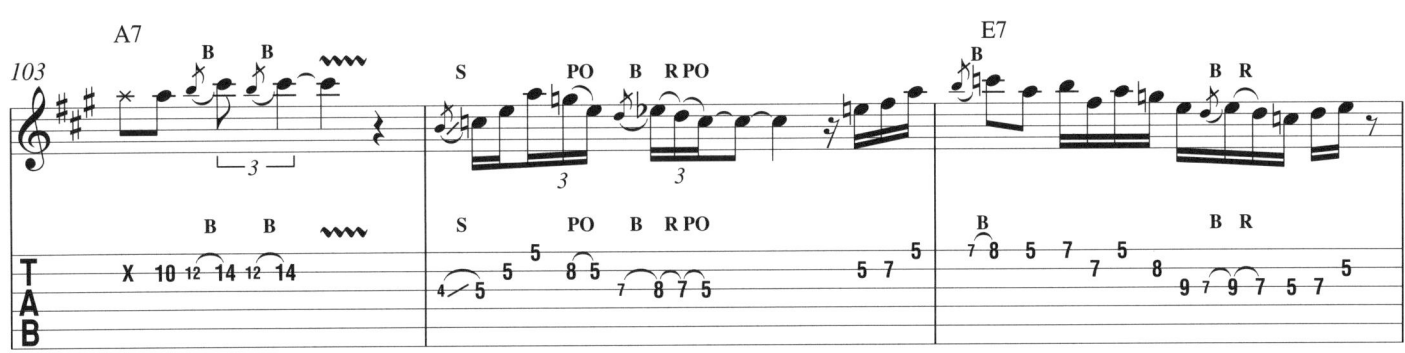

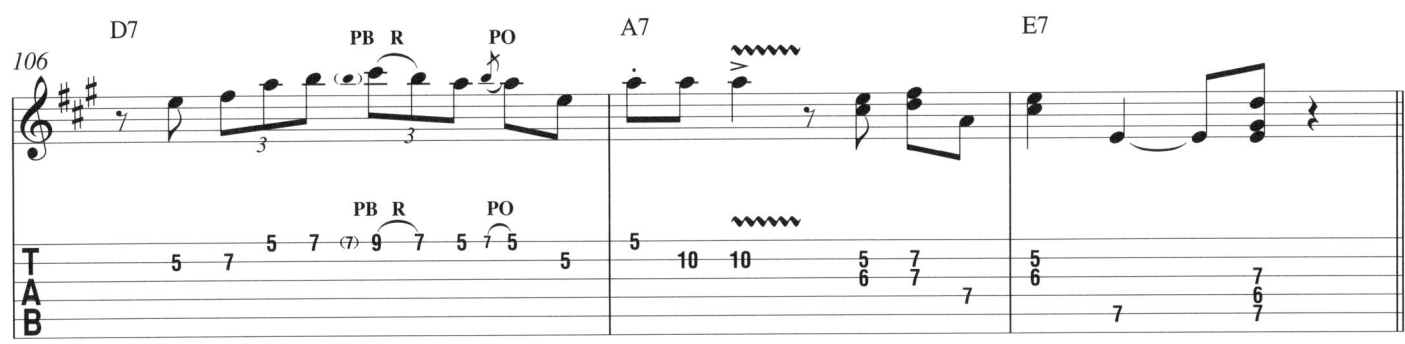

Chorus 10
(chords behind vocals - see additional lyrics)

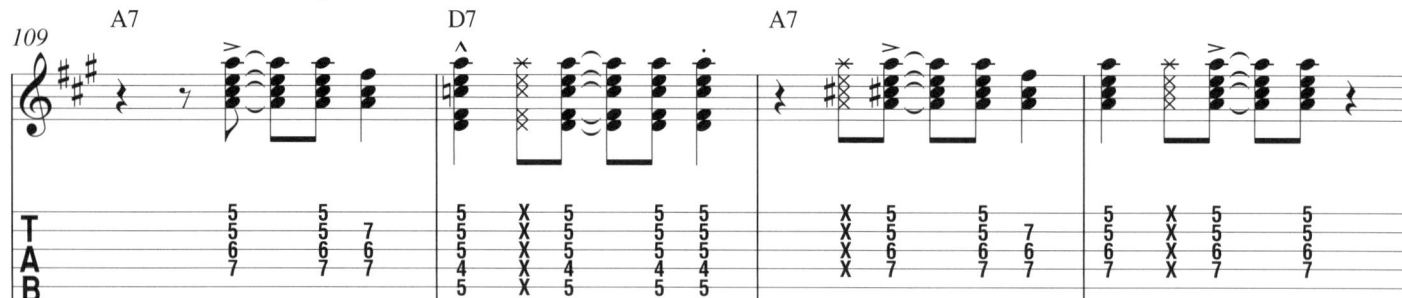

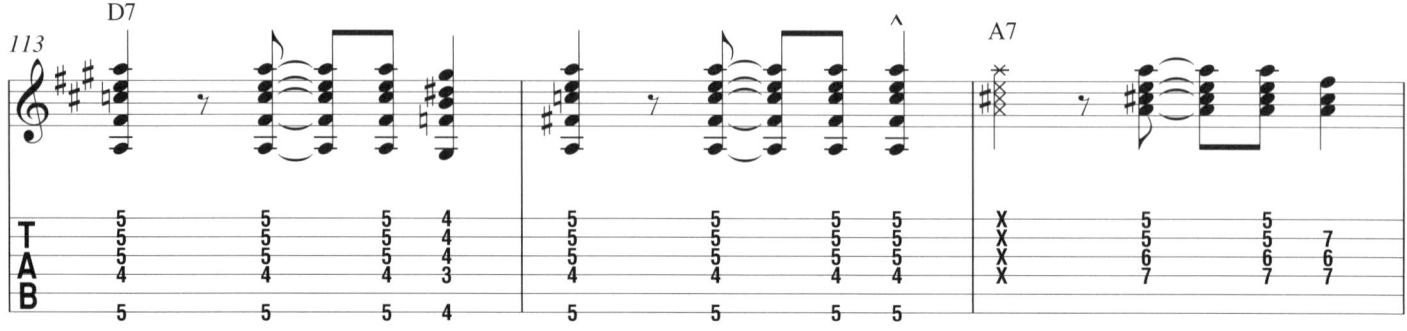

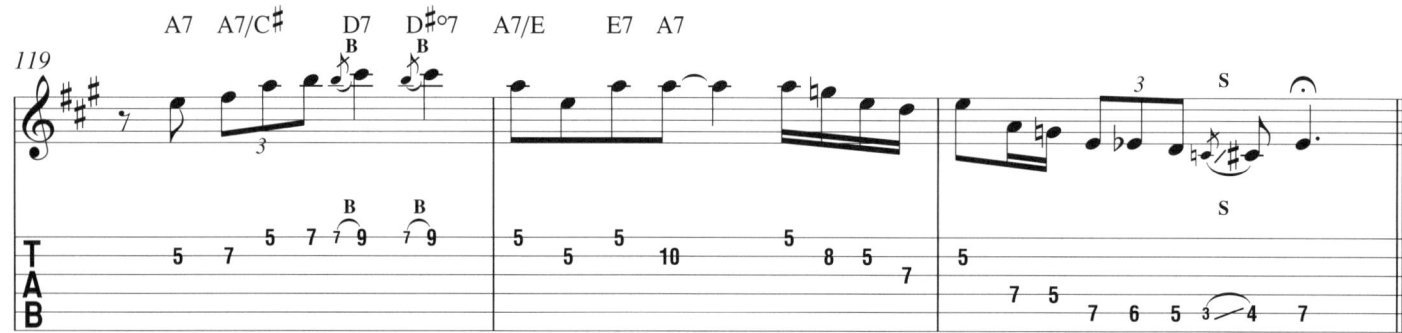

Additional Lyrics

7. I know my luck has been bad
   It's been bad so many days
   Yes my luck has been bad,
   It's been bad so many days, yeah
   Oh, please come to me baby
   Please don't turn my love away

8. Oh baby I need you so
   Oh baby, honey I don't know, I need you so
   Well, look right at me and say you'll take me
   So I can live just once more
   Oh yeah

10. Oh babe I need you so
    Yes baby, honey I don't know, I need you so
    Well, look right at me and say you'll take me
    So I can live just once more

CHAPTER 3

"The Last Time (I Get Burned Like This)" Robert Cray

Robert Cray's stinging and soulful attack and sound is instantly recognizable; it's unmistakable, after just two or three notes. In the midst of thousands of blues guitarists and vocalists performing around the world today, Robert Cray has managed to find his own distinctive and very personal voice, and that puts him on a very short list of modern blues artists.

Robert Cray was born in Columbus, Georgia in 1953. His father was in the military, and his family moved around quite a bit in his early years. After living in Germany and a few states around the U.S., Cray and his family eventually landed in Tacoma, Washington in 1968.

Inspired by artists such as Sam Cooke and Ray Charles from an early age, Robert Cray's first instrument was piano. He switched to guitar in the early '60s. While still in high school, Cray met one of his major inspirations and mentors for guitar, Albert Collins, when Collins was hired to perform at Cray's high school graduation.

In 1974, Cray formed the Robert Cray band along with longtime friend and bassist Richard Cousins, and not long after that, Cray and the band began backing up Albert Collins on tours up and down the west coast. Cray recorded his first album, *Who's Been Talking*, in 1979. Six years later, in 1985, after many tours and two more records in his own name, he was awarded his first Grammy for the record *Showdown*, recorded with fellow guitarists Albert Collins and Johnny Copeland. With a number of highly successful recordings and tours to his credit since then, Cray has gone on to win five Grammys (to date), and to become one of the most prolific and important artists in contemporary blues.

"The Last Time (I Get Burned Like This)" was released on *False Accusations* by HighTone Records in 1985, and with subtle and swinging triplet-based strumming patterns, arpeggiated chords, and Memphis-soul inspired double-stops throughout, this slow 12/8 ballad features a rhythm part that masterfully supports Cray's soul-drenched vocals. On ballads such as this, it's essential for the rhythm part to leave plenty of room to breathe, in order to support the lyrics, and Cray pulls that off exceptionally. Along with Jimi Hendrix, Stevie Ray Vaughan, and a few others, Robert Cray is among the very best at singing and playing at the same time, and this rhythm part is a perfect example of what to play (as well as what not to play) in order to support the vocals, for maximum impact.

PERFORMANCE TIPS

Rhythm Part

Cray's intro (figure 3.1) is the instrumental "hook" of the song. It repeats in several places throughout the track, so it's a great place to start. Cray begins the intro with pickup notes on beat 4, played as a triplet up the notes E, G, and A (5, ♭7, and 1), to set up the A minor triad on beat 1.

In bars 1–2 of the intro, Cray mixes Memphis-soul-influenced double stops on the top two strings (e.g., the triplets in bar 1, beat 2, and in bar 2, beats 2 and 3) with a series of thirds that are diatonic to the key of A minor on the 2nd and 3rd strings (e.g., bar 1, beats 3 and 4 and bar 2, beat 1 and the triplet on beat 4). To wrap up the intro in bar 3, Cray arpeggiates a B minor triad on the top 3 strings, then he descends down notes F E D C B (from an A minor scale), to set up his vocal verse at letter A.

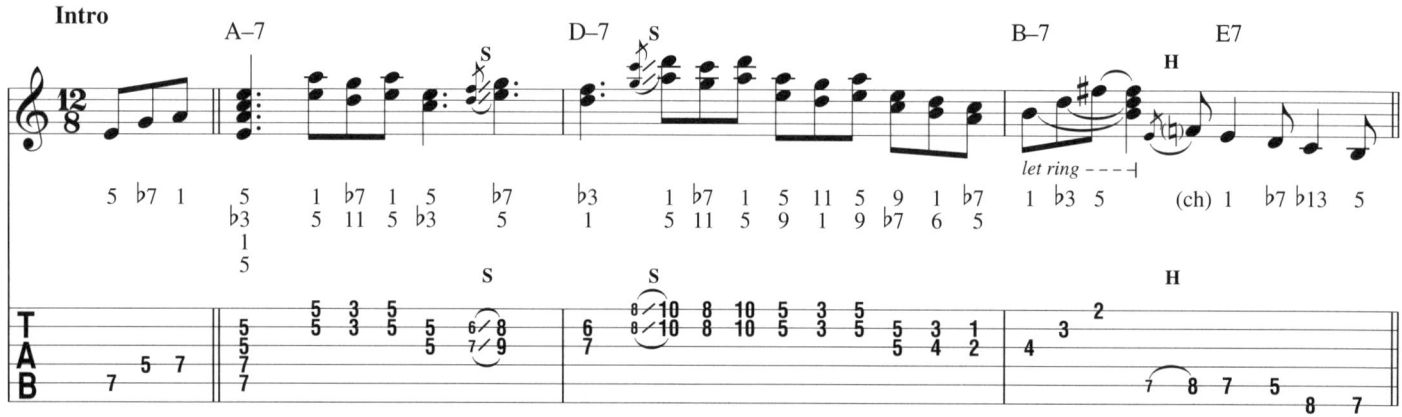

Fig. 3.1. "The Last Time…" Excerpt Bars 1–3

Next, to support his vocal verses at letters A, B, and D, Cray combines a few different strumming patterns and arpeggios through the chord changes. The A minor chord on beat 1 of each verse is played in position 5, as is the D–7 chord on beat 2. The chord changes that follow are within just a few frets; the E7(♯9) and F6 chords are played in position 6, and the FMaj9 chord is in 7th position.

If you listen carefully to Cray's rhythm part, you'll notice that his sixteenth-note strums throughout the track are played with a triplet/swing feel, similar to his sixteenth strums on the F6 in bar 5, on E7(♯9) in bar 6, and over the FMaj9 and F6 chords in bar 7. To internalize nuances such as the swinging sixteenth-note strums, it should be helpful to listen repeatedly to the demonstration track. As with all of the transcriptions in this book, I strongly recommend listening and playing along with Robert Cray's original recording.

Letter B is an excellent example of Cray's mix of arpeggios and strumming patterns through the chord changes. This 6-bar section is similar to his part behind his first verse at letter A, except that Cray plays arpeggios through a few more of the chords, such as in bars 11 and 12.

Note: Cray approached the F6 in bar 12 chromatically from above, with a (passing) G♭6 chord on the last eighth note of the triplet in beat 2. He repeated that G♭6 chord in the same place of the next verse, in letter D (bar 28).

Note that the chorus (which begins at letter C in bar 17) moves to the key of C; that's the "relative major" to the rest of the song, which is in the key of A minor. Cray played arpeggios throughout the chorus, beginning on the C chord for beats 1–3, and then he moves up to position 7 to strum notes from the E–7 chord on beat 4.

Bars 18–20 feature a few interesting "upper-structures" played as arpeggios, which are voice-led from chord to chord. Over the FMaj7 (for beats 1 and 2 of bar 18), Cray arpeggiates though an A minor triad in 5th position, and lets the bass player provide the (low) root sound for the chord. Combined with the bass player's low F note, Cray's upper structure A minor triad (ACE) creates a great sounding FMaj7 chord. Next, on beats 3 and 4, Cray changes the E notes (on the second string) to Fs, to arpeggiate through an F triad. In bar 19, he includes the note D (on the 5th string) below the F triad (on strings 432), voice-leading into a D–7 arpeggio for the entire measure. In bar 20, he changes the F to an E (on the B string) to bring the chord change back to A minor.

Bars 21 and 22 are similar to bars 17 and 18, and to finish off the chorus in bars 23 and 24, Cray smacks four high-impact E7(♯9) chords (played as the first two eighth-notes in each triplet) on beats 1 and 3, followed by a line (in bar 24) that descends down the notes EE DD CC BB from the A minor scale, to set up his third vocal verse at letter D.

Cray's rhythm part at letter D is similar to his verses at letters A and B, except for an interesting variation on the E7(♯9) chord: in bar 27, Cray arpeggiates through an E7(♭9) as a substitution, instead.

Solo

Robert Cray's solo "The Last Time (I Get Burned Like This)" is a powerful lesson in "less-is-more." Rather than using the song as a vehicle to feature lightening-fast soloing chops, Cray chose instead to let the solo serve the song; his phrases perfectly convey the emptiness, emotion, and story line of the lyrics. His solo phrases emerge as sparse long tones, soulful string bends, and vibrato-laden minor triads, which then morph into brittle flurries of blue notes to signal the end.

With no wasted notes, Cray's phrases on this brief, 8-bar solo show maturity and restraint. Yet, while listening to his original track (for perhaps the hundredth time), I have to wonder if it's *humanly possible* to shake, squeeze, or coax more soul from the strings of a Stratocaster.

Cray's solo is played over alternating A–7 and D–7 (I–7 and IV–7) chords, and his "pickup notes" to the solo begin on beat 4 of bar 31 with a sparse, funky triplet. Notice that each note in the triplet is preceded with a hammer on. Cray's phrases are full of subtle nuances such as this, and they are essential for conveying the solo's intensity and impact.

Several notes throughout this solo seethe with Cray's brand of slow, intense vibrato. With that much vibrato, it's easy to make the notes sound sharp (out of tune), so be aware of your pitch as you shake/rock the strings back and forth!

Cray shakes more than one note at a time in several places. In bar 34, over the A–7 chord, he shakes E and G notes (chord tones 5 and ♭7) together on the 2nd and 3rd strings. In bar 35, he shakes a D minor triad on the top three strings. Likewise, in bar 36, Cray shakes an A minor triad on the top three strings. Notice that he played the phrase with a strong "2 against 3" triplet feel throughout beats 1–3. Cray ramps up the intensity level in bar 37, with a phrase featuring two mighty powerful string bends on the high E string in 8th position.

Nearing the end of his solo in bar 38, Cray again lays on the vibrato, as he ascends through A minor and G triads (on strings 321), followed by a colorful D–9 chord on the top four strings on beat 1 of bar 39. For that voicing, Cray taps into another upper-structure; he plays a close-position FMaj7 chord. Combined with the bass player's D note sounding below, it creates a powerful D–9 chord.

For his last few notes in bar 39, Cray returns to 5th position (where he began the solo), to ratchet up the intensity level to the breaking point, with a flurry of brittle string bends, releases, and pull-offs, based around the A minor pentatonic scale.

Cray's mastery of nuances, such as string bends, vibrato, hammer-ons, pull-offs, and slides, combined with all of the space between his phrases at this slow, dramatic tempo, makes this solo *much* more difficult to play than it sounds. So good luck with Cray's rhythm part and solo. I hope you enjoy this track as much as I have.

CHAPTER 3 "The Last Time (I Get Burned Like This)" Robert Cray 27

ABOUT THE CD

"The Last Time" Full Band

"The Last Time" No Guitar

Tracks 5 and 6 for "The Last Time (I Get Burned Like This)" follow the same song form and format as Robert Cray's original recording.

The Last Time (I Get Burned Like This)
As Played by Robert Cray

Words and Music by
Robert Cray

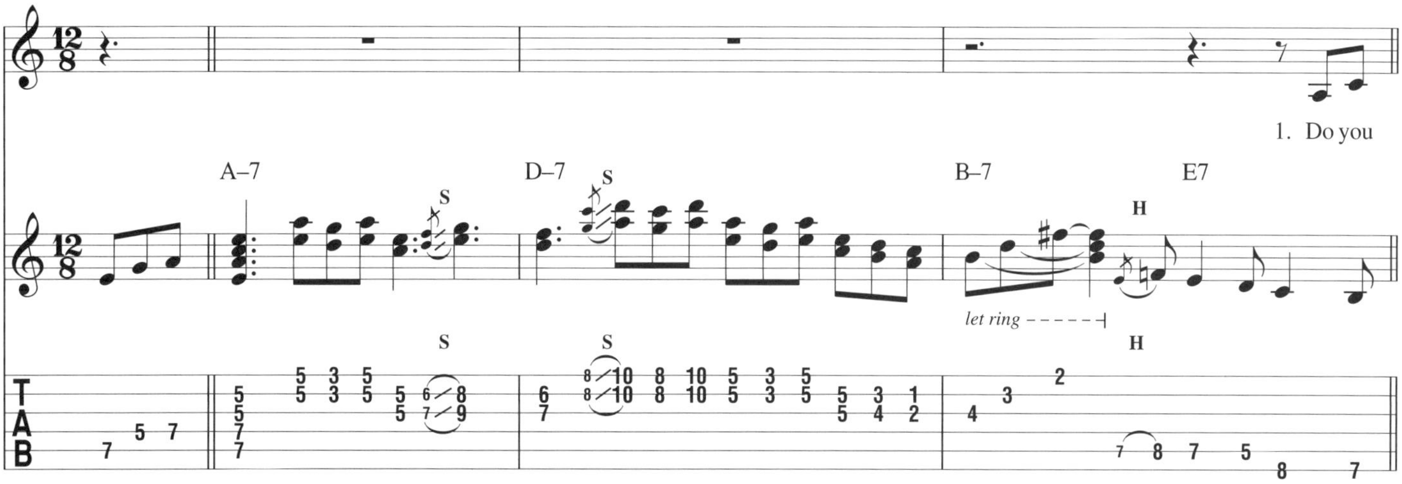

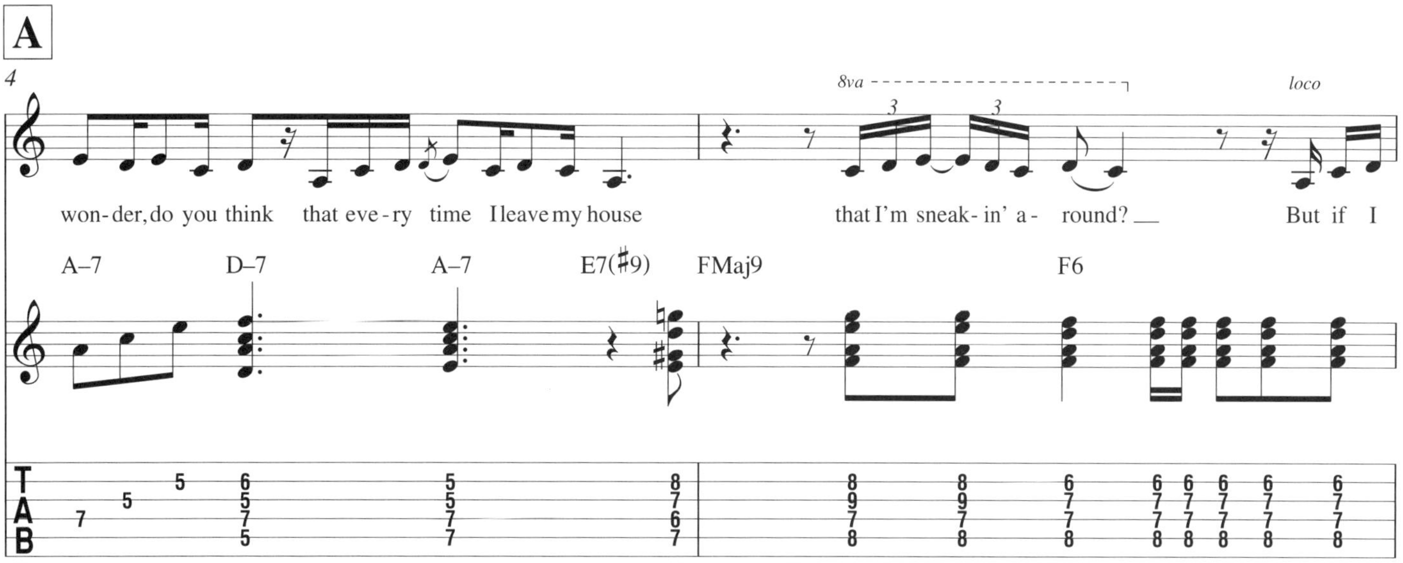

© 1985 BUG MUSIC (BMI) and BUG MUSIC-SONGS OF WINDSWEPT (BMI)/Administered by BUG MUSIC
All Rights Reserved Used by Permission

CHAPTER 3 "The Last Time (I Get Burned Like This)" Robert Cray 29

C

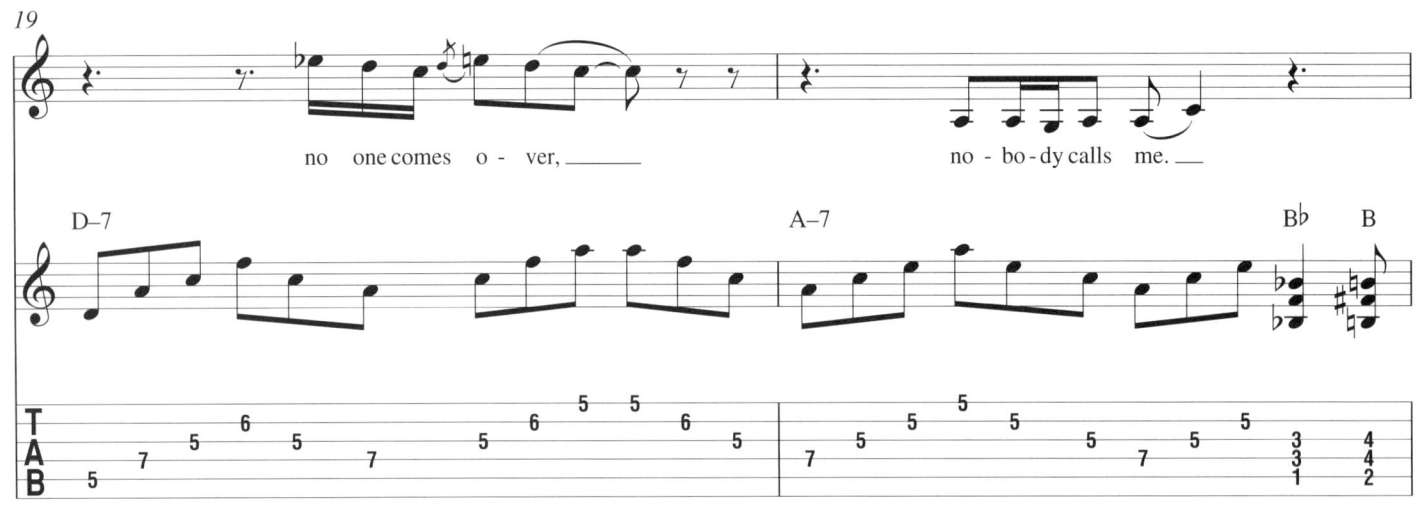
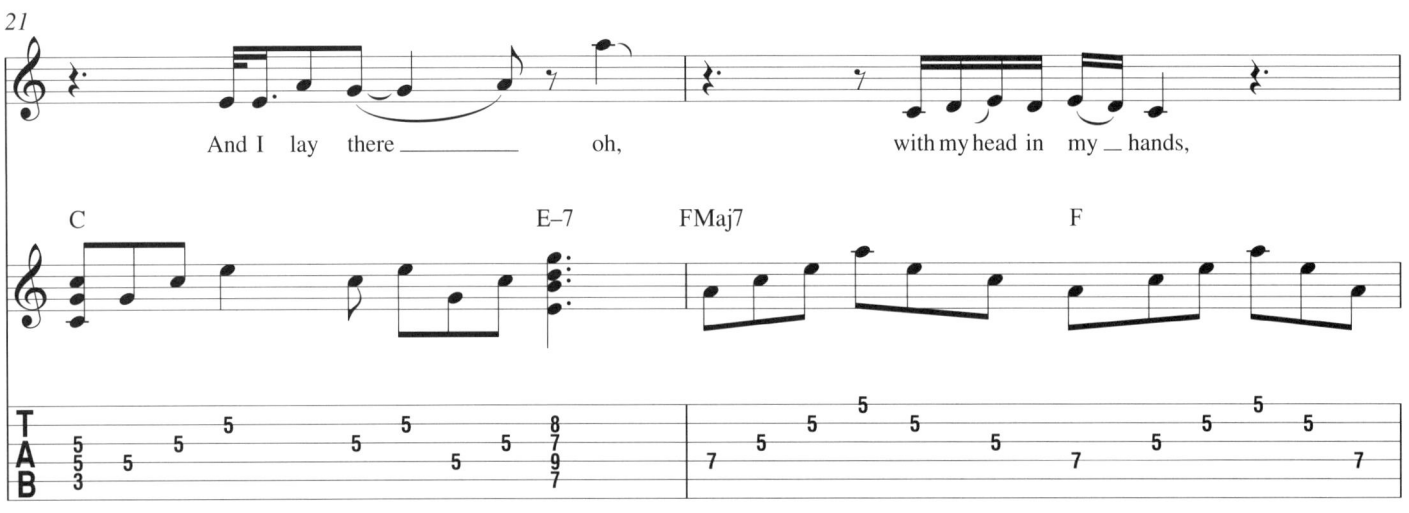
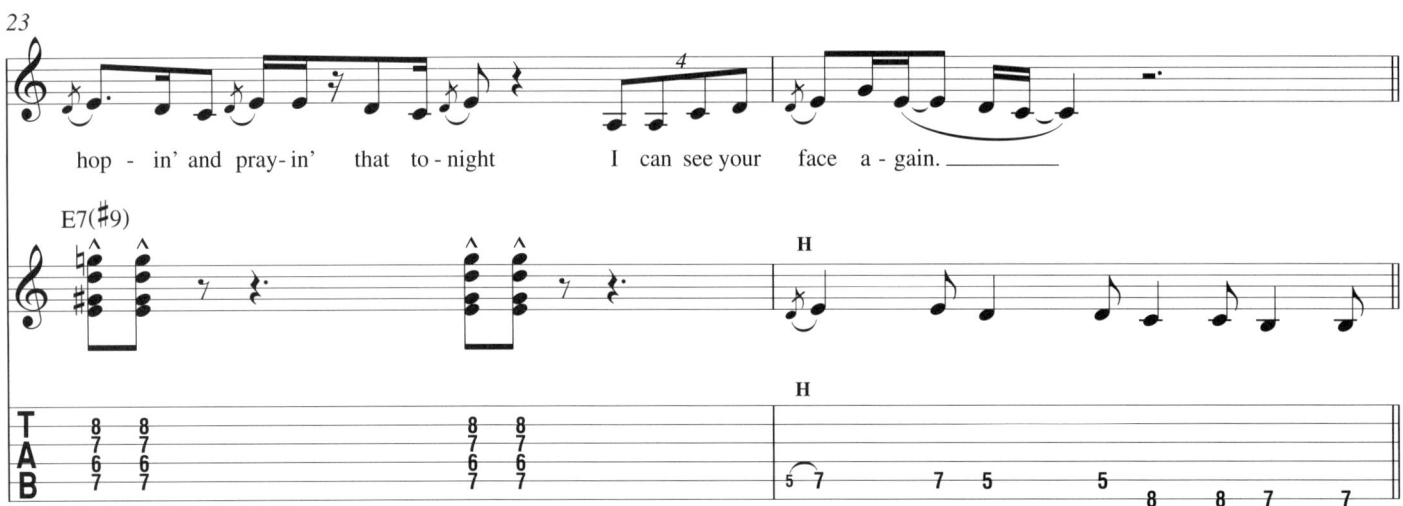

CHAPTER 3 "The Last Time (I Get Burned Like This)" Robert Cray

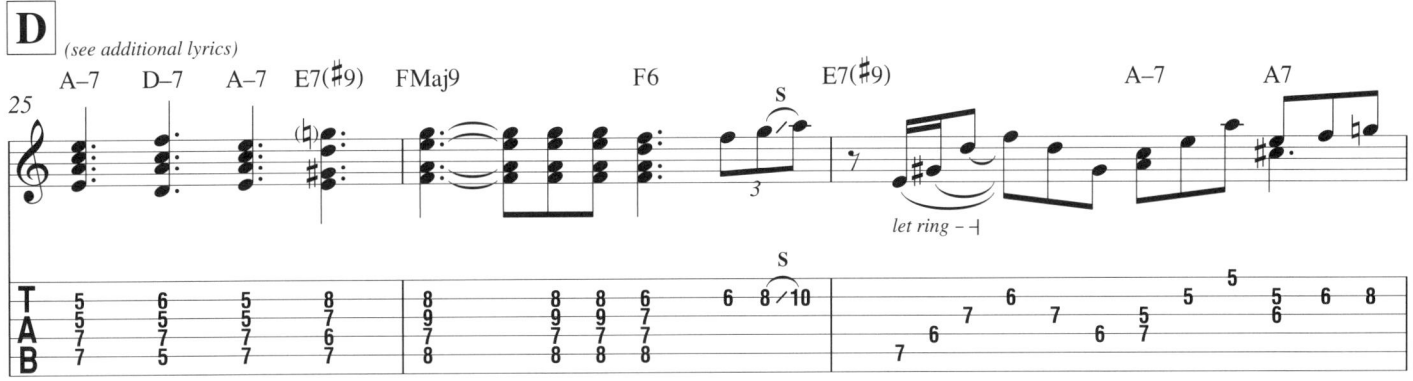
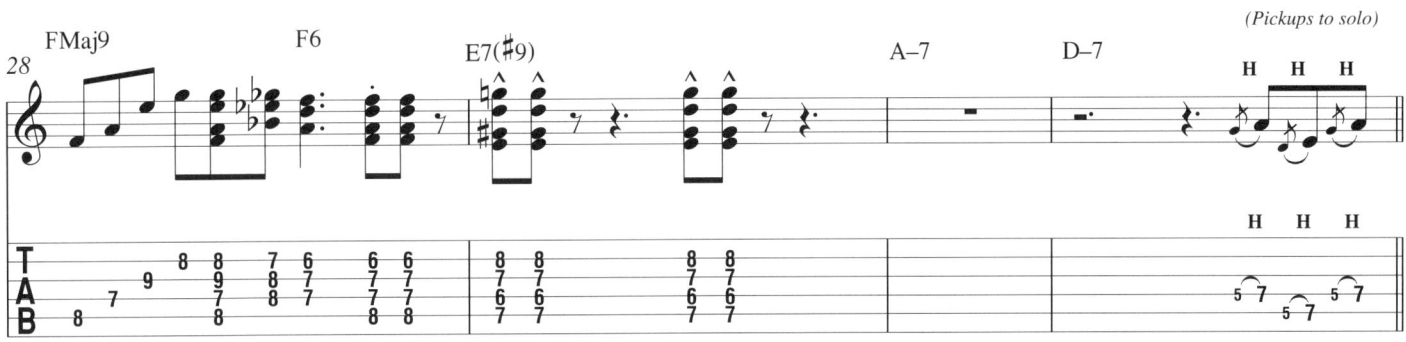
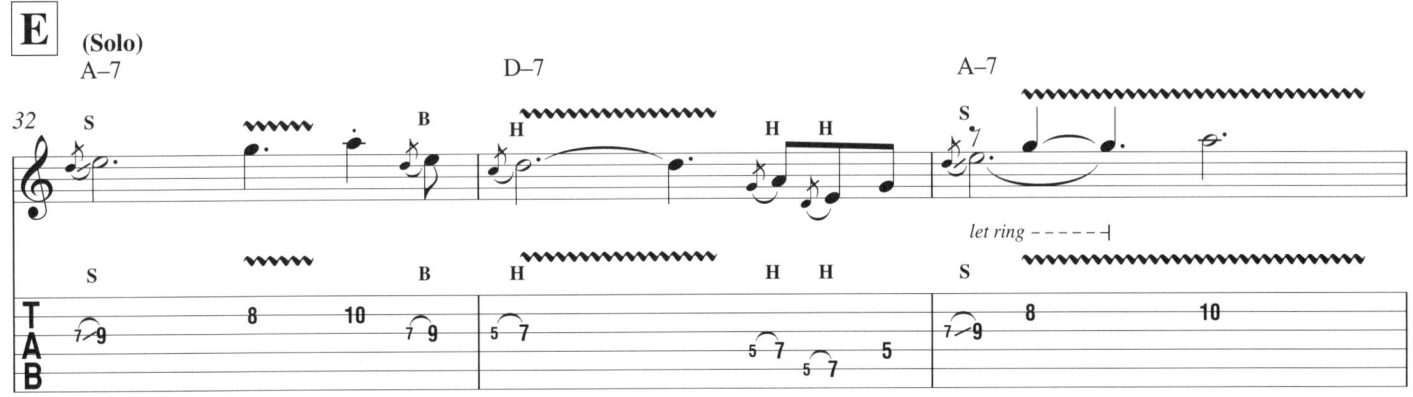
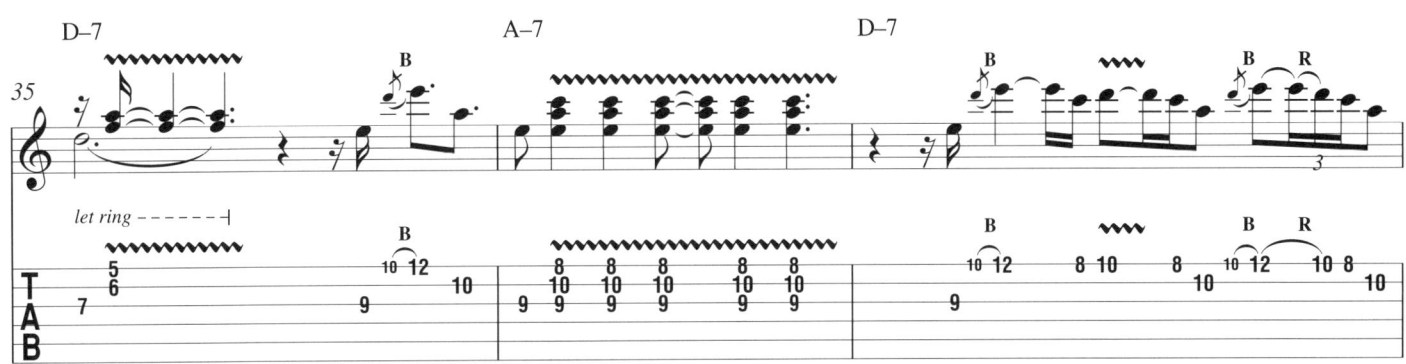

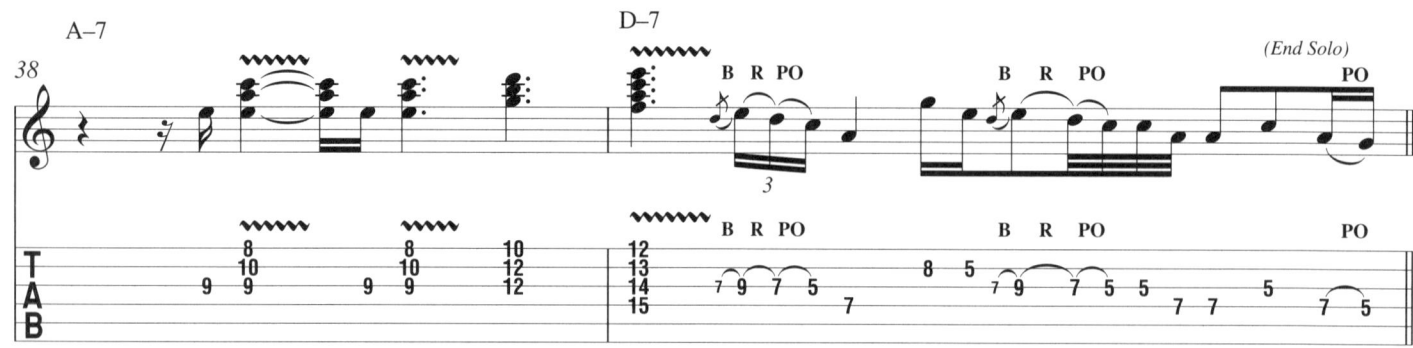
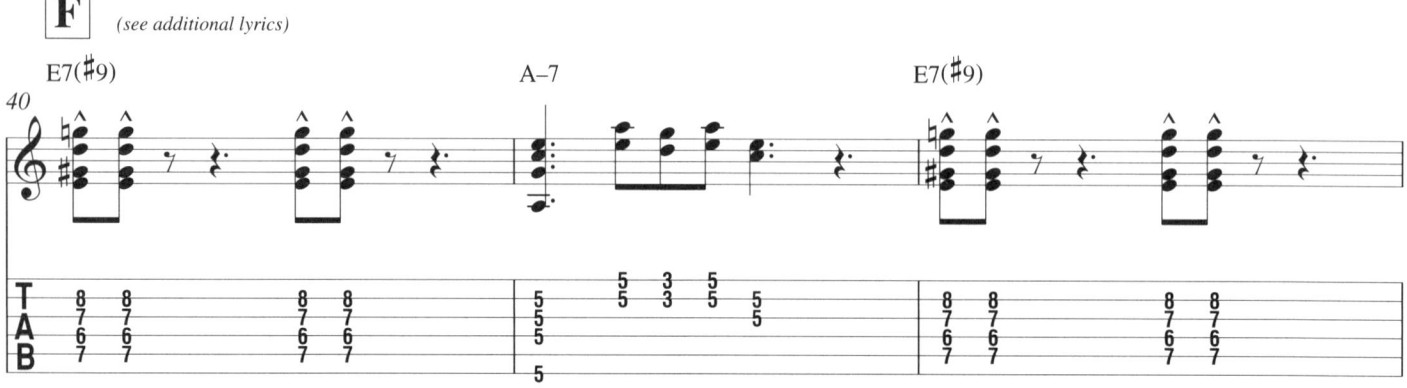
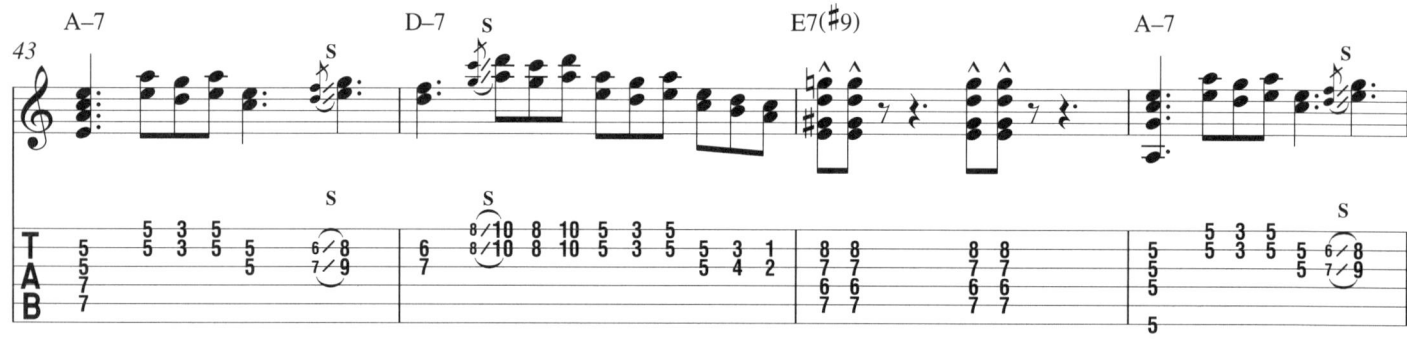
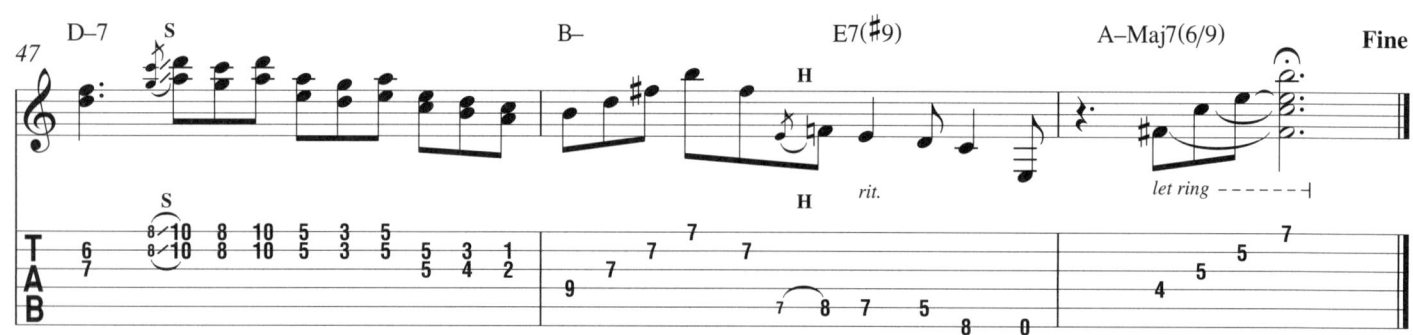

Additional Lyrics:

Vocal verse at **D**

Tomorrow's the start
Of a brand new day
And all the lessons that I've learned
Will help to pave my way
And it'll be the last time
That I get burned like this

Chorus and tag at **F**

It'll be the last time
That I get burned like this
The last time
That I get burned like this
I swear ohhh
The last time
That I get burned like this

CHAPTER 4

"Okie Dokie Stomp" Clarence "Gatemouth" Brown

Clarence "Gatemouth" Brown (1924 to 2005) has played a prominent role in the history of Texas blues and roots music, and he was one of the most unique and original guitarists to ever come from the Lone Star State. In addition to his highly respected skills as a blues guitarist and vocalist, Brown was very proficient on a number of other instruments, including fiddle, mandolin, harmonica, bass, and drums.

Throughout his sixty-year career, Brown's live performances and recordings reflected his diverse and eclectic influences, which ranged from blues, country, Cajun, and zydeco, to big band, swing, and r&b. Never content to be "pigeonholed" as a bluesman however, Brown defied being categorized, and instead referred to his music as "American music, Texas style."

Clarence "Gatemouth" Brown was born in Vinton, Louisiana, and moved with his family to southeastern Texas when he was very young. His earliest musical influence was his father, who played fiddle and guitar in Cajun and bluegrass bands. By the early/mid 1940s, T-Bone Walker's jazz-inflected phrases and big-band styled horns and arrangements had a powerful impact on Brown's music, and T-Bone's influences are particularly noticeable in some of Brown's early recordings.

Brown was adamant about finding his own voice on the instrument, however, and he eventually found it. With his "home-grown" finger-style right-hand technique, along with a capo—and his unique approach of parking/resting his first finger *behind* the capo when playing in open position (next to the capo)— Brown developed a very personal and easily recognizable sound, style, and vocabulary on guitar. Over his fifty-eight-year recording career, "Gate" was a major influence to many well-known guitarists, including Albert Collins, Guitar Slim, Johnny "Guitar" Watson, and Frank Zappa.

PERFORMANCE TIPS

"Okie Dokie Stomp" (by Pluma Davis, aka Plummer "Ivory" Davis) was originally recorded in 1954 on Peacock Records, and this jumping medium/up tempo instrumental became Brown's "signature" showcase for the decades that followed. Right from bar 1 of "Okie Dokie Stomp," Brown's eighth-note and triplet-based phrases careen forward with an onslaught of hammer-ons, pull-offs, and slides. Gate picks up momentum chorus after chorus, as he weaves in and around the big-band style horns with a rock-solid rhythmic feel and picking attack.

While listening along with Brown's original recording, you'll notice that all nine choruses are filled with call and response. His phrases connect with each other like rapid-fire conversation. Brown's high-intensity phrases sound vocally inspired, much like a blues lyric. Chorus 6 is a challenge, since it has fewer breaths/pauses between phrases, but for most of the track, Brown left plenty of room to breathe between his phrases.

Note: Brown played "Okie Dokie Stomp" in standard tuning, with a capo on the 11th fret. However, since this instrumental also plays and sounds great without the capo, I've written the music and tab to play in standard tuning without the capo.

Brown's phrases on "Okie Dokie Stomp" are rooted mostly in the E♭ blues scale, combined with the major 3rd (G), 6th (C), and 9th (F) from the E♭ major pentatonic scale. Since Gate's phrases are laced with quick and subtle nuances (such as hammer-ons, pull-offs, and slides in bars 3–6 of chorus 1), they're tricky in places!

Brown lays out for the 4th chorus; that's played as an interlude or "shout-chorus" for the horn section. Chorus 3 and chorus 7 are very similar (chorus 7 is basically a restatement of chorus 3).

The beginning of choruses 8 and 9 feature 4-bar stops by the band. Gate barrels right through both stops, as his scorching eighth-note and triplet-based fills take the intensity level to new heights.

"Okie Dokie Stomp" closes with another one of Brown's signature fills, as he descends right down the E♭ blues scale.

This roadhouse classic is a ton of fun to play. I hope you enjoy it!

ABOUT THE CD

 "Okie Dokie Stomp" Full Band
TRACK 7

 "Okie Dokie Stomp" No Guitar
TRACK 8

Tracks 7 and 8 for "Okie Dokie Stomp" are based on Clarence "Gatemouth" Brown's original recording, so they're nine choruses in length.

CHAPTER 4 "Okie Dokie Stomp" Clarence "Gatemouth" Brown

Okie Dokie Stomp
As played by Clarence "Gatemouth" Brown

Words and Music by
Plummer "Ivory" Davis

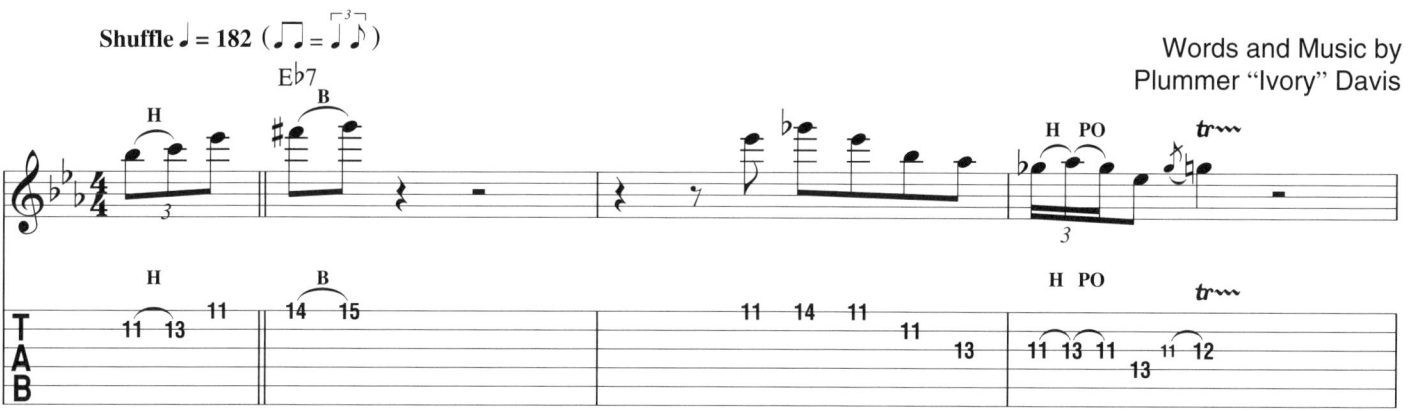
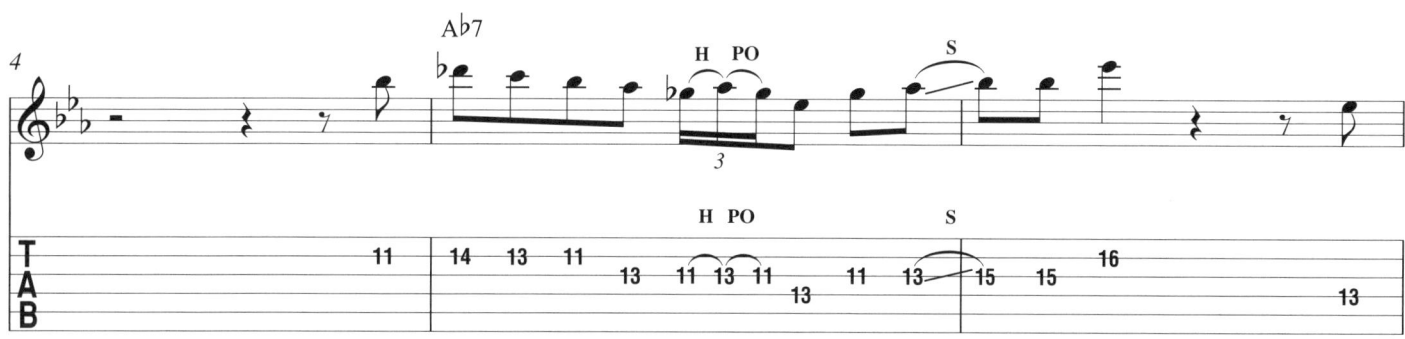
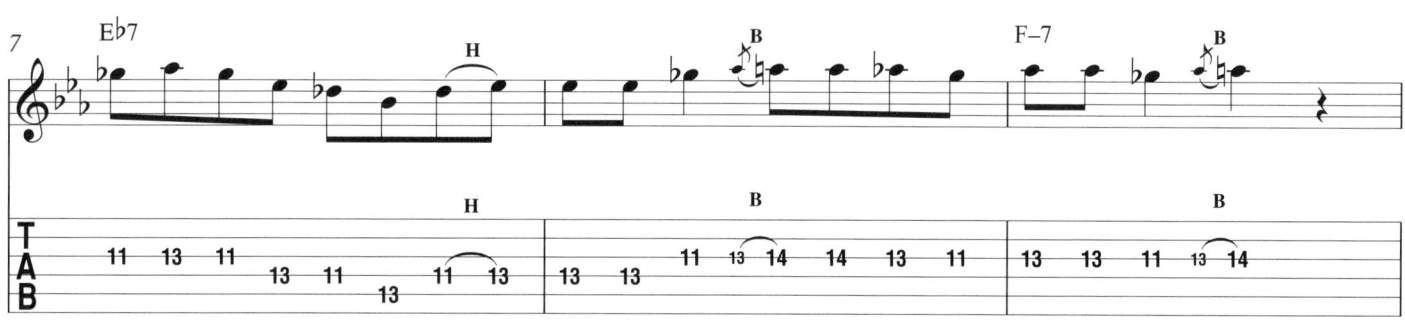
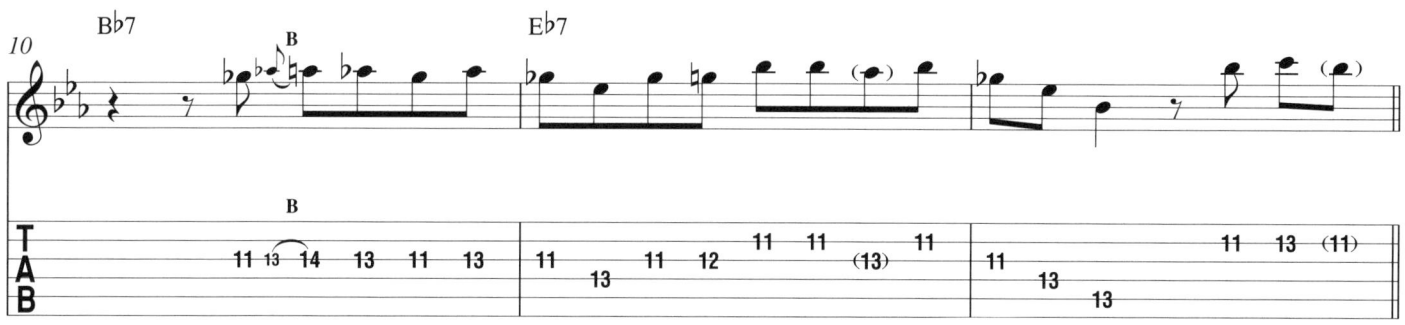

Copyright © 1954 SONGS OF UNIVERSAL, INC.
Copyright Renewed
All Rights Reserved   Used by Permission

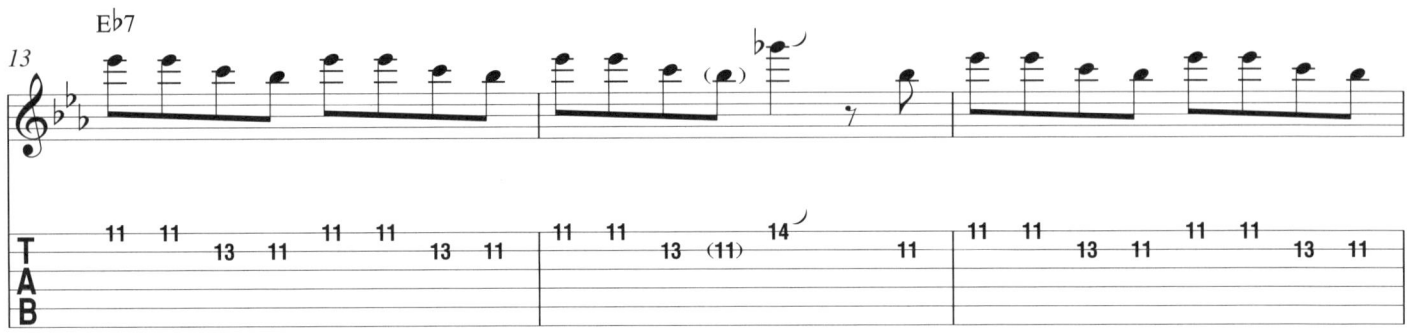

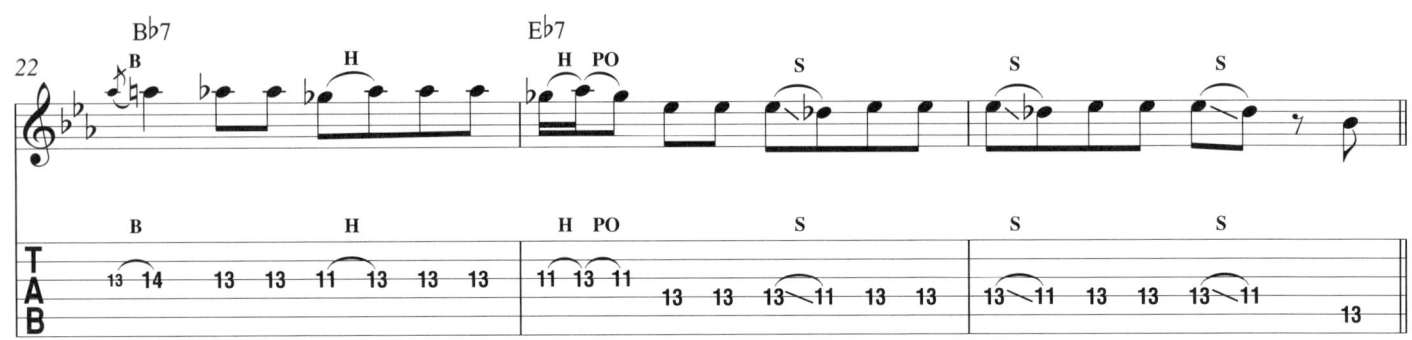

CHAPTER 4 "Okie Dokie Stomp" Clarence "Gatemouth" Brown

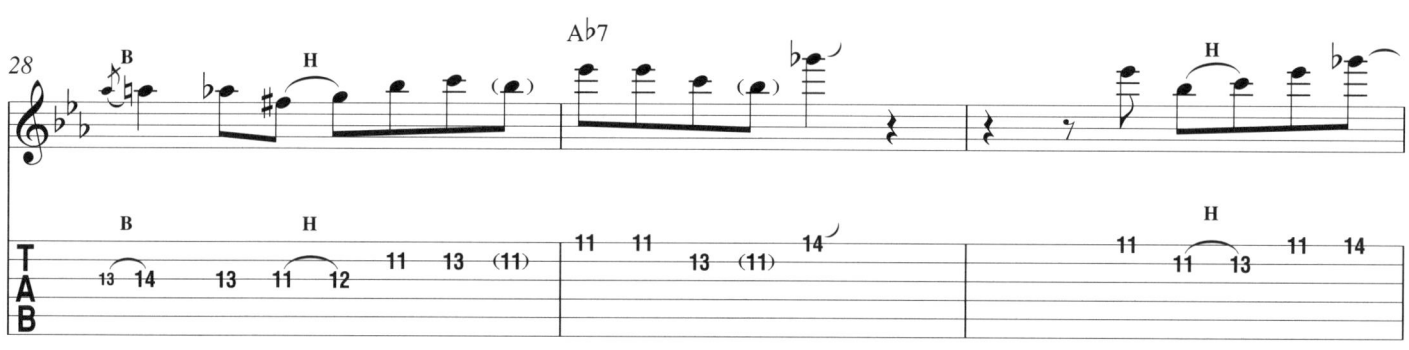
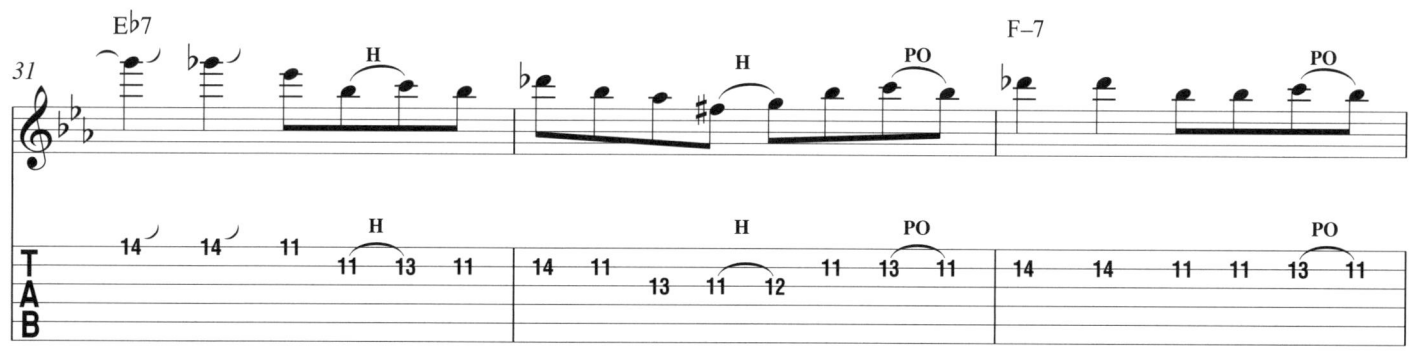
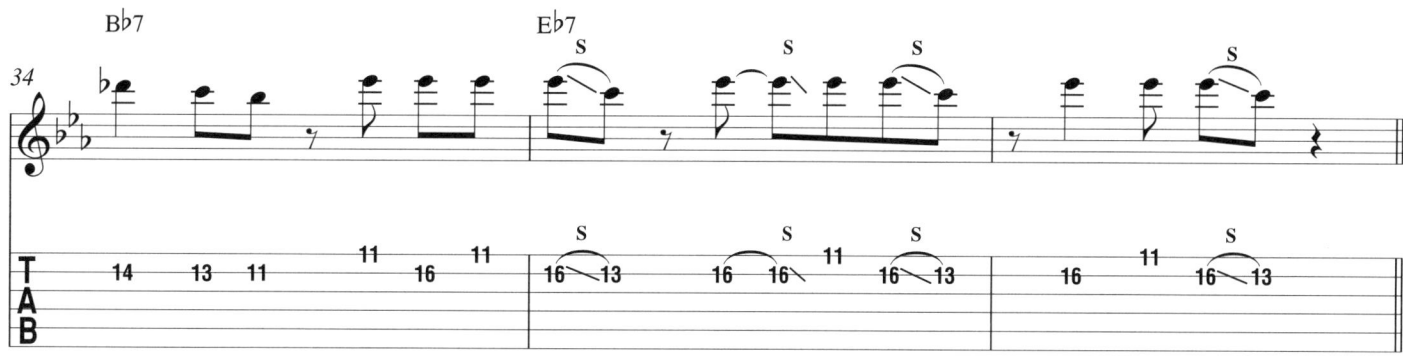

(horns and rhythm section only; guitar tacet this chorus)

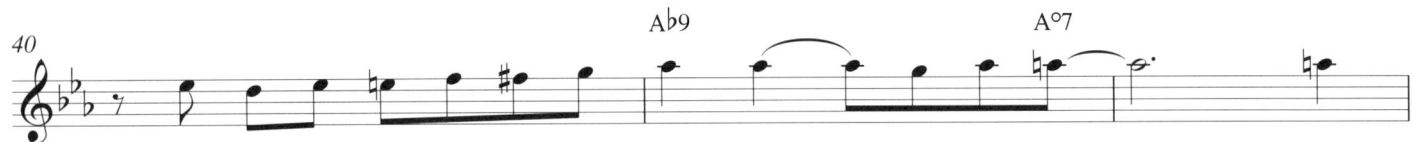

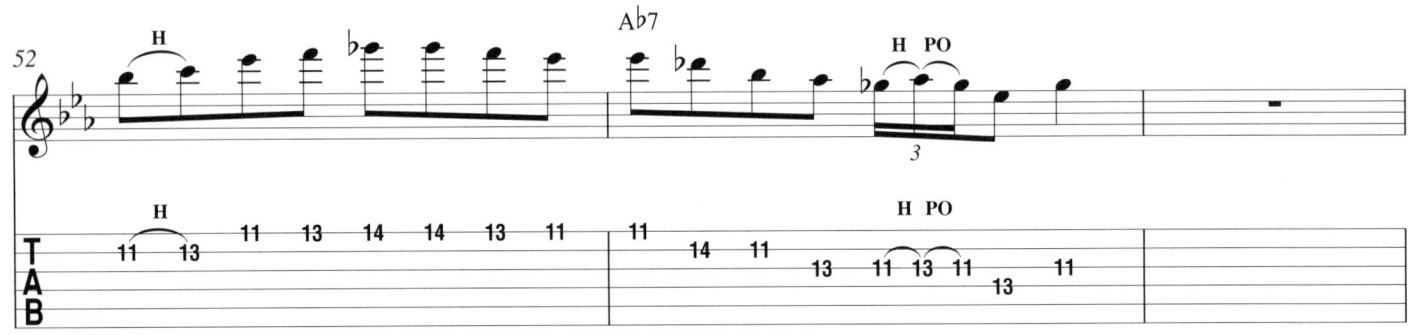

CHAPTER 4 "Okie Dokie Stomp" Clarence "Gatemouth" Brown

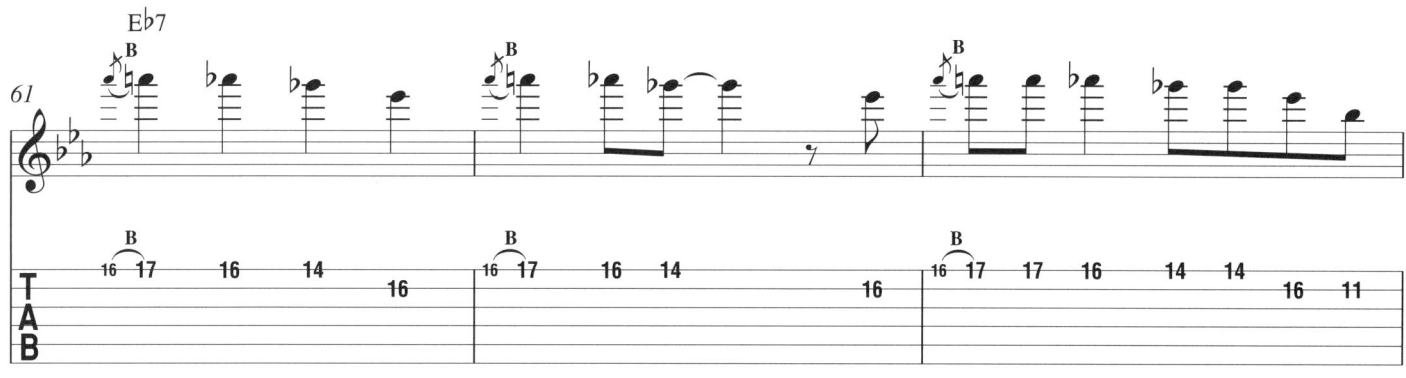
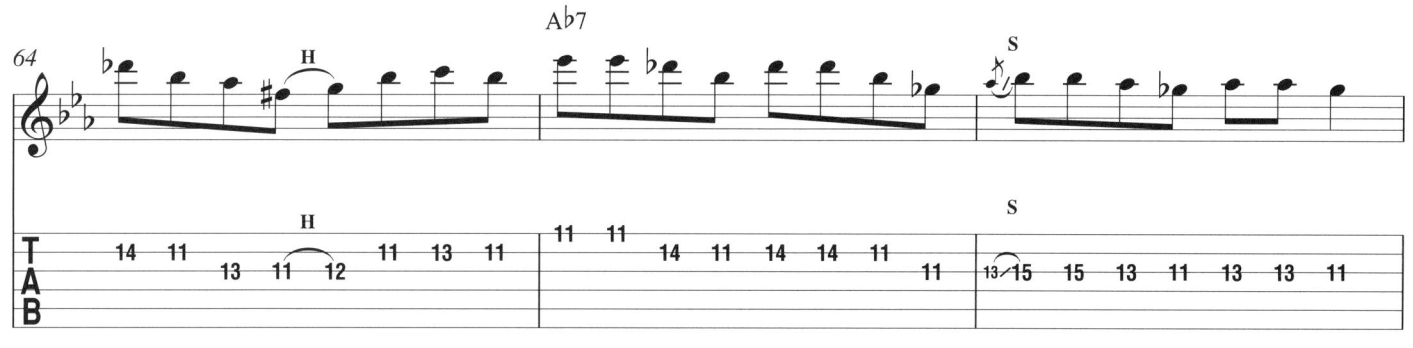

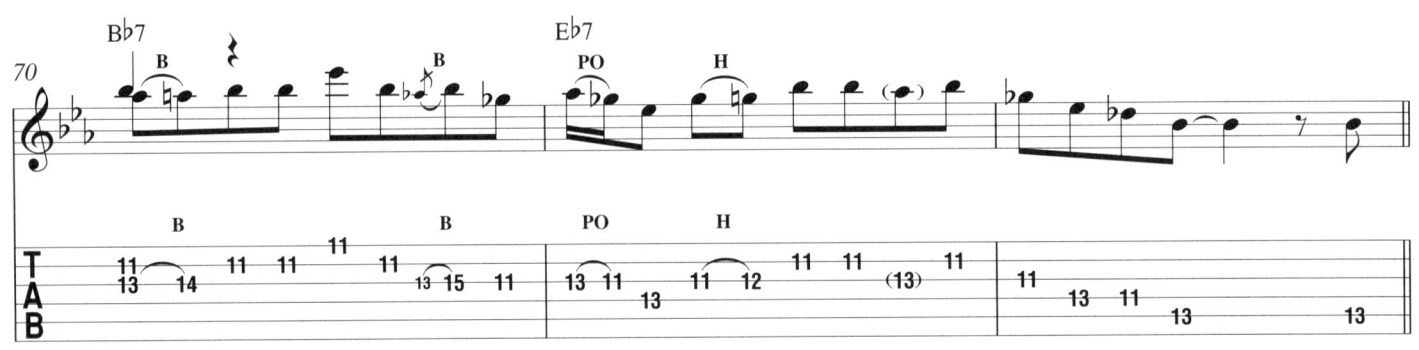

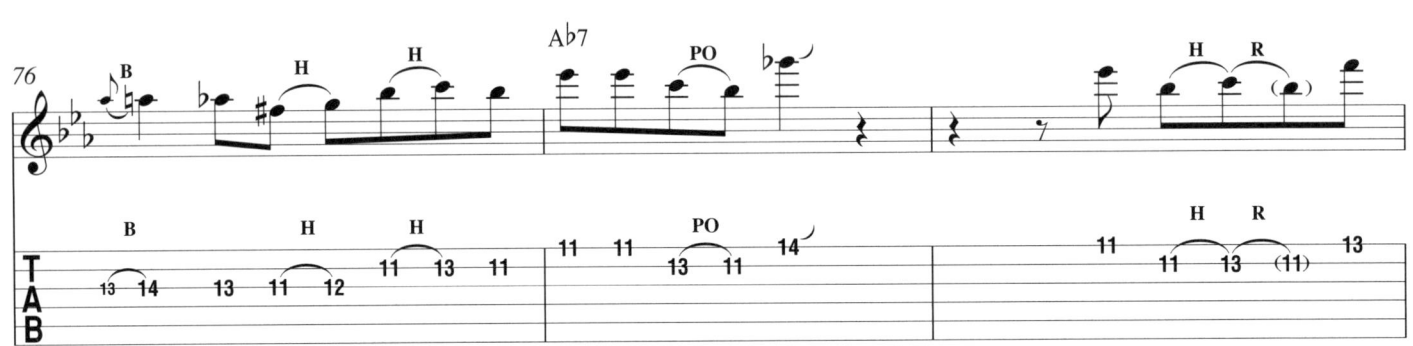

CHAPTER 4 "Okie Dokie Stomp" Clarence "Gatemouth" Brown

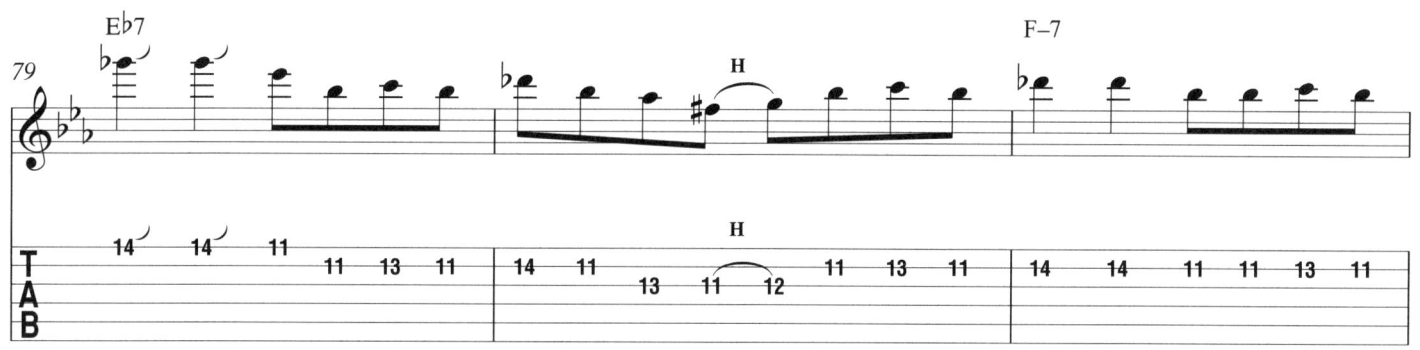
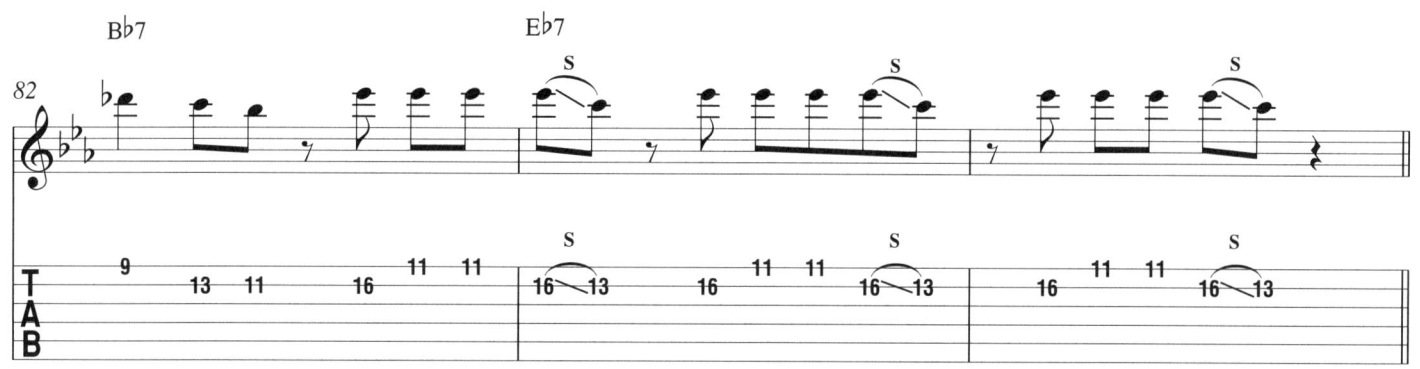
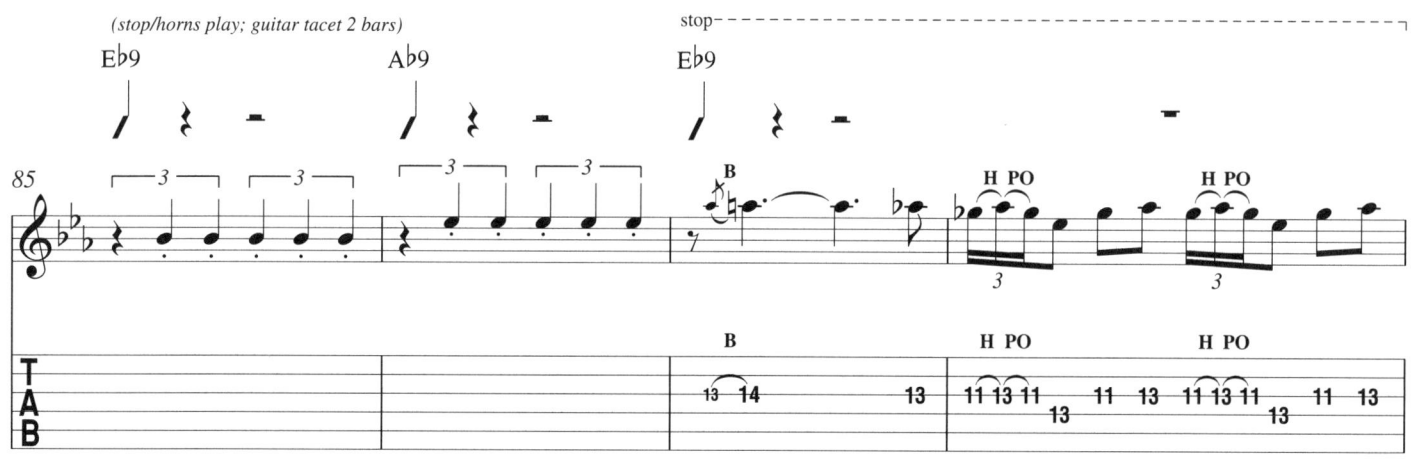
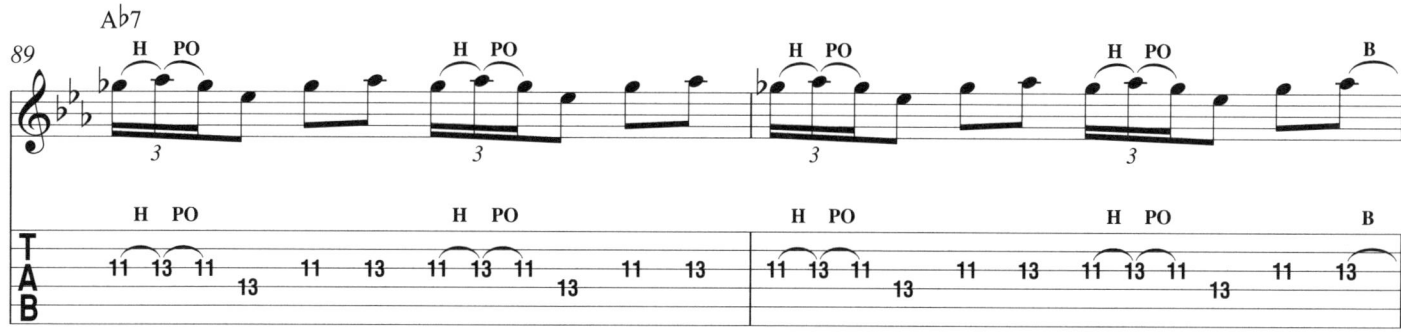

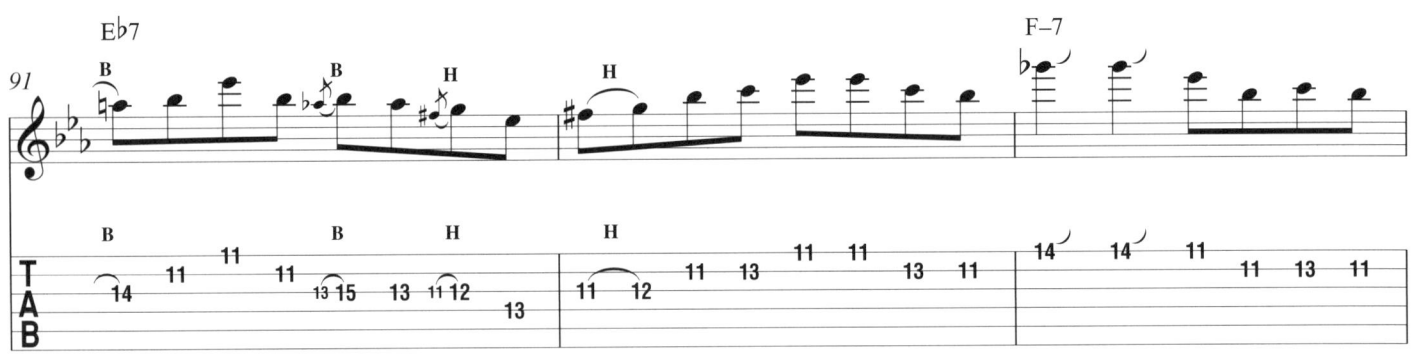
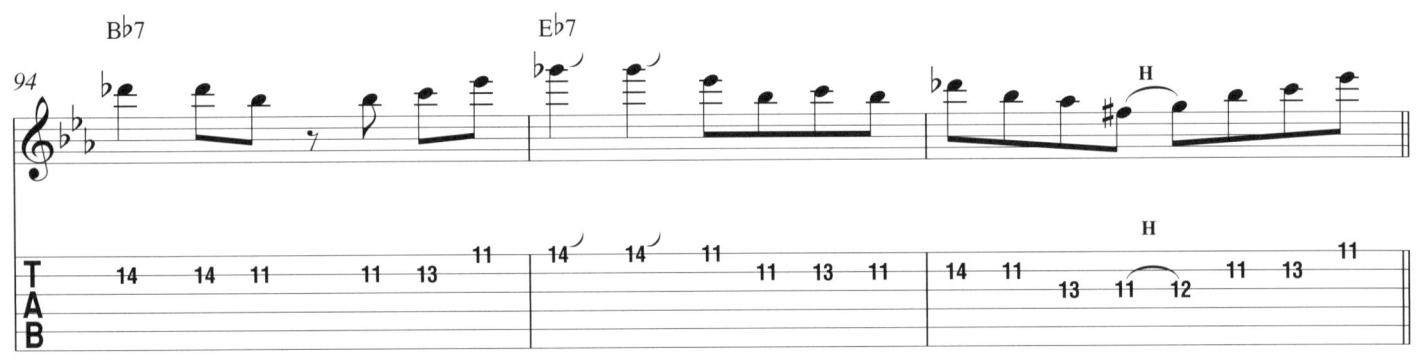

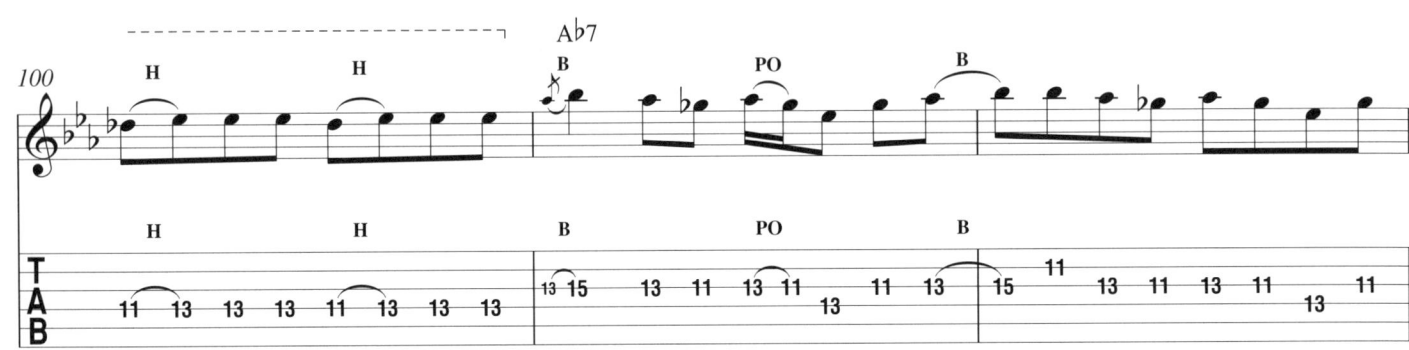

CHAPTER 4 "Okie Dokie Stomp" Clarence "Gatemouth" Brown

CHAPTER 5

"Papa Ain't Salty"
T-Bone Walker

Aaron Thibeaux Walker (1910 to 1975) was one of the true pioneers of the electric guitar, and his legacy and musical influences run vast and deep throughout the worlds of blues and rock. T-Bone Walker's impact on modern blues guitar's vocabulary and phrasing is easily recognizable in many greats that followed: B.B. King, Clarence "Gatemouth" Brown, Chuck Berry, Buddy Guy, Jimi Hendrix, Eric Clapton, Stevie Ray Vaughan, and so many others "went to school" on T-Bone.

Originally released on his classic *T-Bone Blues* in 1959 on Atlantic, T-Bone's phrases on the intro to "Papa Ain't Salty" (by T-Bone Walker and Grover McDaniel) are the very first notes you'll hear on the record.

PERFORMANCE TIPS

Both of T-Bone's solos from "Papa Ain't Salty" are comprised entirely of notes and phrases from the G blues and G pentatonic scales, and both solos are played in the 3rd position. (To play in the 3rd position, place your left-hand fingers [1 to 4] on frets 3, 4, 5, and 6.) This fingering for the blues scale is considered to be "home base" for most blues soloists, and as you'll notice, it's also home base for both choruses of T-Bone's solo.

The excerpt below from bars 6–8 of T-Bone's intro on "Papa Ain't Salty" features phrases that are derived from the G blues scale, combined with the 3rd (B), the jazzy/colorful 6th (E) and 2nd or 9th (A), from the G pentatonic scale. The phrase that starts on beat 3 (of the first bar) may sound familiar to you, because many other blues guitarists, including Stevie Ray Vaughan, have adapted it note-for-note into other keys, tempos, and musical contexts, for their own solos!

CHAPTER 5 "Papa Ain't Salty" T-Bone Walker

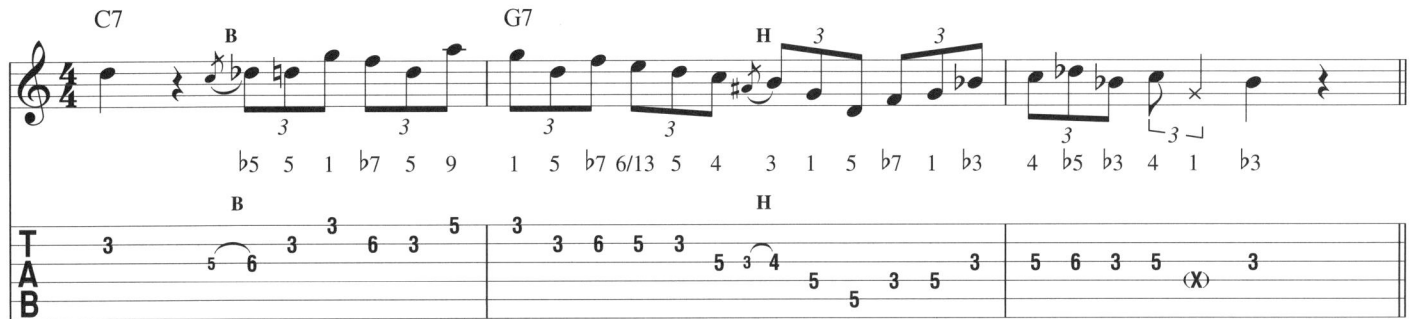

Fig. 5.1. "Papa Ain't Salty" Bars 6–8. Analyzed against a G7 chord.

The analysis (1 3 5 ♭7 etc.) included below the notes illustrates the relationship to both scales used in this solo.

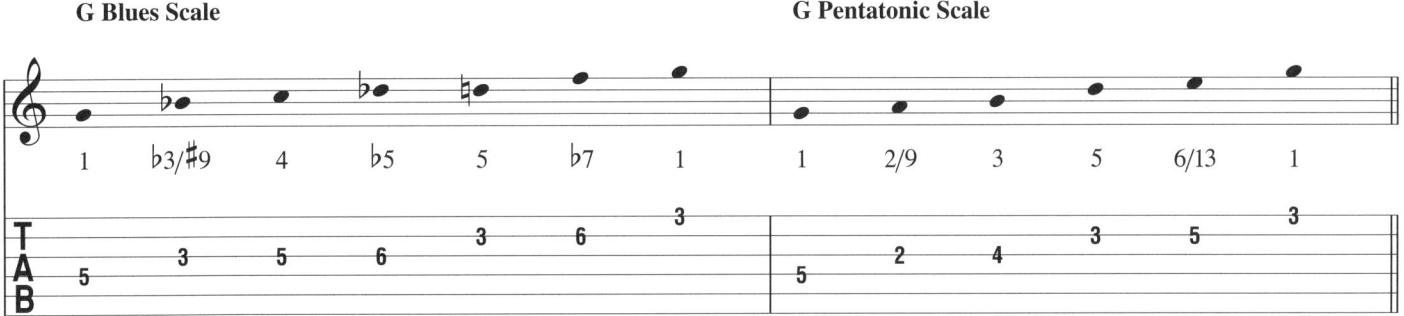

Fig. 5.2. Scales Used in "Papa Ain't Salty"

> ### STRING BENDS IN THE T-BONE STYLE
>
> T-Bone played with heavy strings, so for string bends in the "T-Bone style," avoid over-bending the notes. To get deeper inside the mind-set for T-Bone's sound and style (particularly if you're playing anything lighter than an .011 set), imagine that you're playing on heavier strings. Play them as half step, instead of whole step bends. As an example/illustration of T-Bone's frequent half step string bends, take a look and listen to his very first note(s) from both solos; both choruses begin with half step bends from C to D♭. Also try moving your picking hand back toward the bridge to create the sound and feel of a heavier set of strings; since there's more string tension right next to the bridge, it creates somewhat of a "thicker" sound. Avoid adding fast vibrato to the notes as well, since that wasn't a part of T-Bone's phrasing or sound on this track.

The intro solo to "Papa Ain't Salty" is a great project to tackle first, since it's chocked full of T-Bone's classic and influential phrases. Plus, it's quite a bit easier to play than his second chorus. T-Bone's intro phrases are based on eighth notes and triplets, and although his lines are not particularly fast, his phrases get longer and longer as the solo progresses. That makes this solo very challenging to work up to tempo.

On T-Bone's second solo, his phrases are faster, much denser, and rhythmically more active. Right from bars 2–3, his lines are based on more of a double time feel, with sixteenth notes and triplets, and several of his phrases fall rhythmically "between the cracks." These phrases are much more difficult to feel and to play. To master either of these solos, I strongly recommend playing along with T-Bone's original track to "Papa Ain't Salty" repeatedly.

After the intensity of his second chorus, T-Bone relaxed the pace with a chorus of his vintage sliding 9th chords. On the original recording, the rhythm guitarist "answered" T-Bone's sliding 9ths by repeating them; those answers are included on my play-along track as well.

Following the sliding 9ths chorus is a rhythm guitar part that's played throughout much of T-Bone's original track. Similar to a bass line, this single-note part is based on notes 1, 3, 5, and 6 of the G major scale (G, B, D, E). Finishing off the chorus—and the track—is one of T-Bone's signature ending licks.

Good luck with "Papa Ain't Salty," and remember to listen and play along with T-Bone!

ABOUT THE CD

For this book, four choruses of T-Bone's performance on "Papa Ain't Salty" are formatted into two separate tracks:

Full Band
TRACK 9

No Guitar
TRACK 10

Tracks 9 and 10 are T-Bone's intro solo (12 bars).

Tracks 11 and 12 are three choruses in length, with T-Bone's second 12-bar solo, followed by a chorus of his signature "sliding 9th" chords, and then one chorus of a sample rhythm part with T-Bone's ending.

Note: These tracks begin with a 2-bar intro, so count seven beats before playing the pickup notes to T-Bone's solo.

Full Band
TRACK 11

No Guitar
TRACK 12

CHAPTER 5 "Papa Ain't Salty" T-Bone Walker

Intro Solo

Papa Ain't Salty
As played by T-Bone Walker

Words and Music by Grover McDaniel
and T-Bone Walker

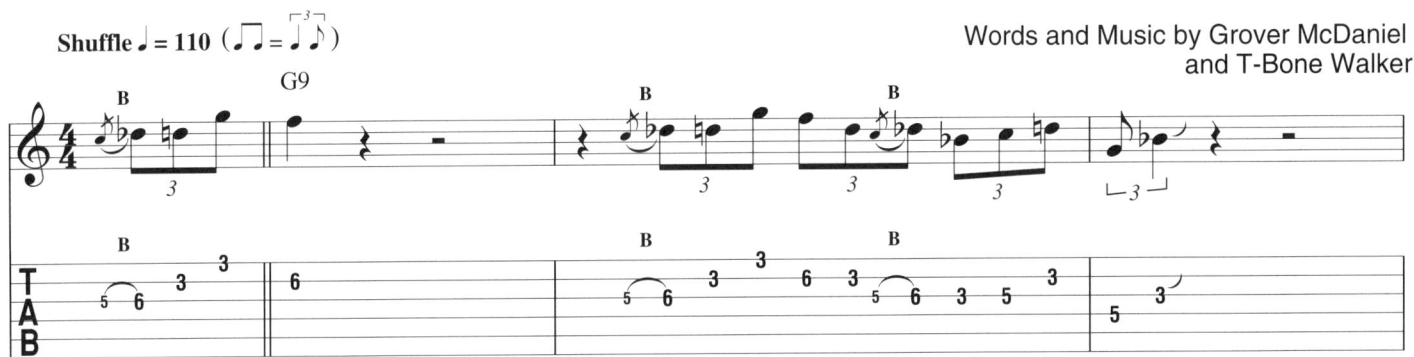

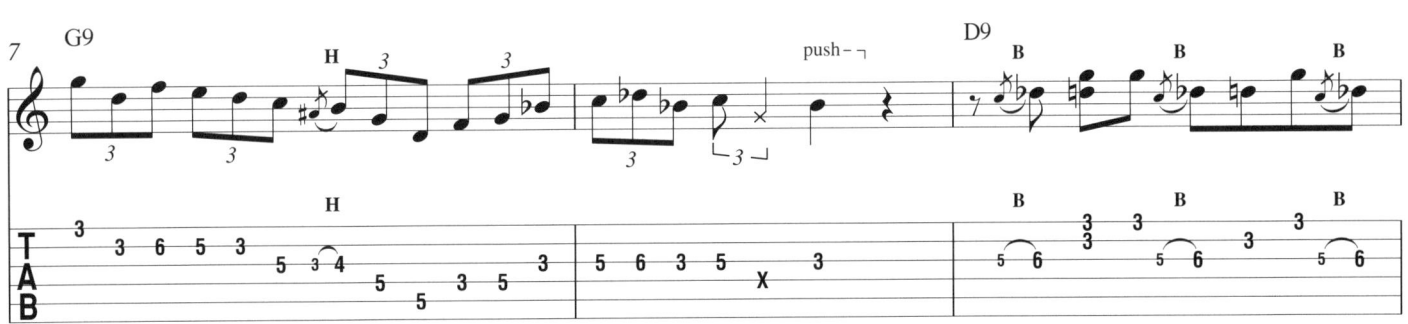

Copyright © 1955 by Unichappell Music Inc.
Copyright Renewed
International Copyright Secured   All Rights Reserved

2nd Solo

Papa Ain't Salty
As played by T-Bone Walker

Words and Music by Grover McDaniel
and T-Bone Walker

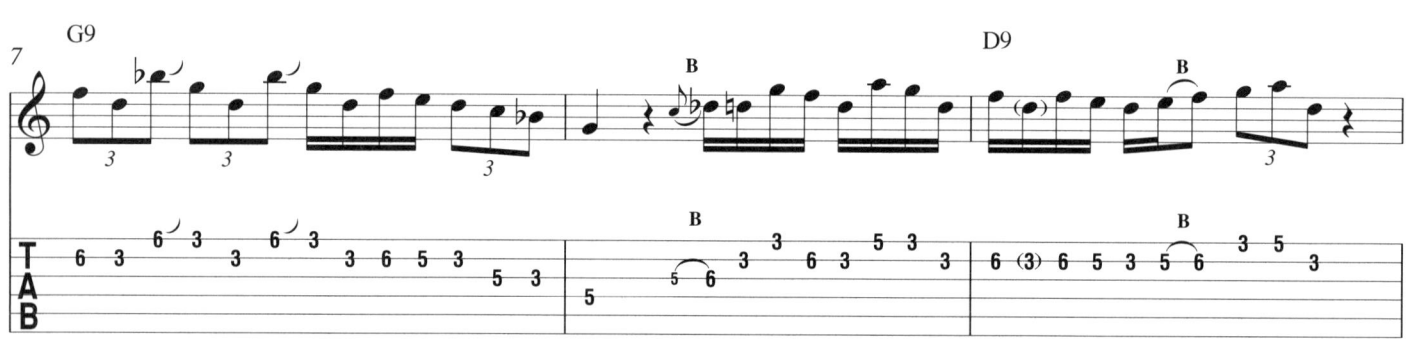
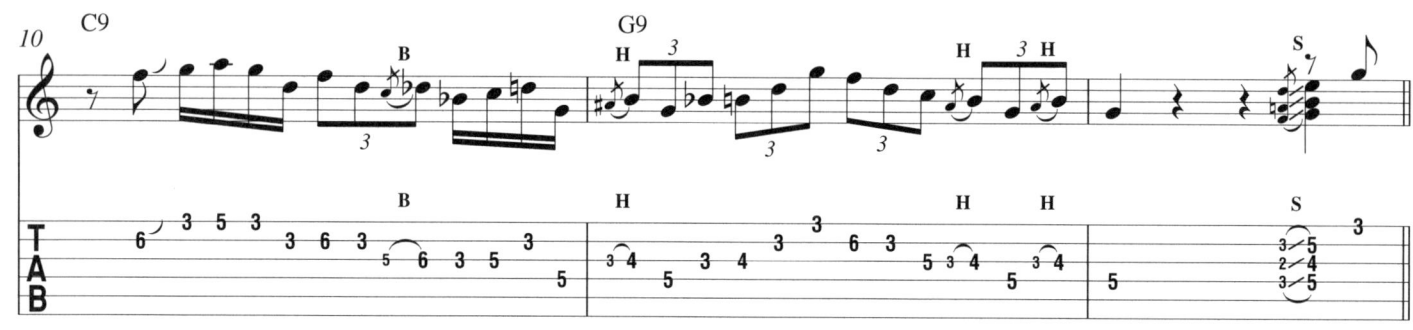

Copyright © 1955 by Unichappell Music Inc.
Copyright Renewed
International Copyright Secured All Rights Reserved

CHAPTER 5 "Papa Ain't Salty" T-Bone Walker

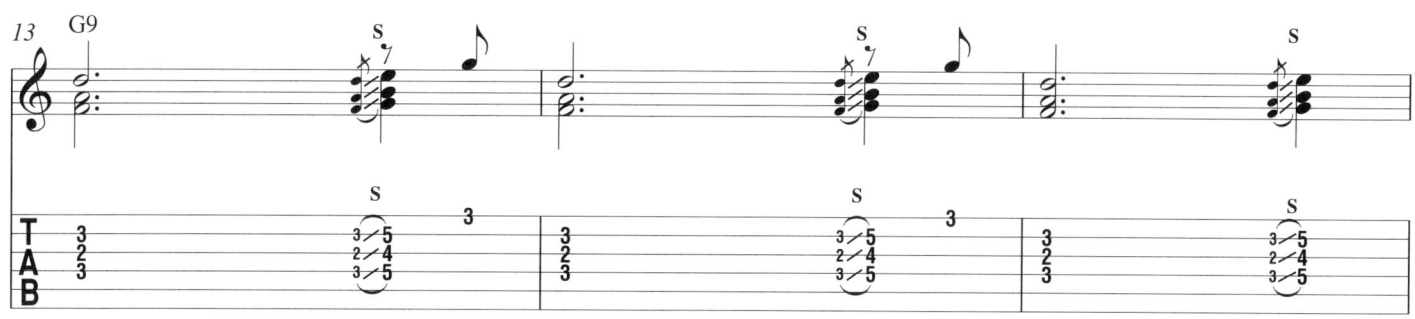
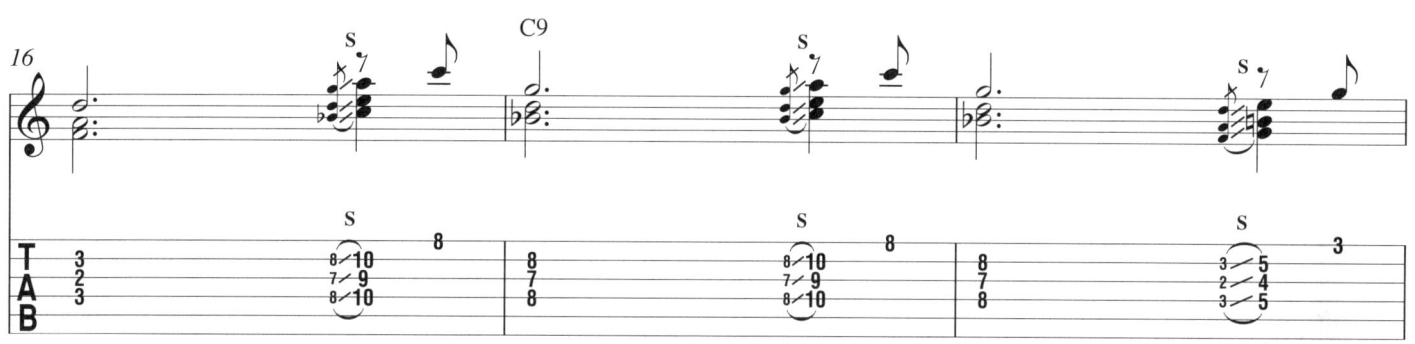
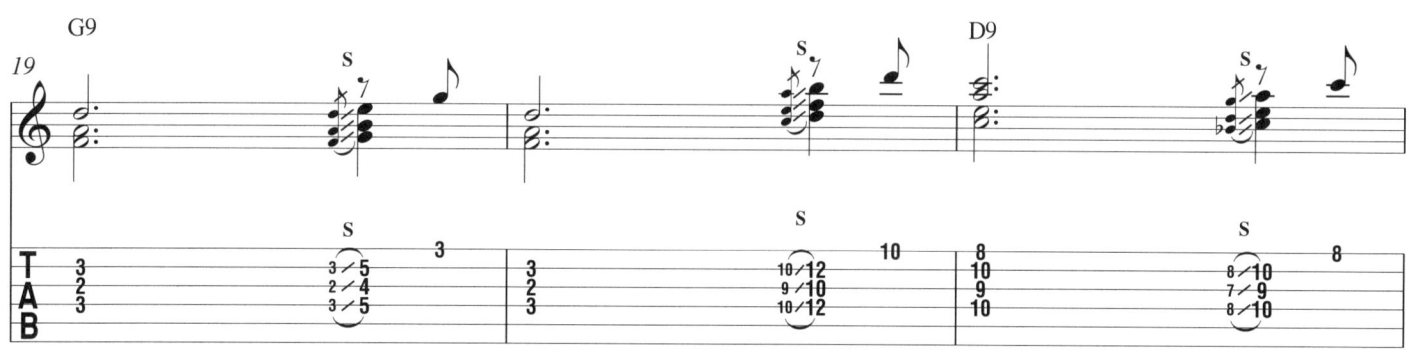
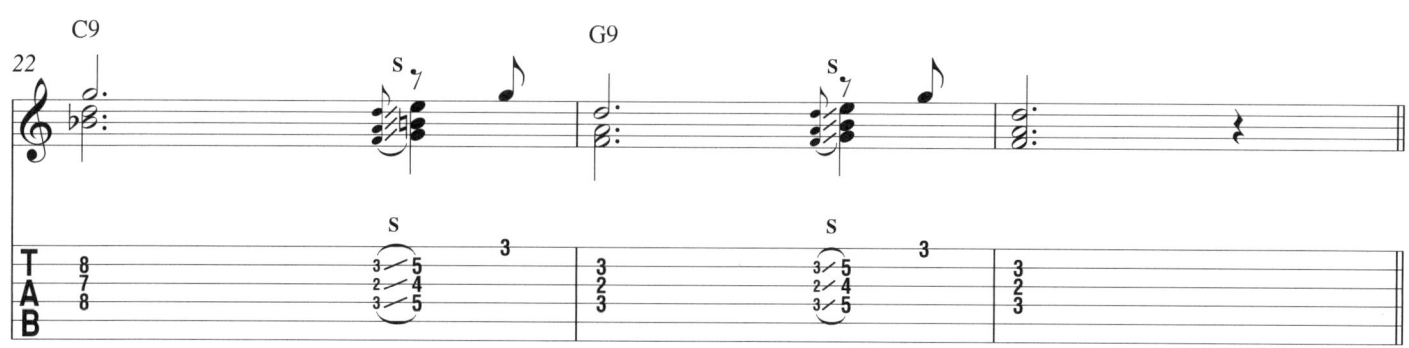

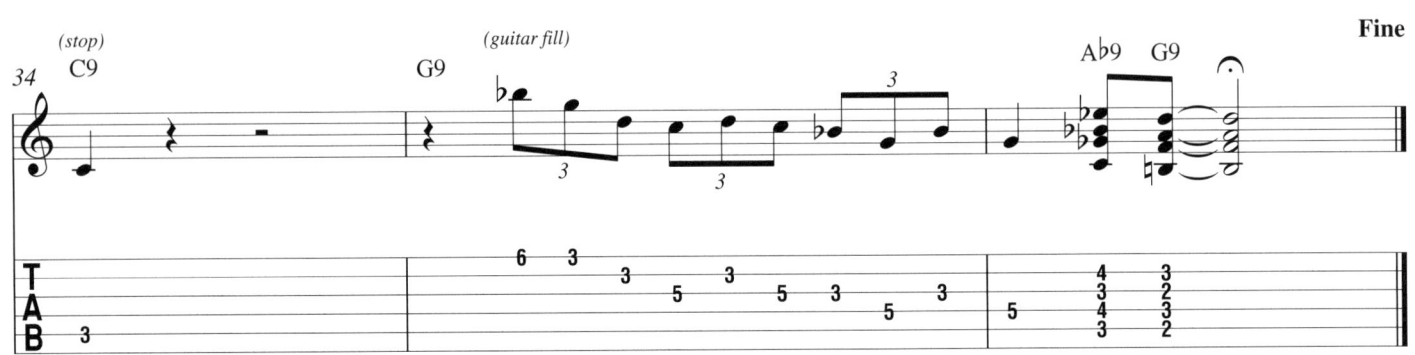

CHAPTER 6

"The Sad Nite Owl" Freddy King

Originally from Texas, Freddy King (1936 to 1976) moved to Chicago in 1949, and not long after that, he began making his mark on audiences around the city's south and west sides. Known as the "Texas Cannonball," King developed his personal sound and style while playing with a plastic thumb pick and a metal pick on his index finger. By the early 1960s, Freddy King had become a singer, guitarist, and composer—a musical force to be reckoned with. With a reputation of playing intense and impassioned solos, and more than two dozen popular guitar instrumentals to his credit, Freddy King made a huge impact on many up-and-coming blues and rock greats, including brothers Jimmie and Stevie Ray Vaughan, along with their British counterpoints such as Eric Clapton, Peter Green, Jimmy Page, and Jeff Beck.

"The Sad Nite Owl" (by Freddy King and Sonny Thompson) was originally recorded on his second all-instrumental record, *Freddy King Gives You a Bonanza of Instrumentals*, released on King Records in 1965. Pianist Sonny Thompson collaborated on most of Freddy King's instrumentals from this time period, and he is credited as cowriter of the instrumentals on this record, as well as his earlier hits on King records, such as "Hideway" and "San-Ho-Zay" (chapter 7).

PERFORMANCE TIPS

Slow 12-bar blues guitar instrumentals from the 1960s are rare, so that makes this vintage tune somewhat unique. The head (melody) to "Sad Nite Owl" is sparse and very simple. With its strict 12/8 piano accompaniment and groove, it sounds (by today's standards) somewhat corny—and very cool, at the same time. The head is tightly harmonized in close triads (3-note chords), with Freddy King on the top note; pianist Sonny Thompson fleshes out the harmony of each chord, just below King's melody.

Freddy King's brief, 12-bar solo is restrained and very soulful. There are no wasted notes in this chorus! On first listen, it sounds fairly simple. However, once you begin playing it, you'll realize that's not the case. Slow tempos such as this are deceptively simple. For most of this solo, King's phrases seem to float rhythmically. His notes fall (dangerously) right between the cracks of the beats, throughout this solo. This is classic "deep blues" phrasing, played at a slow tempo, so it's essentially impossible to learn this solo just by reading it. As the saying goes, "You can't learn that in school…" In order to assimilate and eventually internalize King's phrases, along with all of the space between his notes, it's essential to listen and play along with King's phrases repeatedly. For this solo, we're talkin' hundreds of times.

Freddy's string bends are perfectly timed and impeccably in tune. They are extremely challenging to re-create. That fact really hit home when I went to record this solo.

Good luck with "The Sad Nite Owl." I hope you enjoy this classic slow-blues instrumental.

ABOUT THE CD

Full Band
TRACK 13

No Guitar
TRACK 14

No Guitar; extend to five choruses
TRACK 15

King's original recording of "The Sad Nite Owl" is a brief three choruses in length; the in head, solo, and out head. This slow blues in G is a great vehicle to solo over, so an extended version of the song has been included.

Tracks 13 and 14 are three choruses in length, like Freddy King's original track: the in head, solo, and the out head. Track 15 has been extended to five choruses in length: the in head, three choruses of solo, and the out head.

The Sad Nite Owl
by Freddy King

Words and Music by
Sonny Thompson

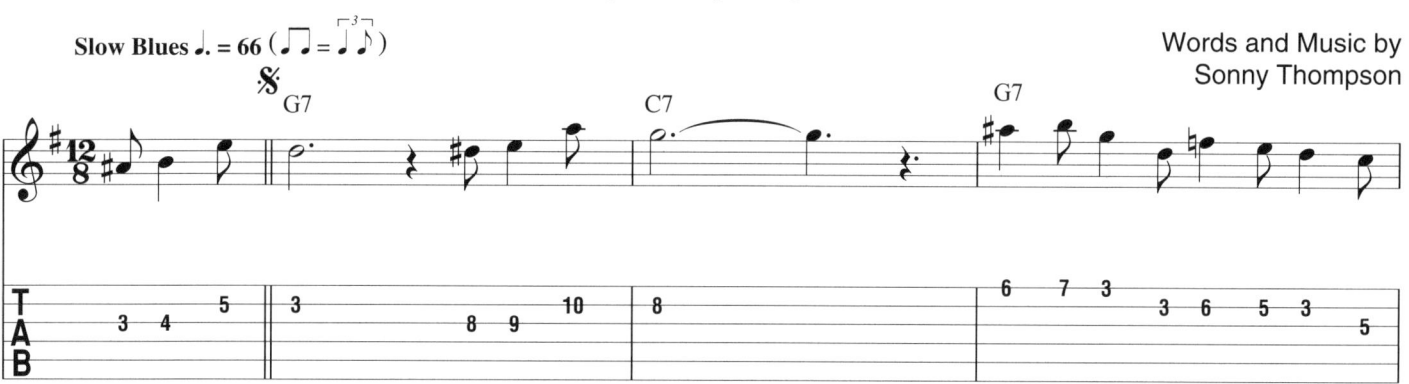

Copyright © 1996 by Fort Knox Music Inc. and Bug Music-Trio Music Company
International Copyright Secured   All Rights Reserved
Used by Permission

BERKLEE BLUES GUITAR SONGBOOK

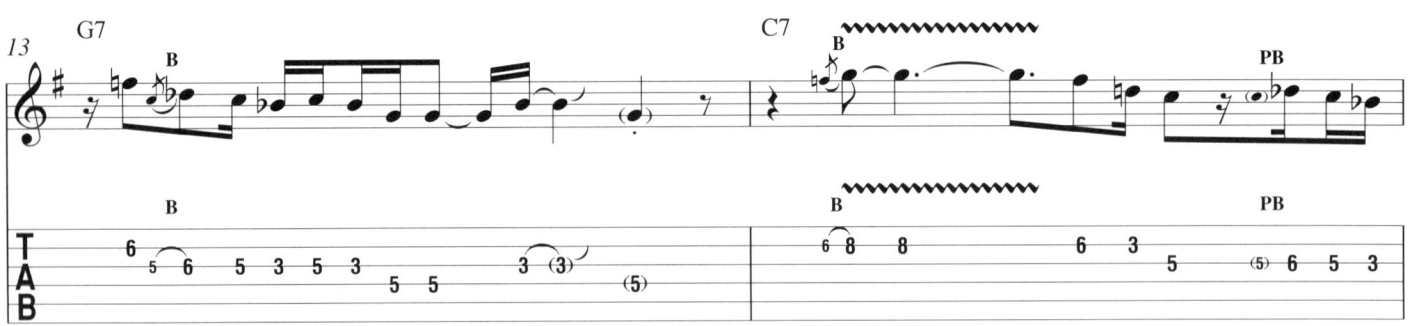

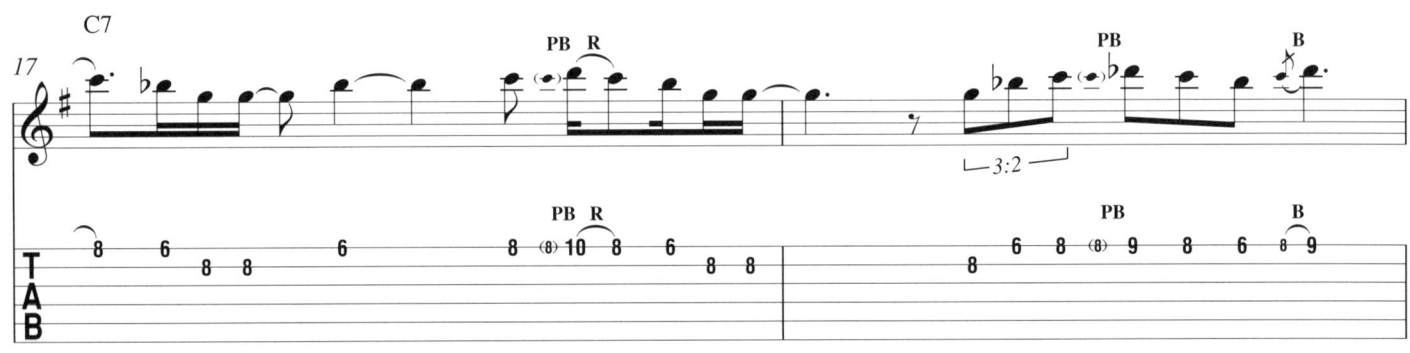
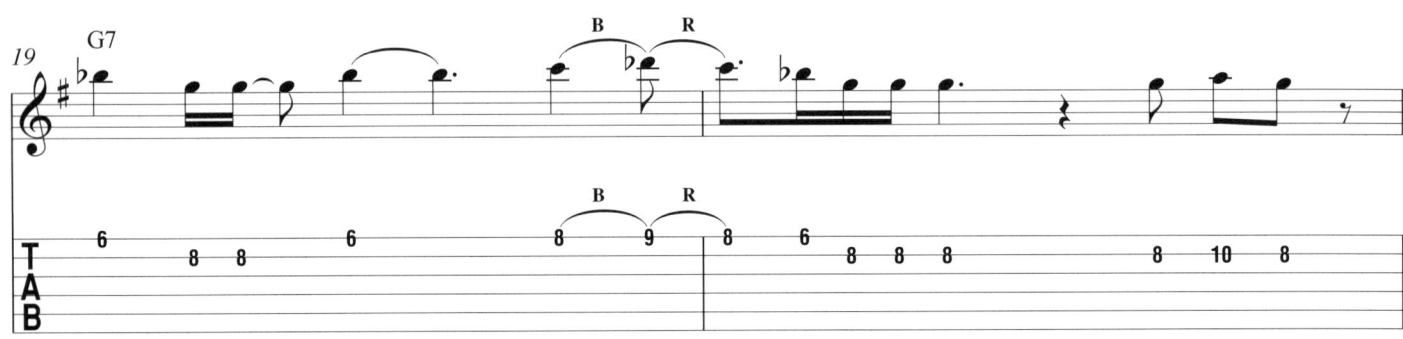

CHAPTER 6 "The Sad Nite Owl" Freddy King

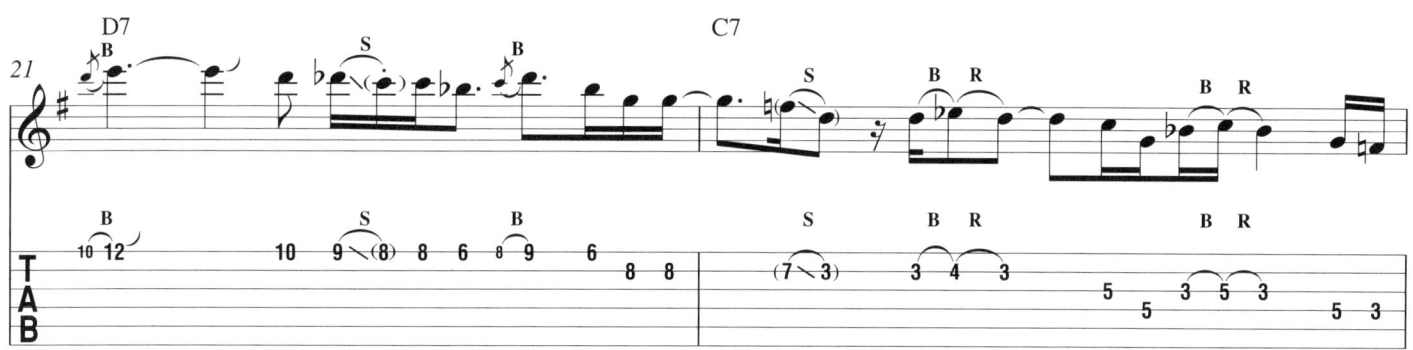

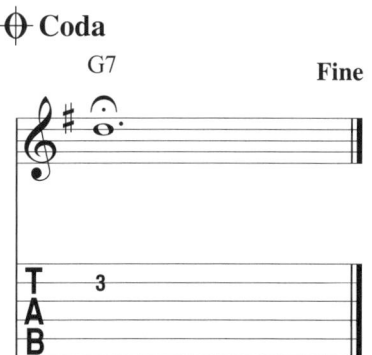

CHAPTER 7

"San-Ho-Zay" Freddy King

With its rockin' straight-eighth groove, and a cool, retro-surf vibe, "San-Ho-Zay" (by Freddy King and Sonny Thompson) has become a standard in many blues guitarists' repertoires. "San-Ho-Zay" was released by King Records in 1961, on *Let's Hide Away and Dance Away with Freddy King,* along with several other classic instrumentals, including "Hide Away," "Side Tracked," and "The Stumble."

PERFORMANCE TIPS

"San-Ho-Zay" features a slightly unusual song form for the head (melody). Because of that, on more than one occasion I've witnessed "train wrecks" during live performances such as blues jams when one (or more) of the players got lost on the form (arrangement). So let's take a look at Freddy King's arrangement to "San-Ho-Zay." The tune begins with three choruses of the head, followed by two solo choruses, and then it ends with two more choruses of the head.

The "in head" (beginning melody) to "San-Ho-Zay" is three choruses long. The first chorus is twelve bars, and the second and third choruses are sixteen bars long. Both 16-bar choruses feature an extended I (C7) chord; it's eight bars in length, instead of four. Also, both choruses feature a "stop" in bars 7–8. King jumped in with powerful, perfectly timed fills through both stops, and then brought the band back at the IV (C7) in bar 9, to finish out both choruses. King's two solo choruses (discussed below) were played over the 12-bar form, and for the out head he played a 16-bar chorus followed by a 12-bar chorus to end the tune.

The mix of 12-bar and 16-bar forms on the head to "San-Ho-Zay" makes this a little trickier than a standard 12-bar blues to pull off during unrehearsed performances, such as blues jams. It can be done, however the key is (quickly and effectively) communicating the arrangement to others in the band before counting off the tune.

Here's how to briefly explain the form to others in the rhythm section. If they understand song form, you'll be off and running in seconds. Also, in order to keep it simple for blues jams etc., it helps to play the same arrangement "going in" (beginning the tune) as when ending the tune, or "taking it out."

ARRANGEMENT NOTES

Chorus 1: 12 bars

Choruses 2 and 3: 16 bars. Extended with a long I chord (eight bars), with a "stop" on beat 1 of bar 7, and guitar fills through bars 7–8. The band comes back in on the IV chord. (Remind the others to watch for visual cues…then cue the stops, etc.!)

Freddy King played much of the head to "San-Ho-Zay" with a very staccato feel, by picking many of the notes with heavy right-hand palm muting. It's tough to phrase the melody with that staccato of a feel, but Freddy King made it sound easy.

As you listen to King's solo and read along with the music, notice that King's string bends and vintage blues/rock phrases keep coming, one after the other, nearly nonstop throughout both choruses. He played long phrases and paused (only briefly) every few bars, as if coming up for a quick breath between phrases. King's phrases throughout both choruses are based on a very cool mix of the C blues and C major pentatonic scales. And with his unrelenting, finger-twisting string bends, his intensity level doesn't let up.

"San-Ho-Zay" is classic go-for-the-throat Freddy King. It's a challenging study in string bends and intonation; King's pitch on all string bends is dead-on. Plus, it's a great lesson in playing with (and maintaining) intensity, so focus on that as you practice his solo.

ABOUT THE CD

 Full Band

TRACK 16

 No Guitar

TRACK 17

Tracks 16 and 17 for "San-Ho-Zay" are based on Freddy King's original recording, so they're seven choruses in length.

Good luck with Freddy King's "San-Ho-Zay." His classic and influential blues/rock phrases are worth the extra practice!

San-Ho-Zay
As played by Freddy King

Words and Music by Freddie King
and Sonny Thompson

Straight Eighths/Rock (♩ = 138)

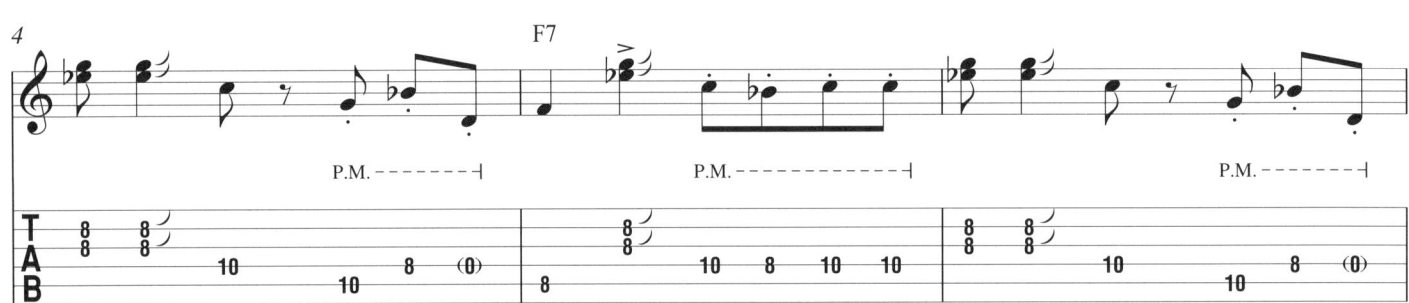

Copyright © 1961 by Fort Knox Music Inc. and Bug Music-Trio Music Company
Copyright Renewed
International Copyright Secured   All Rights Reserved
Used by Permission

CHAPTER 7 "San-Ho-Zay" Freddy King

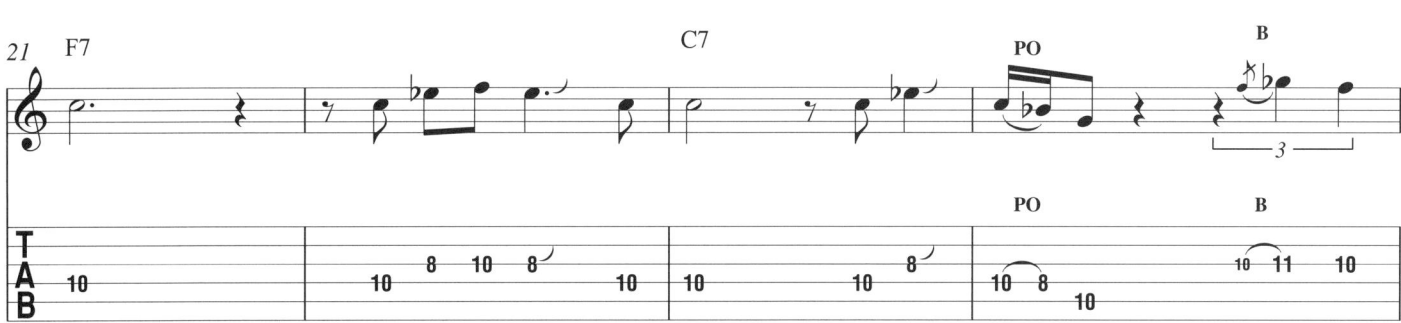

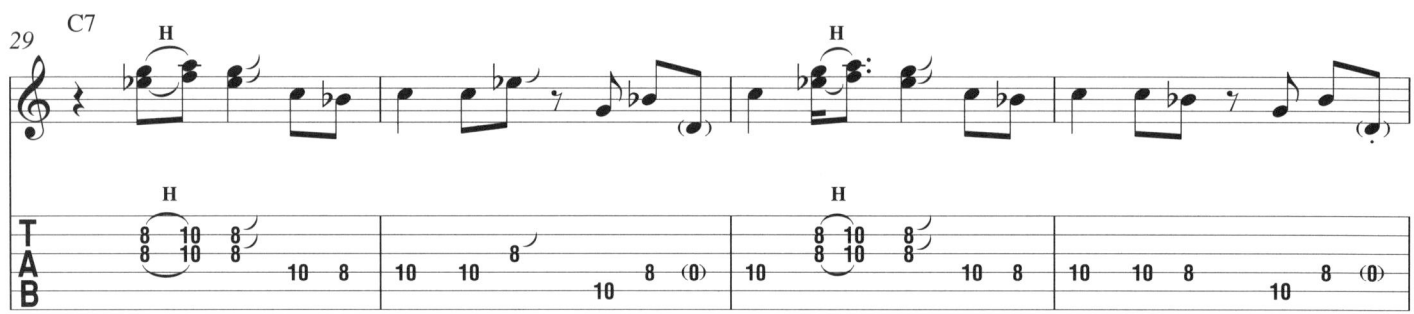
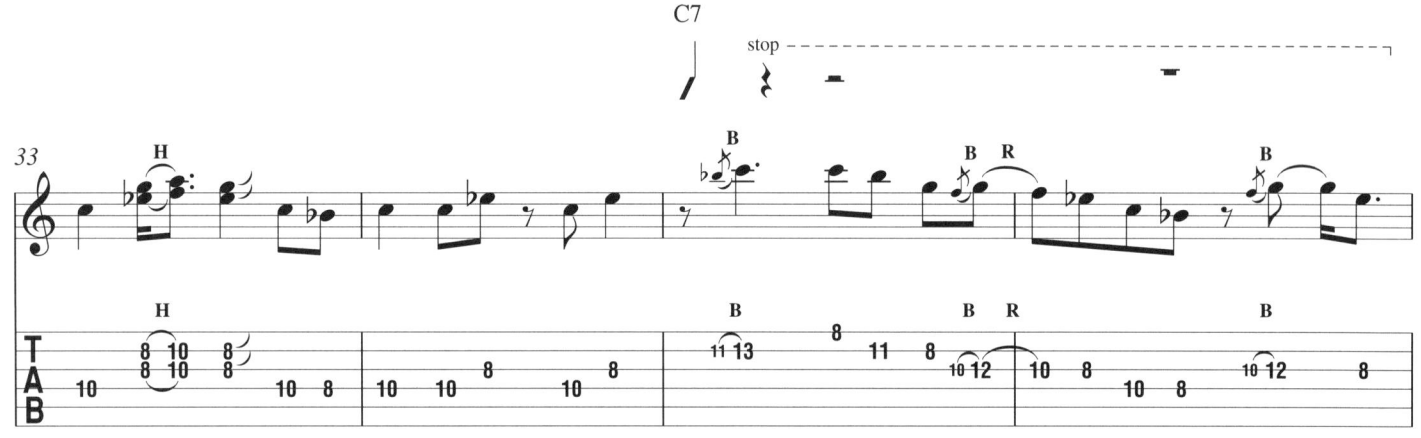
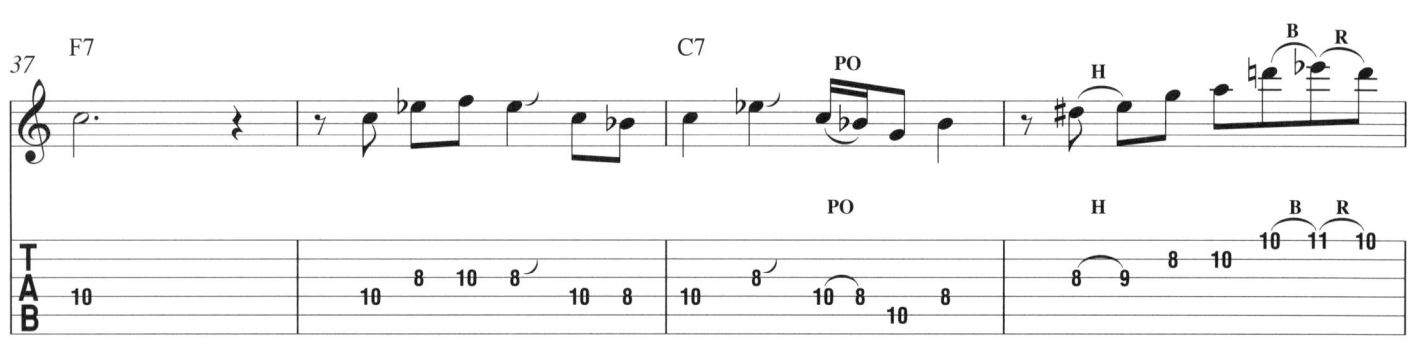
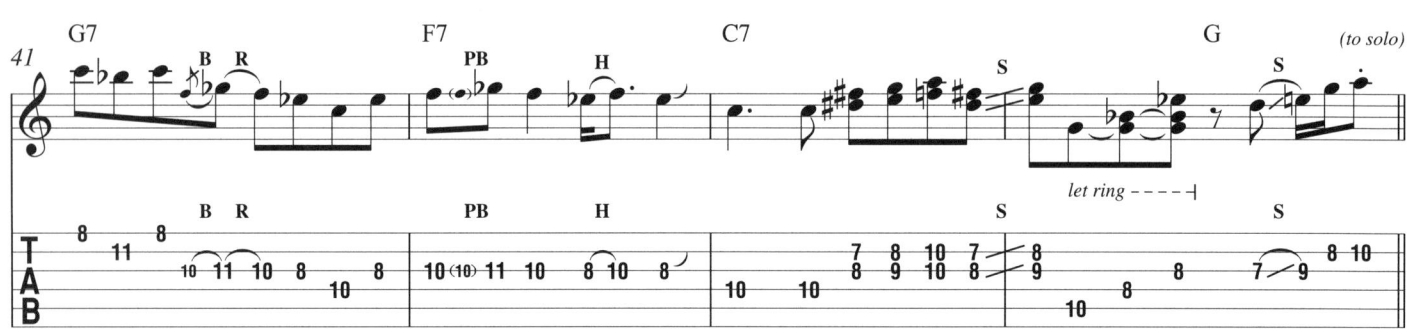

CHAPTER 7 "San-Ho-Zay" Freddy King

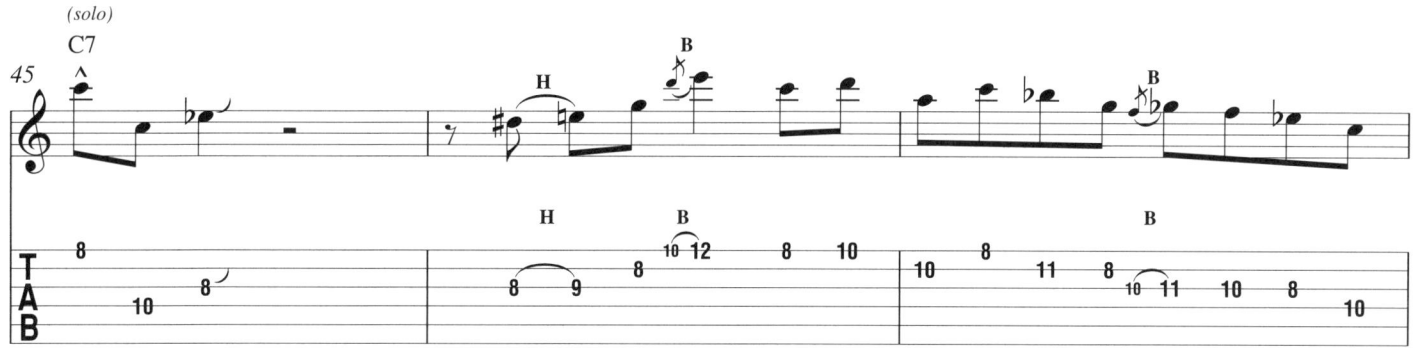
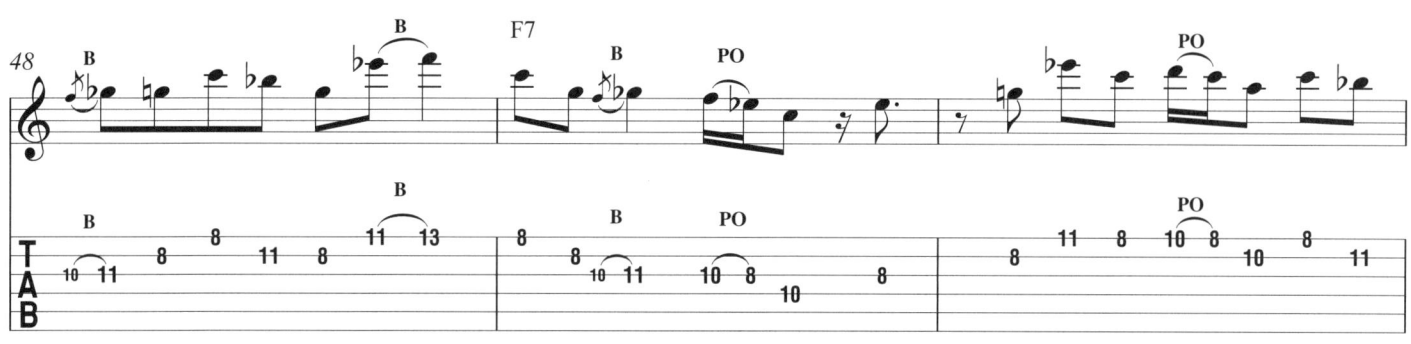
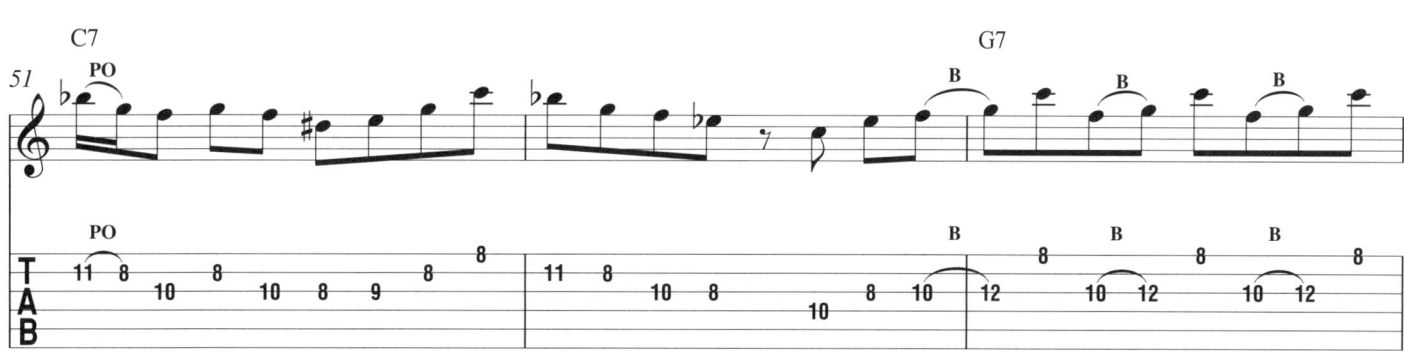
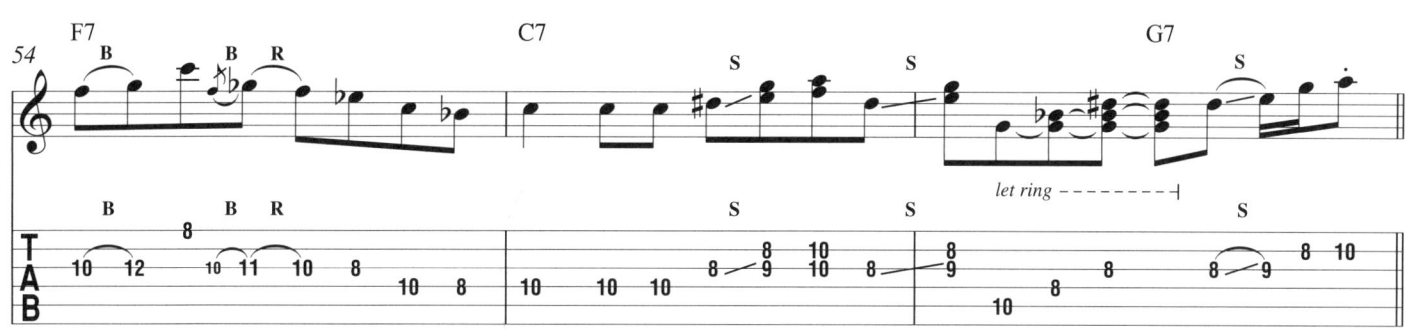

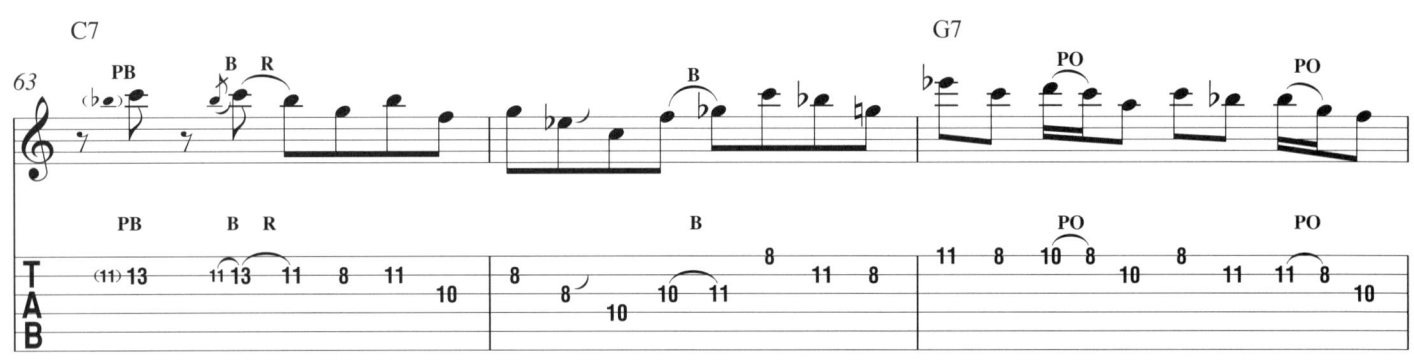
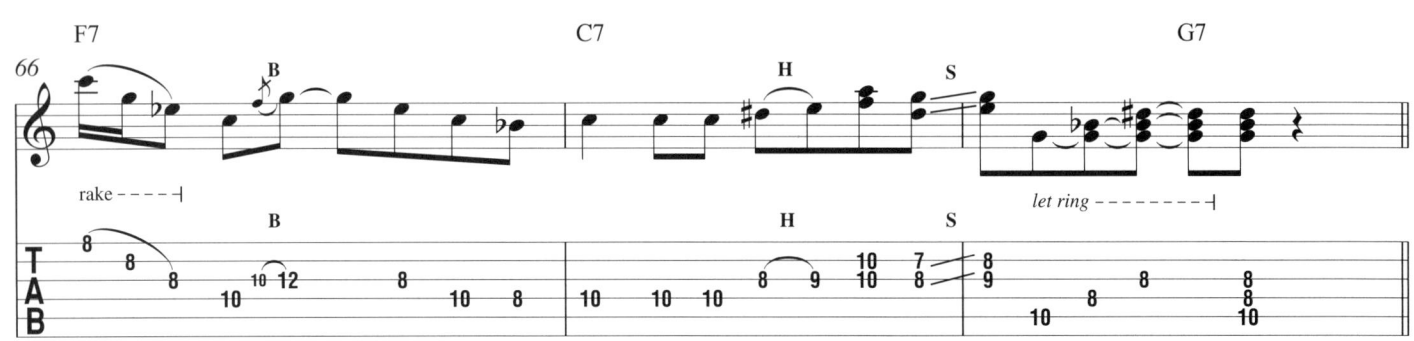

CHAPTER 7 "San-Ho-Zay" Freddy King 63

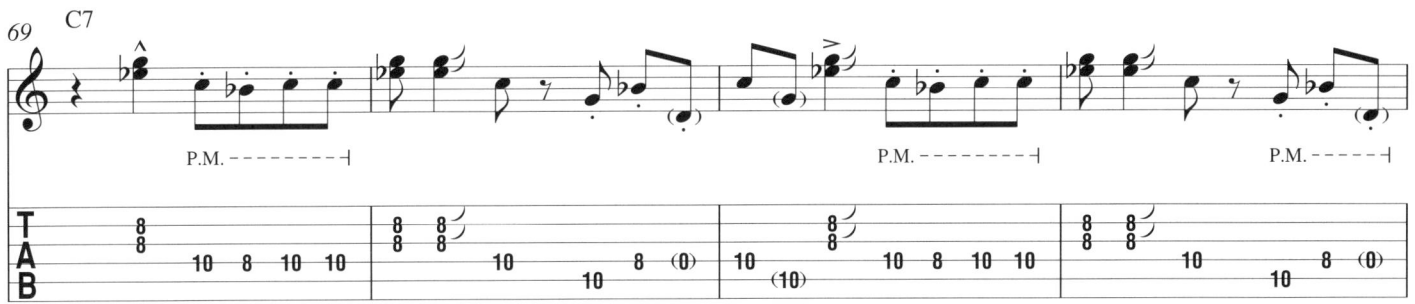

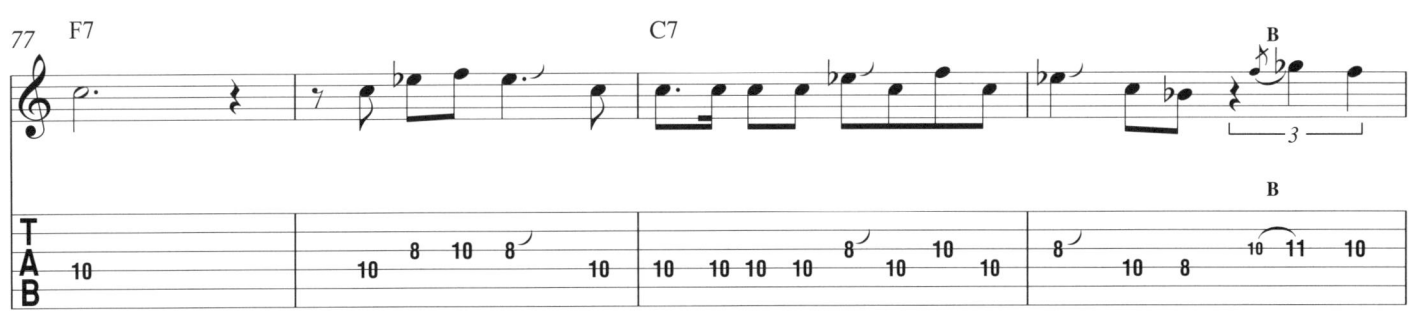
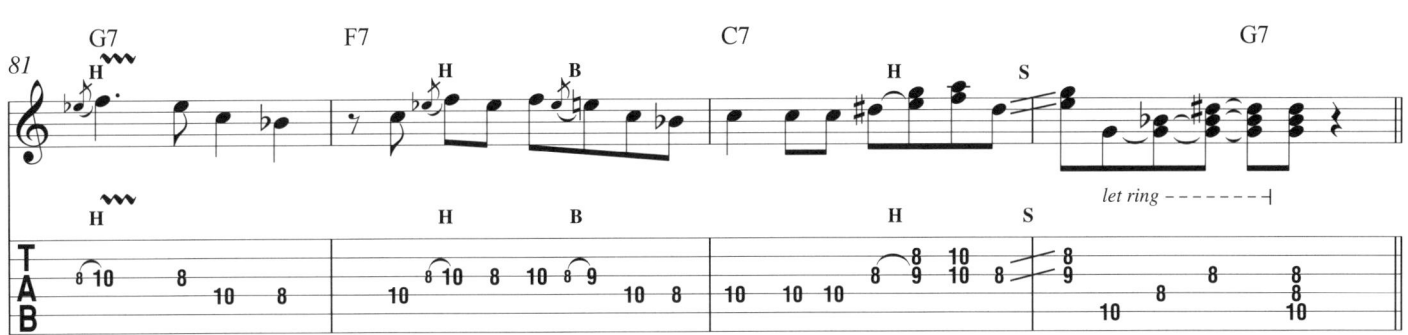

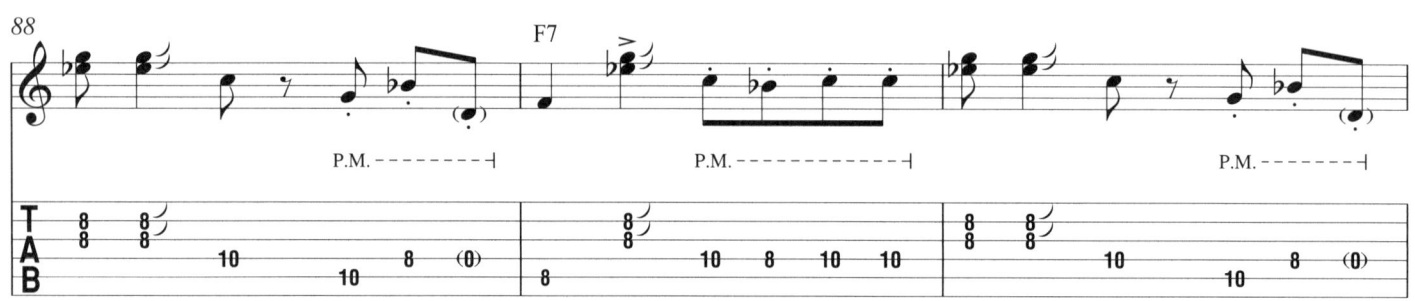

CHAPTER 8

"Wait on Time"
Jimmie Vaughan

Jimmie Vaughan is widely respected as a master of rhythm guitar styles, techniques, and nuances that span the history of the blues. Known for getting to the point without wasting any notes, his playing style conjures descriptions such as "lean-and-mean," "economical," and "down-to-the-bone." Vaughan's solos have inspired (and been imitated by) thousands of blues guitarists, and among his biggest admirers was his younger brother, Stevie Ray Vaughan—who, throughout his career, credited Jimmie as his biggest inspiration and influence.

Jimmie Vaughan was born in 1951 and raised in Oak Cliff, Texas, just south of Dallas. His earliest influences came from a melting pot of American roots styles such as blues, rock 'n' roll, top 40, r&b, and jazz that he was exposed to from popular radio stations around Dallas. Vaughan picked up guitar at the age of thirteen and began playing clubs around Dallas just a couple of years after that. Vaughan formed the band Texas Storm in 1969, playing r&b and soul. In 1970, at the age of nineteen, he moved to Austin.

In 1975, Jimmie Vaughan and harmonica player/vocalist Kim Wilson formed the Fabulous Thunderbirds, which soon garnered a large, loyal following and a reputation as a hard-hitting Texas-style blues band. Soon after that, the "T-Birds" became the house band at Antone's, Austin's best-known blues club, where they played alongside Muddy Waters, B.B. King, Albert King, and many other great blues artists.

Vaughan performed as a member of the Fabulous Thunderbirds until 1989, when he left the band to pursue other musical projects, such as making the record *Family Style*, along with his brother Stevie Ray Vaughan, for Epic records. Tragically, just weeks before *Family Style* was released, Stevie Ray Vaughan's life was cut short from a helicopter crash. Since 1993, Jimmie Vaughan has toured and recorded in his own name, and performed on stage regularly with blues legends such as B.B. King, Buddy Guy, Eric Clapton, Robert Cray, and others.

"Wait on Time" (by Kim Wilson) was originally released on *Girls Go Wild*, on Chrysalis/Tacoma Records in 1978. This greasy, medium tempo shuffle is the perfect vehicle for Vaughan's lean-and-mean style. Vaughan's rhythm part is stripped way down, right to the essential chord hits, bare-bones turnarounds, and hard-hitting solo phrases. "Wait on Time" showcases Vaughan's sublime soloing skills, such as his timing and feel, his impeccable intonation on string bends, and his pacing throughout the rhythm part and solos.

In more recent years, Vaughan has performed exclusively with a capo. However, this track was recorded in the days before Vaughan began using the capo (exclusively). As you listen to the Fabulous Thunderbirds' original recording, notice that Vaughan's solo phrases reflect a strong musical connection to two of his biggest musical mentors, B.B. King and Freddy King.

PERFORMANCE TIPS

Vocal lyrics are included in the music, since Vaughan's rock-solid chord hits, turnarounds, and fills around the vocals essentially make up choruses 2, 3, 6, 7, and 8. With punchy guitar hits (chords) on beats 1 and the "and" (upbeat) of 2, and no-nonsense turnarounds, Vaughan's rhythm part has a sparse overall feel, yet it perfectly supports Kim Wilson's vocal lyrics, and creates tons of rhythmic momentum for the track.

Vaughan's turnaround phrases in (vocal) verses 2, 3, and 6 are very similar. In bar 11, he plays the B9 (I9) chord hits on beats 1 and the "and" of 2, followed by the note F♯ on the "and" of 3 and notes E and F♯ in the triplet on beat 4. On beat 1 of bar 12, he descends down four eighth notes from the B pentatonic and/or blues scale: D B A F♯ (♭3, 1 ♭7, 5).

Note: Vaughan "tweaks" D (the first note) with a quarter string bend, so that it sounds between the flat 3rd and the natural 3rd. These "between-the-cracks" notes, or "tweaks," are notated as quarter-step bends up from D (the ♭3rd). To get the feel for those subtle and essential nuances such as the quarter-step bends, listen repeatedly to Vaughan's phrases, and as you practice through all five vocal choruses, notice the similarities and slight differences of each turnaround. Take the extra time to internalize each of his classic turnarounds.

Vaughan takes those quarter-step string bends a little further, at times. Also, for the intro and chorus 4 turnarounds, he strikes the ♭3rd (D) just before bar 12. Then, while sustaining the note across the bar line, he bends the note up a half step, to sound the natural 3rd (D♯).

For all three solo choruses and for his turnarounds throughout the track, Vaughan's phrases are based *almost exclusively* on the B blues scale (B D E F F♯ A) with the addition of a couple of notes from the B major pentatonic scale (B C♯ D♯ F♯ G♯). As noted in the turnarounds above, at times, Vaughan leans into the major 3rd (D♯), by bending up from the ♭3rd. Vaughan also slides into the D♯ in bar 8 of his intro, and chorus 4. In bar 9 of chorus 5, Vaughan also introduces the note C♯ over the F♯7 (V7) chord. The C♯ is also in the B major pentatonic scale, so like most of the other solos in this book, Vaughan's phrases on "Wait on Time" are a mix of the blues and major pentatonic scales.

Vaughan leans into several more "between-the-cracks" bends throughout his solos. Over the B7 (I7) chord in bars 3–4 of chorus 4, and in bar 10 of chorus 5, he bends up (approximately a quarter step) from A to play notes that sound between A and A# (the b7 and natural 7). Those notes are also notated as quarter-step bends.

Vaughan's opening (intro) solo is the best place to start, since it sounds great, and it's a little easier to get under the fingers than his second and third choruses. Right from his opening notes, Vaughan jumps into the blue flame by firing off a series of whole-step bends and release-bends, with a lean-and-mean sound and feel. Vaughan took his time on this intro; his phrases are not fast or frenzied. However, his razor-sharp string bends, picking attack, and intensity level provide plenty of Texas heat, so this intro solo raises the bar pretty high for the solo that follows in choruses 4–5.

Notice the call and response in his phrasing throughout the intro and throughout his solo in choruses 4–5. Vaughan left plenty of room to breathe between his phrases, and his lines connect throughout the 12-bar form. Just like a conversation, all three choruses are paced like powerful blues lyrics.

Bars 4 and 10 feature a very cool repeated 2-note phrase that alternates between the notes A and F#, which Vaughan played as non-stop triplets, accenting every other note in a repeated triplet figure to create a powerful two-against-three (polyrhythmic) feel. Vaughan's attack on those triplets captures the feel and spirit of several classic recordings such as Freddy King's phrases on the head to "Sidetracked" and parts of Billy Butler's solo on Bill Doggett's r&b hit from 1956, "Honky Tonk."

In bar 10 of chorus 4, Vaughan taps into the deep-blues sound and feel, with a very soulful and powerful (string bend and release) phrase over the F#7 chord, which sounds five of the six notes in the B blues scale. Starting with a whole-step string bend on the high E string, he bends from E to F# on beats 2 and the "and" of 2. Next, the F# (bend) is released a half step to the note F (the b5) on beat "3," and that's followed by the notes D and B. It's difficult to nail the pitches, timing, and intensity of this phrase, but Vaughan makes it sound easy.

Chorus 5 features more classic call-and-response phrases that sound just like a blues lyric. Vaughan starts a phrase (statement) in bars 1–2, and that's followed by a reply in bars 3–4 that continues into bar 5, and beyond. Bars 4–12 of chorus 5 are the most challenging part of the track to learn, by far. To climax the "conversation" and the solo, Vaughan's phrases are faster and much more crowded, as he spits out quick flurries of (dead-on) string bends, releases, slides, hammer-ons, and pull-offs. His phrases in bars 6–7 fall rhythmically between the cracks, so it's tough (or nearly impossible) to capture his timing and feel for those. Again, my suggestion for getting the feel for these phrases is to listen, sing, and play along with Vaughan's solo repeatedly.

Good luck with this solo and rhythm part. When you dig into Jimmie Vaughan's opening string bends, you'll realize just how challenging this is!

ABOUT THE CD

 Full Band

 No Guitar

Tracks 18 and 19 for "Wait on Time" are eight choruses long, to match the length of the Fabulous Thunderbirds' original recording.

Wait on Time
Solo by Jimmie Vaughan

Words and Music by
Kim Wilson

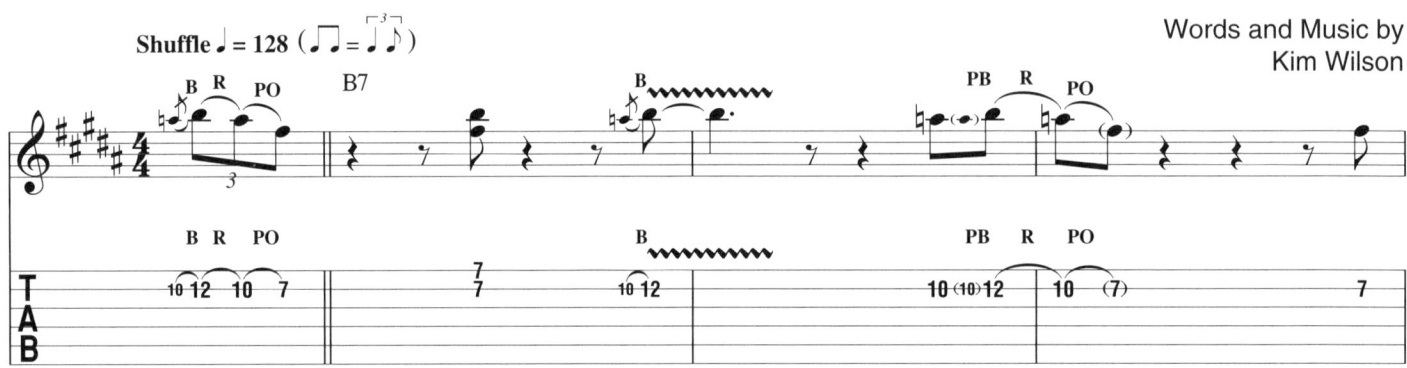

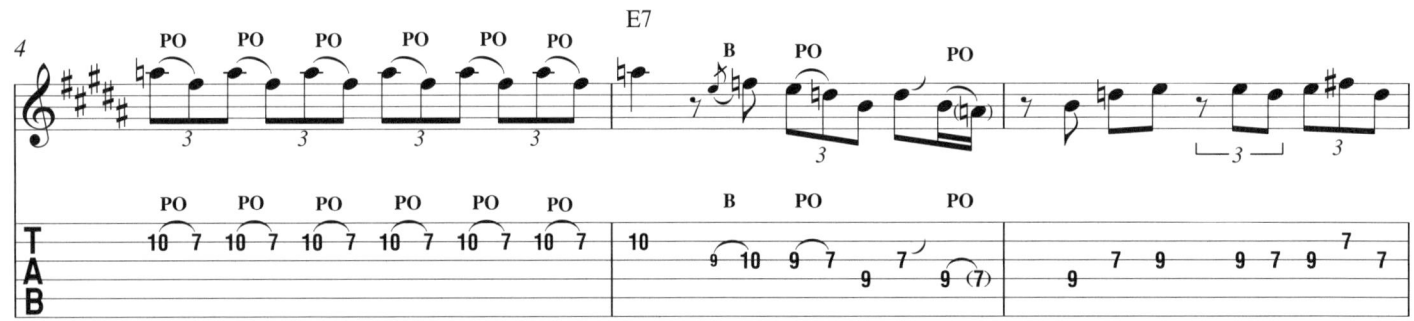

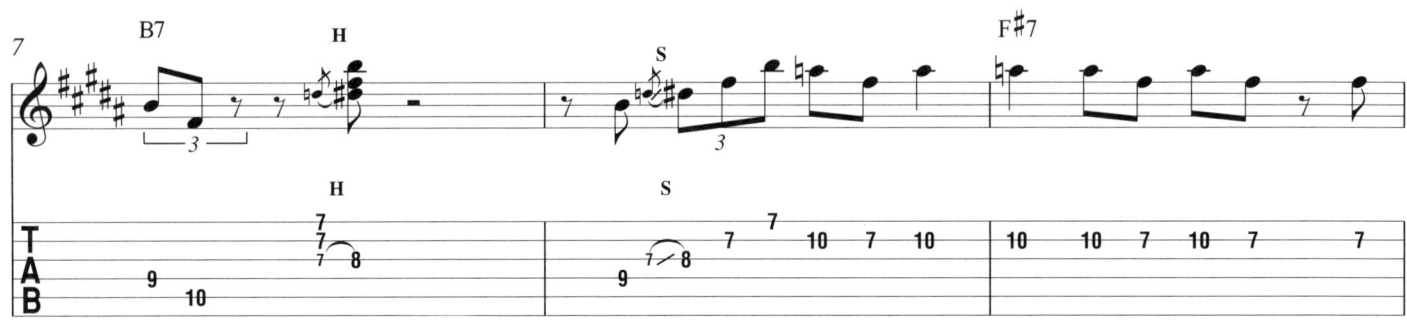

© 1979 BRUCO MUSIC (BMI) and POCKET ROCKET MUSIC (BMI)/Administered by BUG MUSIC
All Rights Reserved   Used by Permission

CHAPTER 8 "Wait on Time" Jimmie Vaughan

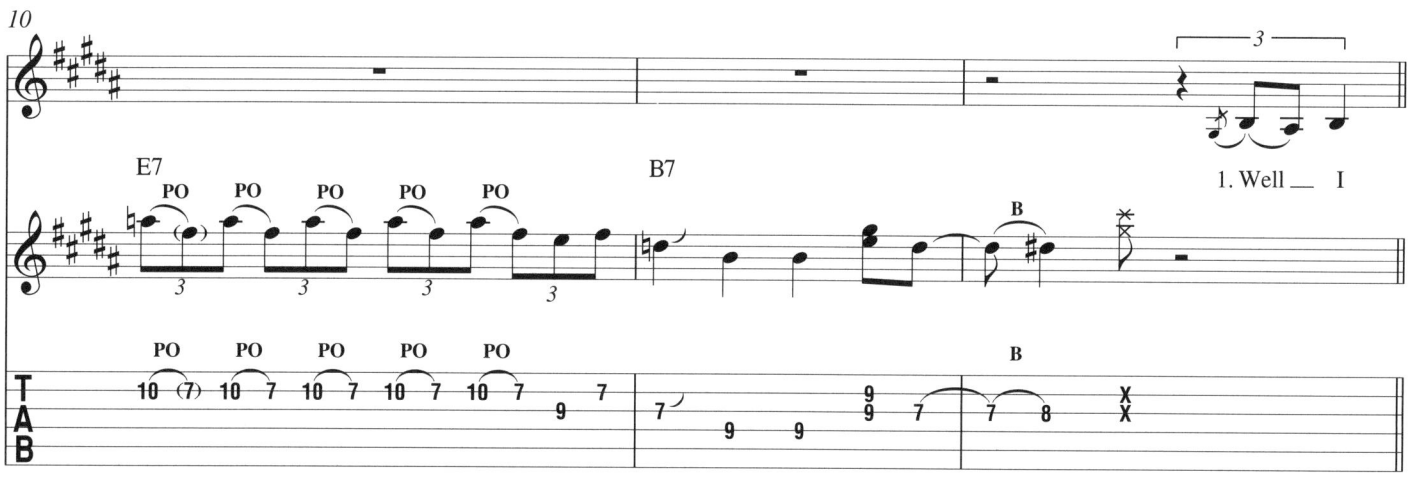

Chorus 2 - Vocal Verse 1

Chorus 3 - Vocal Verse 2

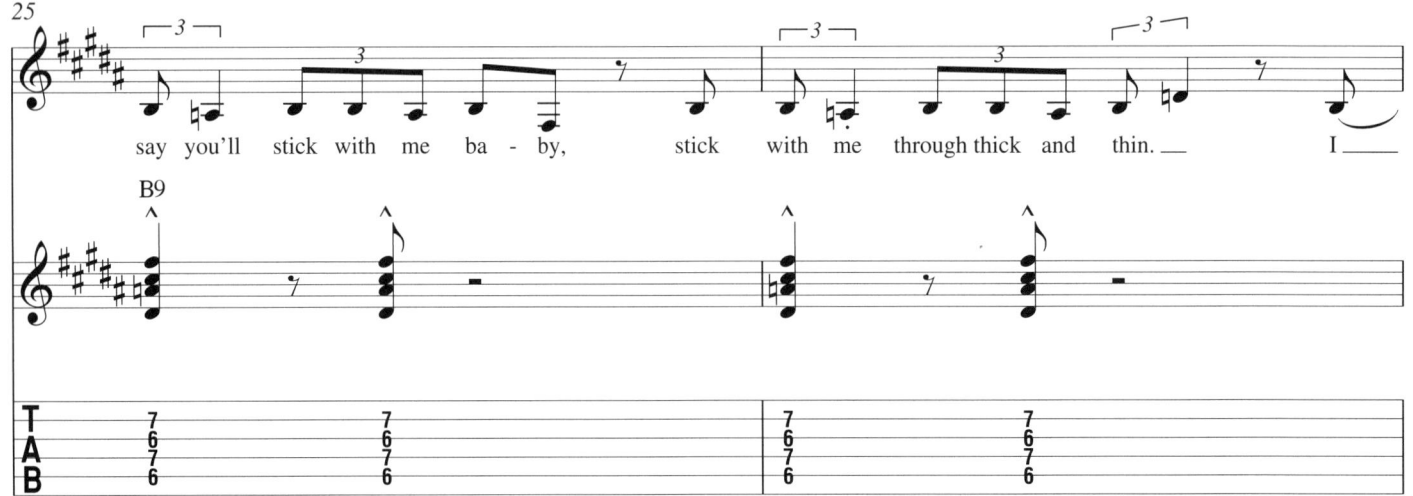

CHAPTER 8 "Wait on Time" Jimmie Vaughan 71

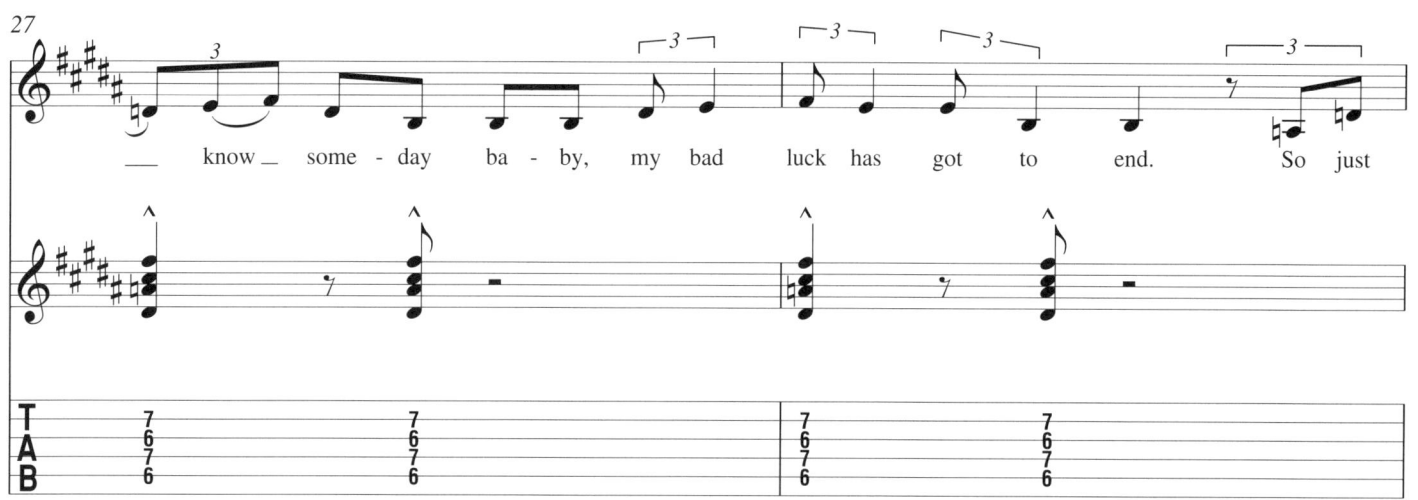

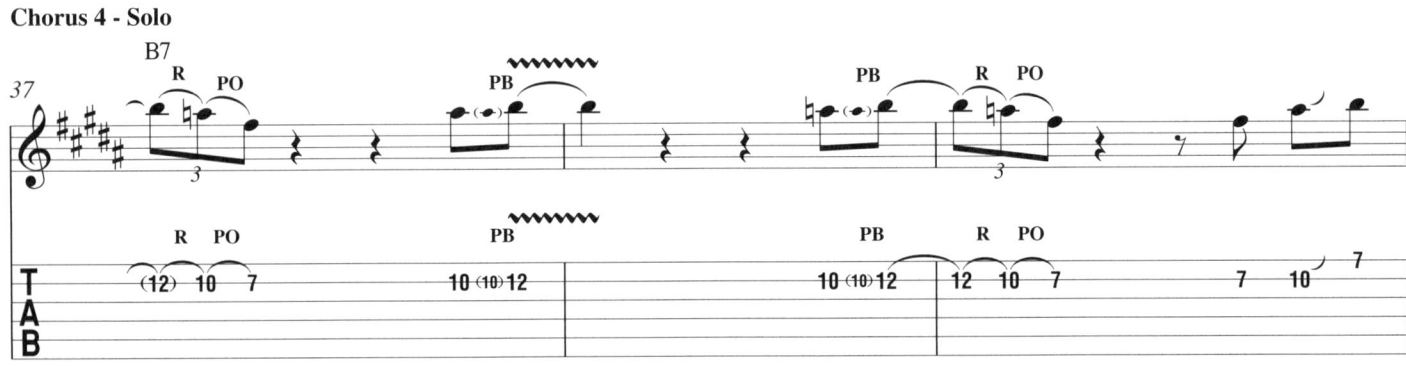

Chorus 4 - Solo

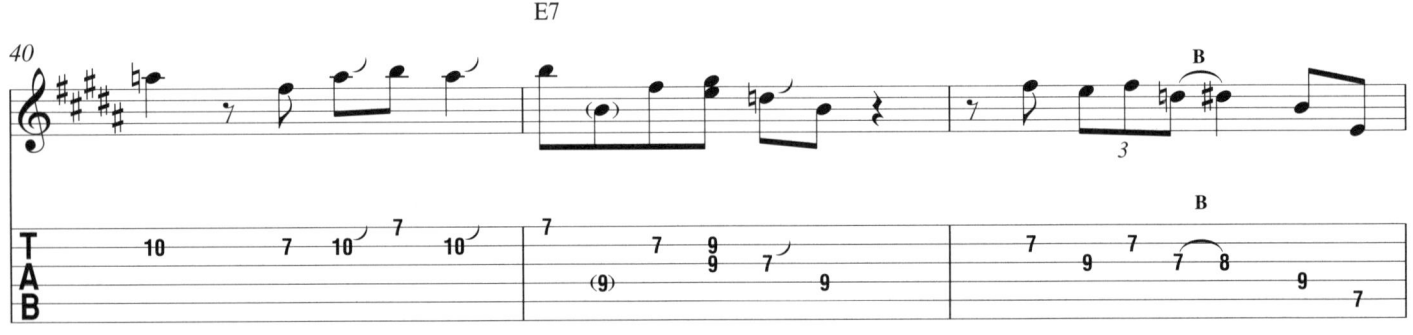

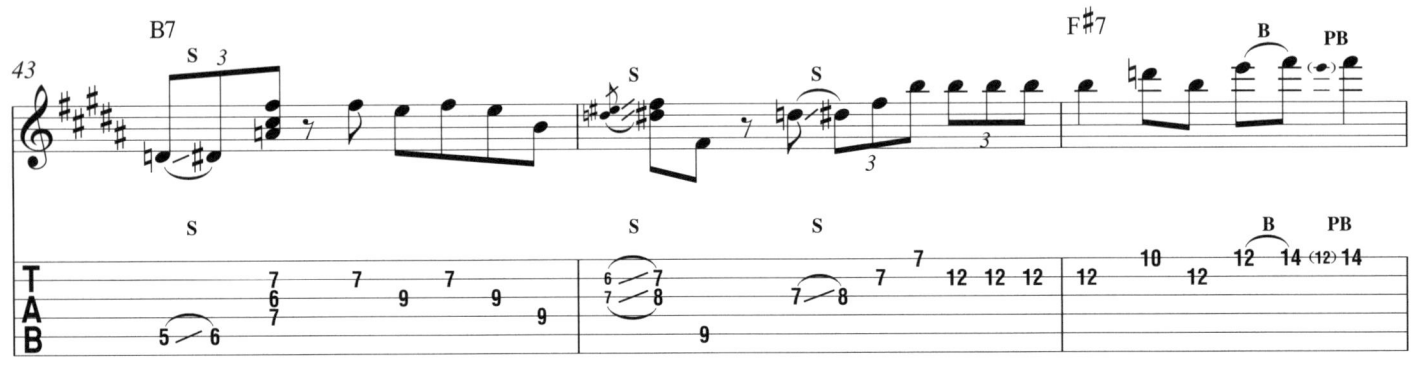

CHAPTER 8 "Wait on Time" Jimmie Vaughan

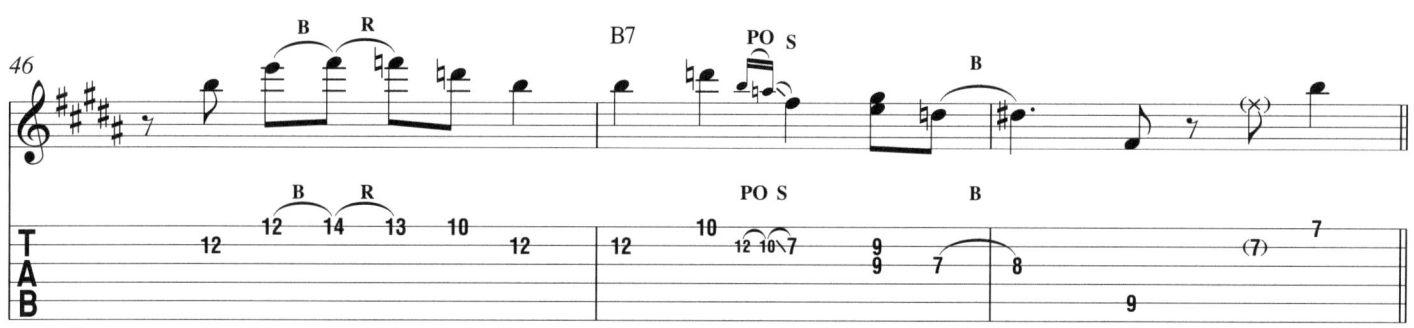

Chorus 5 - Solo (continued)

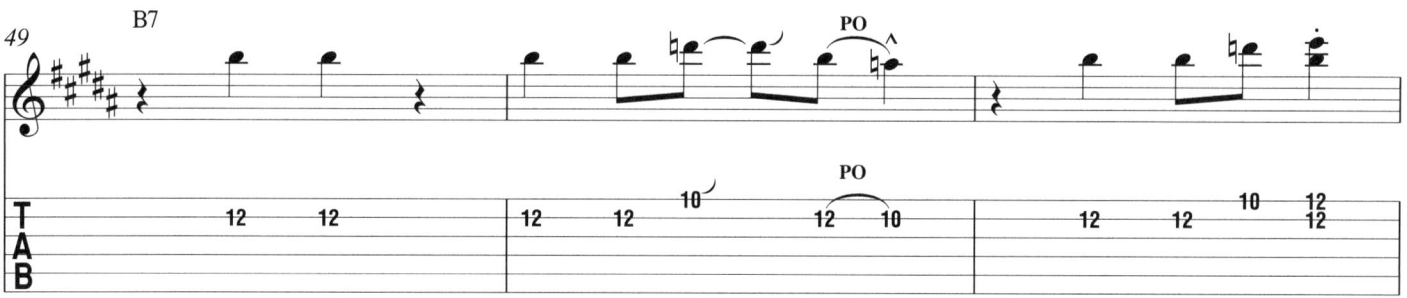

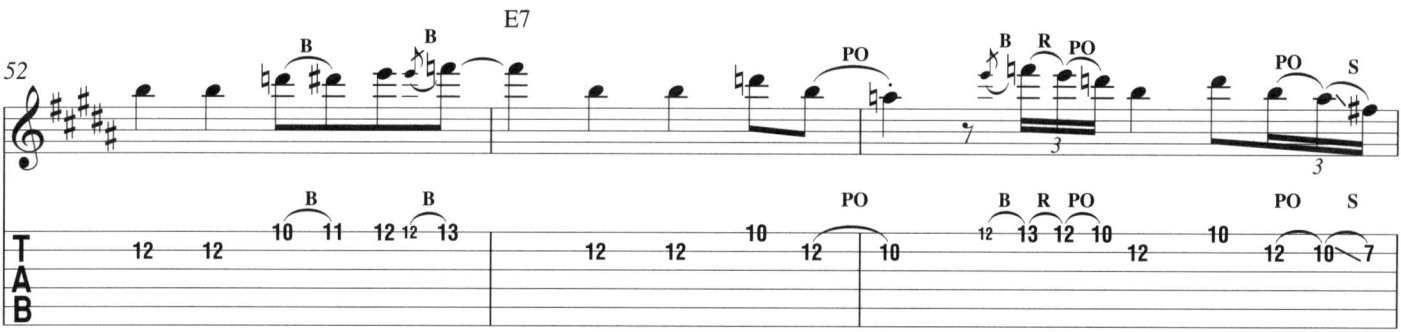

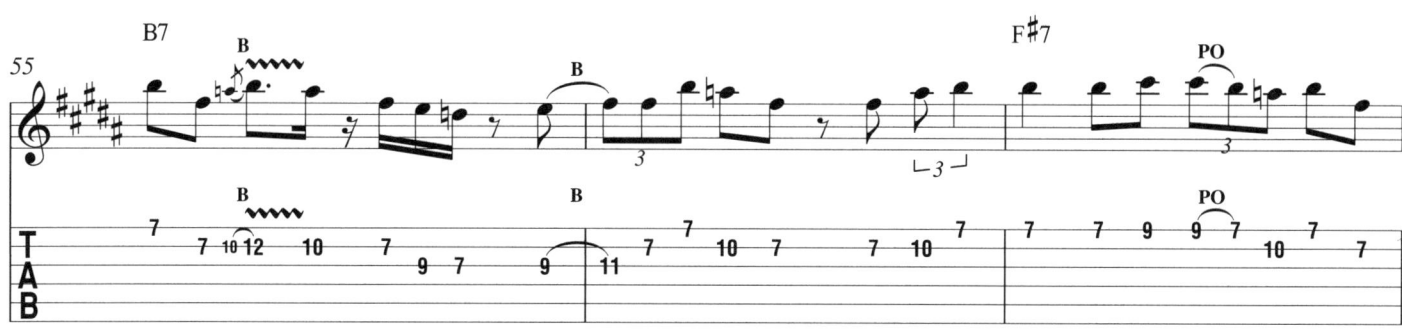

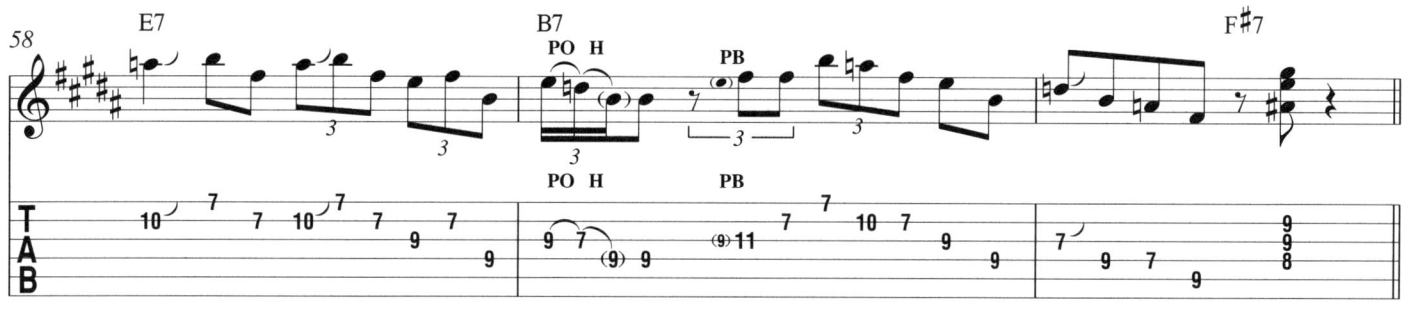

Chorus 6 - Vocals
(see additional lyrics)

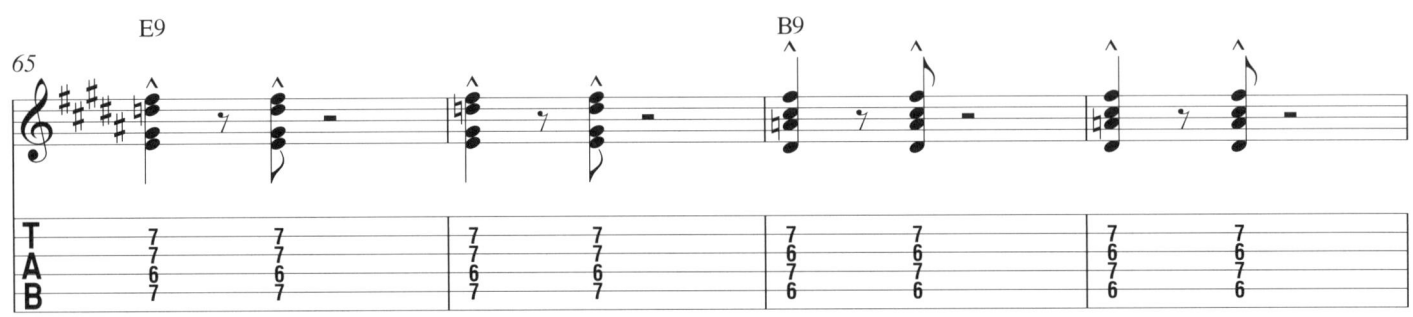

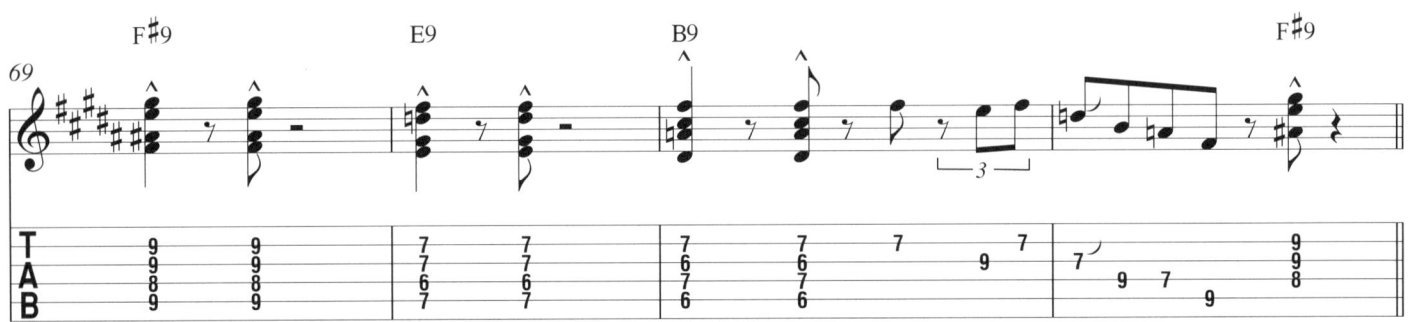

Chorus 7 - Vocals
(see additional lyrics)

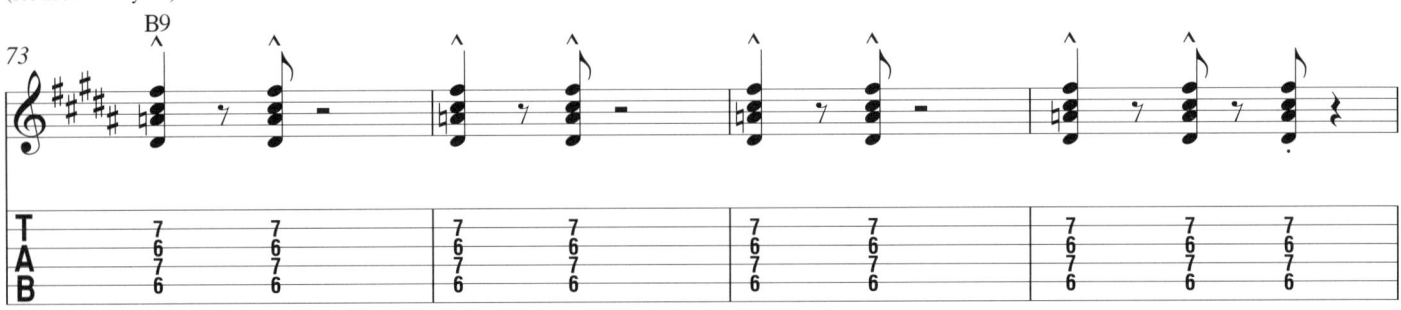

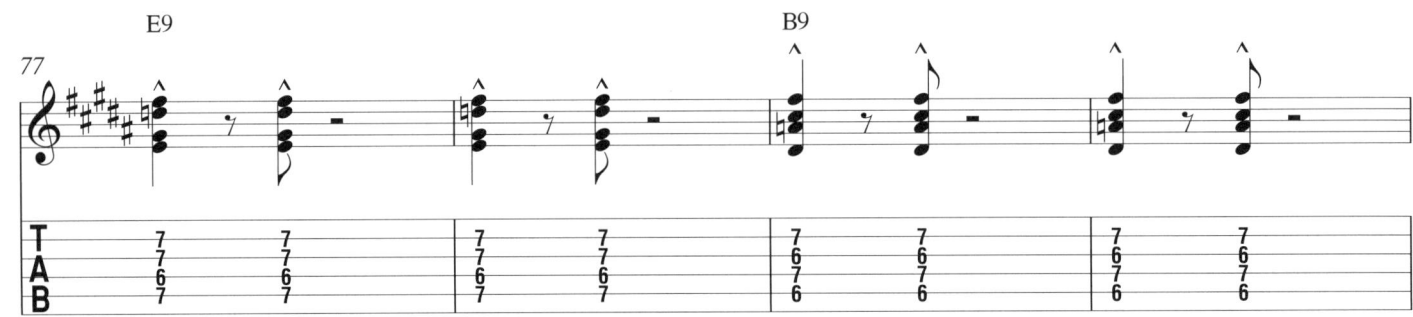

CHAPTER 8 "Wait on Time" Jimmie Vaughan

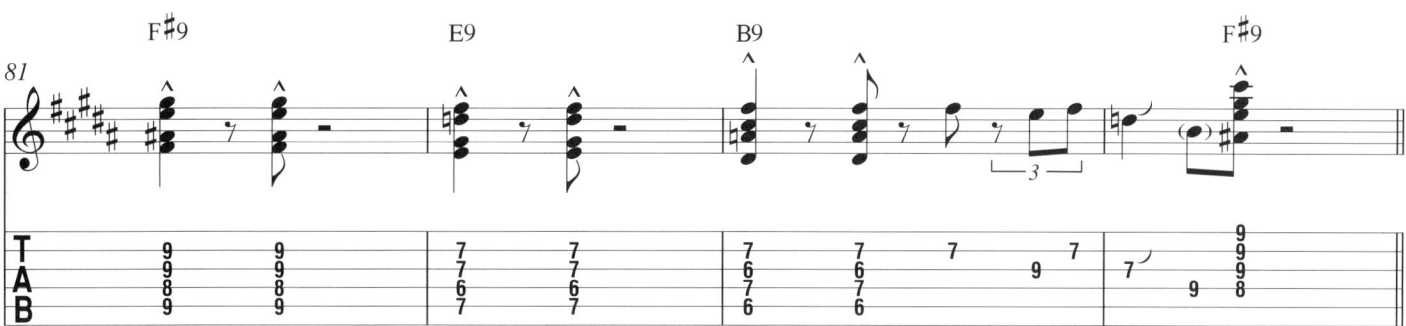

Chorus 8 - Vocals
(see additional lyrics)

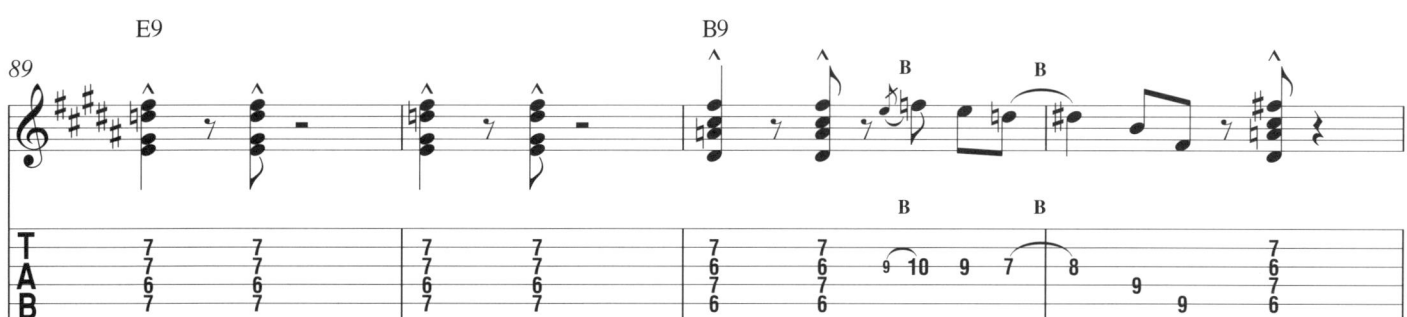

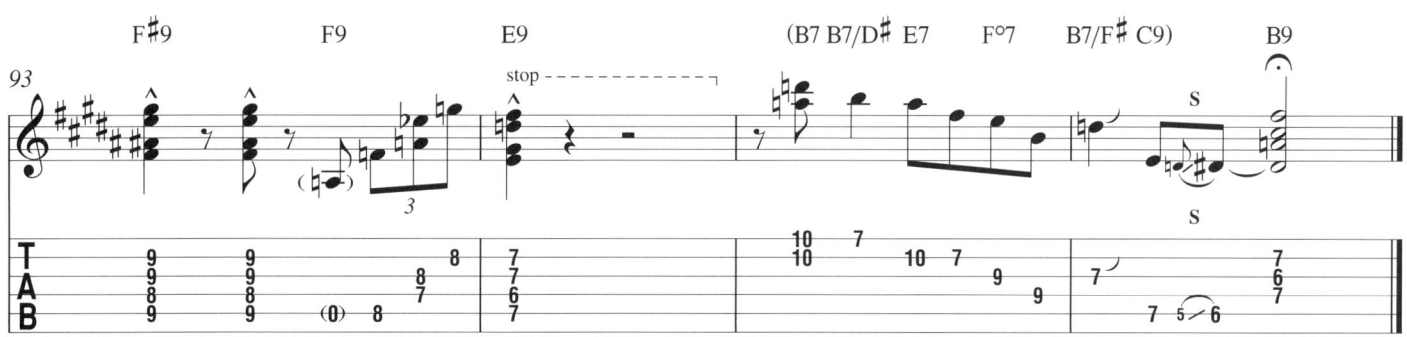

Additional Lyrics

6. Well you say you'll stick with me baby
   Stick with me through thick and thin
   I know someday baby
   My bad luck has got to end
   Now wait on me baby
   I'll be there one day
   Yes, and until I get there baby
   All I can do is hope and pray

7. Well I live the life I love
   And I love the life I live
   The life I have baby
   Is all I have to give
   So just wait on me baby
   I'll be there one day
   Yes and until I get there baby
   All I can do is hope and pray

8. Well you just got to wait on time baby
   Yes, just wait on time now baby
   Yeah, yeah, be good to me baby
   Because until I get there baby
   All I can do is hope and pray

CHAPTER 9

"The Woman I Love"
B.B. King

B.B. King (b. 1925) is unquestionably the world's greatest ambassador of the blues. During his career spanning six decades (and counting), he's performed in at least eighty-eight countries and amassed a huge collection of honors and awards from Grammys and W.C. Handy Blues Awards, to the National Medal of Arts and the Presidential Medal of Freedom. He's performed on many critically acclaimed recordings, and influenced throngs of the greatest guitarists of today. Simply stated, B.B. King has done more for the blues than anyone.

"The Woman I Love" (by B.B. King and Jules Taub, aka Jules Bihari) was originally released as a single in 1954 on RPM records. This medium-tempo shuffle in the key of B♭ is vintage '50s B.B. King, and it showcases his superlative talent as a singer and as a guitarist. King's vast vocal range conveys a mountain of soul with an intensity level that's right on par with his guitar chops, which bristle with vintage '50s tone and intensity.

PERFORMANCE TIPS

"The Woman I Love" features more than a dozen of B.B. King's hugely influential and often-imitated phrases, which have been adopted as essential soloing vocabulary for thousands of blues and rock guitarists.

As with all of the transcriptions in this book, I strongly recommend listening and playing along with B.B. King's original recording of this song. (See the discography/listing of original recordings in the appendix.)

One essential skill for the rhythm guitarist that's often overlooked (or underestimated) is the ability to play effective and inspiring fills around the vocalist's lyrics. So in addition to learning B.B. King's solo phrases, I recommend practicing and eventually memorizing (or "internalizing") his fills throughout these vocal verses.

As you practice B.B. King's phrases on this track, try to match the intensity that he poured into every note. To work this piece "into the ballpark," you'll need to play all single-note lines and string bends with intensity and conviction.

CHAPTER 9 "The Woman I Love" B.B. King

Play them with a punchy, aggressive picking attack. Really lean into the string bends and the notes with vibrato, to make the phrases sing!

B.B. King kicks off the intro of "The Woman I Love" with a six-note motif (up the notes C♯ D F G B♭ B♭), that he repeated three times. The note C♯ (♭3 or ♯9) starts off the phrase, and the notes that follow (D F G B♭) are from the B♭ pentatonic scale: B♭ C D F G, the 1, 2 (or 9), 3, 5, 6 (or 13) from the B♭ major scale. King played most of this 4-bar intro solo, and the band "answered" his phrases in bars 1 and 2 with hits on the "and" of beat 2. King played those hits also—as chords (as shown in the music and tab). His chord hits are difficult to hear though, since they're somewhat buried/obstructed in the mix.

B.B. repeated that opening lick three times (in the first two bars), and then he glided right into another of his "signature" licks. Immediately after striking the B♭ (on the 6th fret, high E string) on the first beat of bar 3, he slid up the B string to nail the B♭ note (root) on the 11th fret a few more times.

Note: Thanks are due to B.B. King for this classic sliding phrase. It's a shame that he never "patented" this lick, because it's been imitated and adopted as essential soloing vocabulary for countless blues and rock guitarists since the 1950s!

King's intro to "The Woman I Love" sets the tone for his phrases that follow. This solo features a powerful mix of the B♭ blues scale, B♭ D♭ E♭ E F A♭ (1 ♭3 4 ♭5 5 ♭7), combined with a few notes from the B♭ pentatonic scale, the D (3rd), G (6 or 13th), and C (9th).

Take a look, and listen to King's 4-note phrase between bars 4 and 5, leading into the E♭7 (IV) chord. On beat 4 of bar 4, B.B. slid into the note G (12th fret, G string) followed by B♭ (11th fret, B string) and then the note D♭ (B string, 14th fret), which he bent one half step up, to D. The notes G, B♭, and D♭ are the 3rd, 5th, and ♭7 of the E♭7 chord, so they outline the sound of the chord very clearly. However, the D (the natural 7th) sounds unusual against the E♭7 (the IV) chord. In certain contexts, leaning into the natural 7th against a dominant 7th chord may sound like a mistake. Yet somehow, with the attitude and "mojo" that King attacked the phrase with, that big, fat D note sitting right on beat 1 of the E♭7 chord sounds right at home; it's one of the coolest notes in the solo!

Bar 6 features another of King's classic phrases that conveys tons of intensity and forward momentum. Starting on the "and" of 1, King struck the high A♭ (16th fret, high E string) twice, then he immediately descended three frets down the string to the note F, followed by (chromatic notes) E, E♭, and D. The phrase ends by striking the note B♭ (B string 11th fret) three times in quick succession. Notice that B.B. played this same phrase again in bar 10, but there he struck the high A♭ once and sustained it instead of hitting it twice, as before.

Back in the '50s, King descended down the string to execute that phrase. In later years, he phrased the same notes around a powerful (minor 3rd) string bend, from the note F up to the A♭, then he released the bend back down to play the F, E, D, and B♭ notes that followed. Employing the minor 3rd string bend creates even more of a vocal quality for the phrase, and over the years, that's become one of King's most recognizable and often imitated licks.

King's phrases in his solo in choruses 4 and 5 create a ton of forward momentum and intensity–such as his (high-note) phrase in bars 46 and 47 of chorus 4. With repeated pull-offs and a slide, and denser/more complex rhythms, this phrase is a much more challenging variation of his descending lines in bars 6 and 10 of his intro chorus.

Leading into his third chorus, King launched into powerful (slide influenced) repeated triplets through bars 49–51, with notes D and F (chord tones 3 and 5) on the top two strings, which create even more momentum and tension, to help climax the solo. Then, in bar 4, King slid up into a high B♭9 chord in the 13th position on the top strings, followed by a B♭13 chord on beat 3, to finish the phrase. King closed out the solo with more classic licks based on the B♭ blues scale.

I recommend learning King's intro chorus first, since it sounds great, plus it's a little easier to play than the choruses that follow. Good luck with B.B. King's solos and fills on "The Woman I Love." I hope you enjoy playing this as much as I have!

ABOUT THE CD

 Full Band
TRACK 20

 No Guitar
TRACK 21

Tracks 20 and 21 for "The Woman I Love" are seven choruses in length; they run the entire length of King's original track.

The Woman I Love
As played by B.B. King

Words and Music by B.B. King and Jules Bihari

Copyright © 1954 by Universal Music - Careers and Powerforce Music
Copyright Renewed
All Rights Administered by Universal Music - Careers
International Copyright Secured   All Rights Reserved

CHAPTER 9 "The Woman I Love" B.B. King

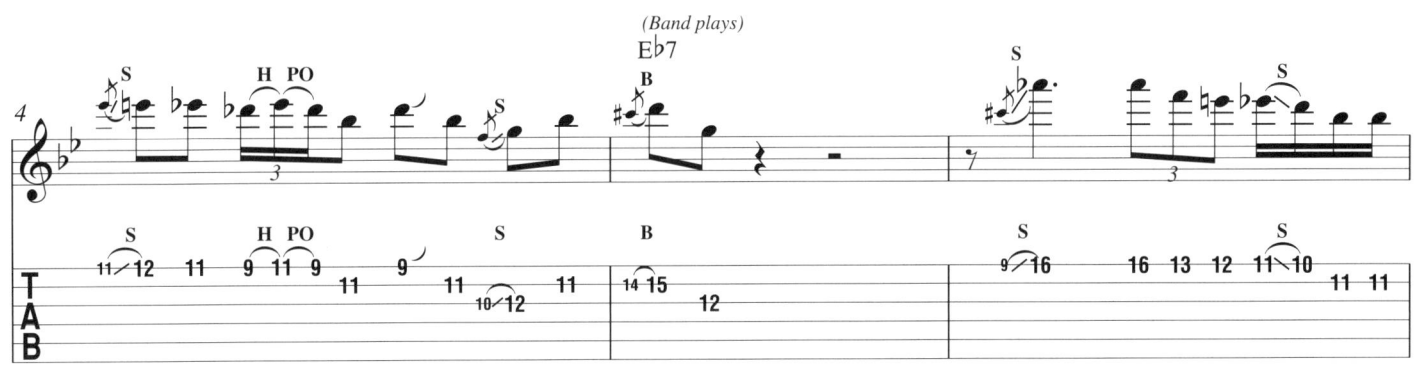

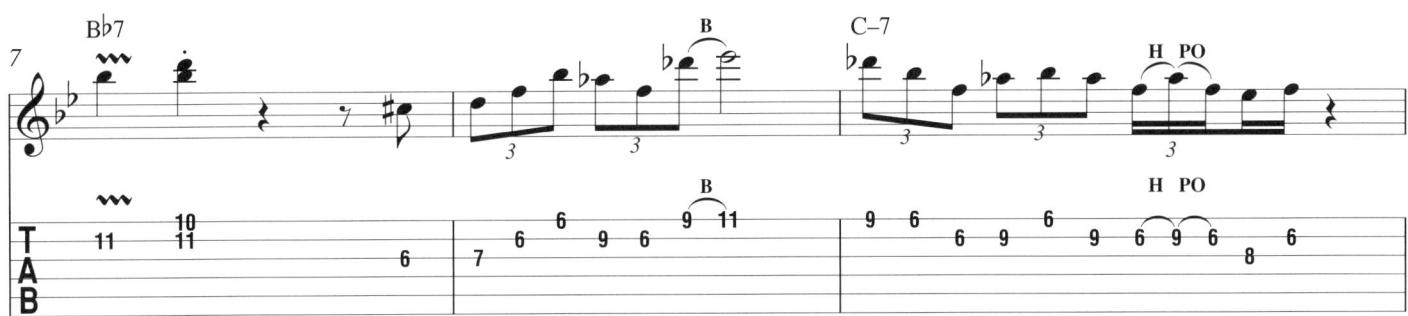

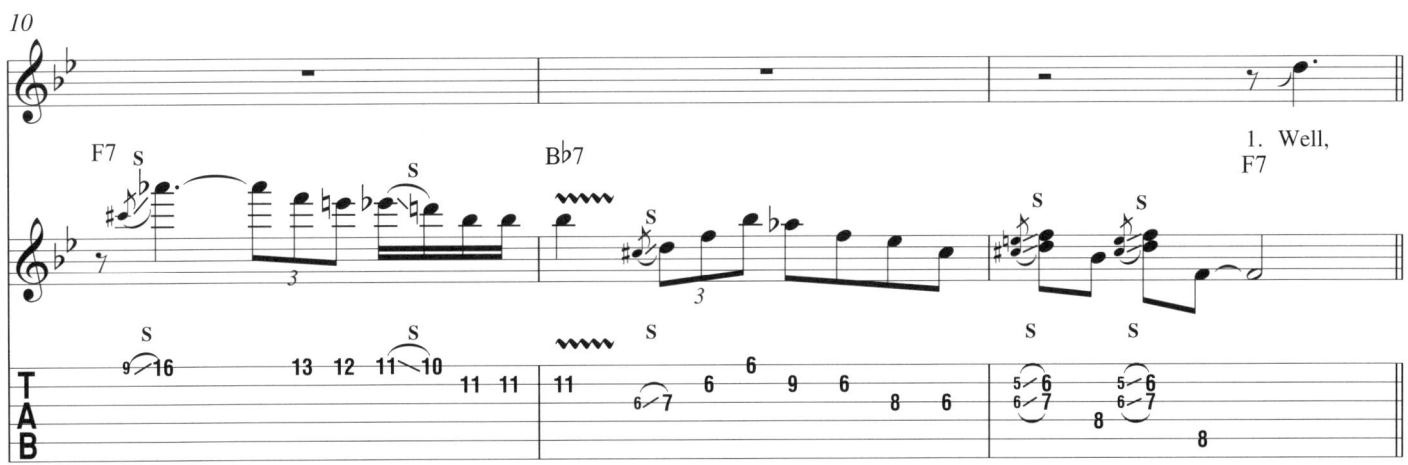

Chorus 2

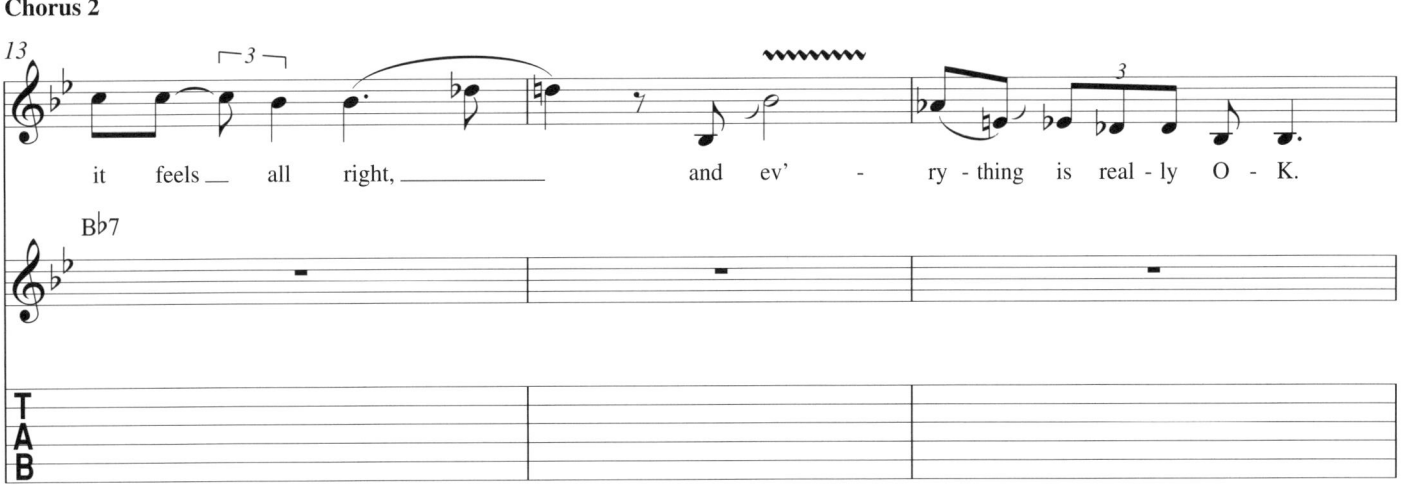

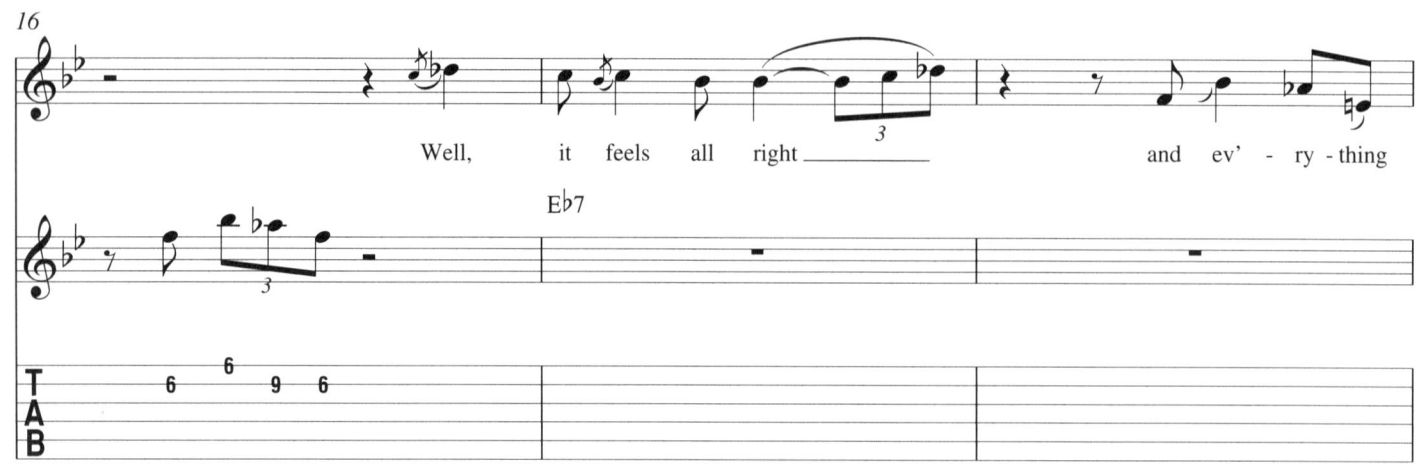
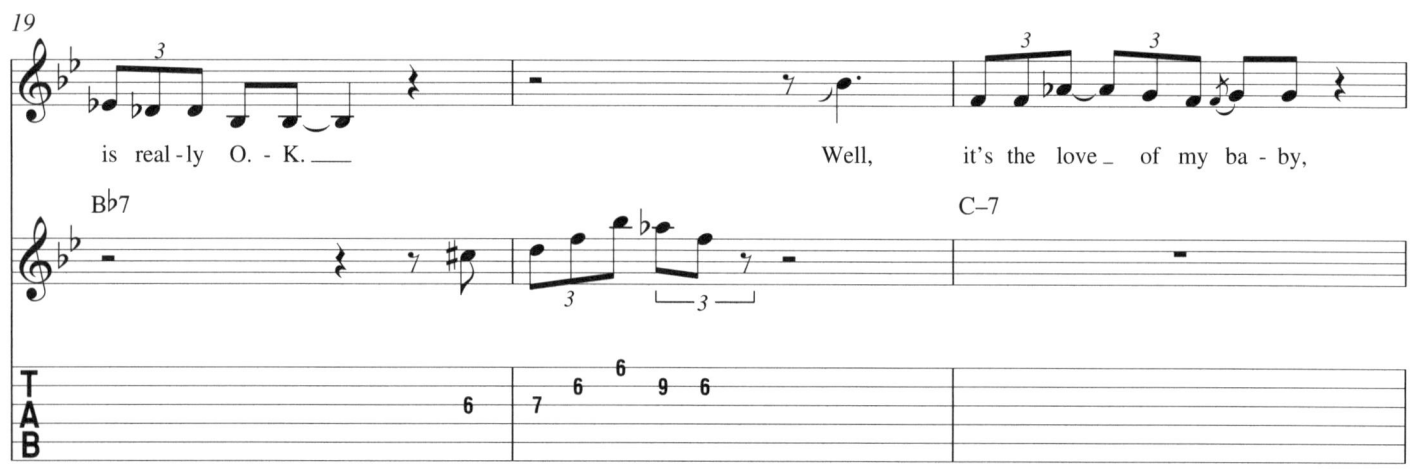
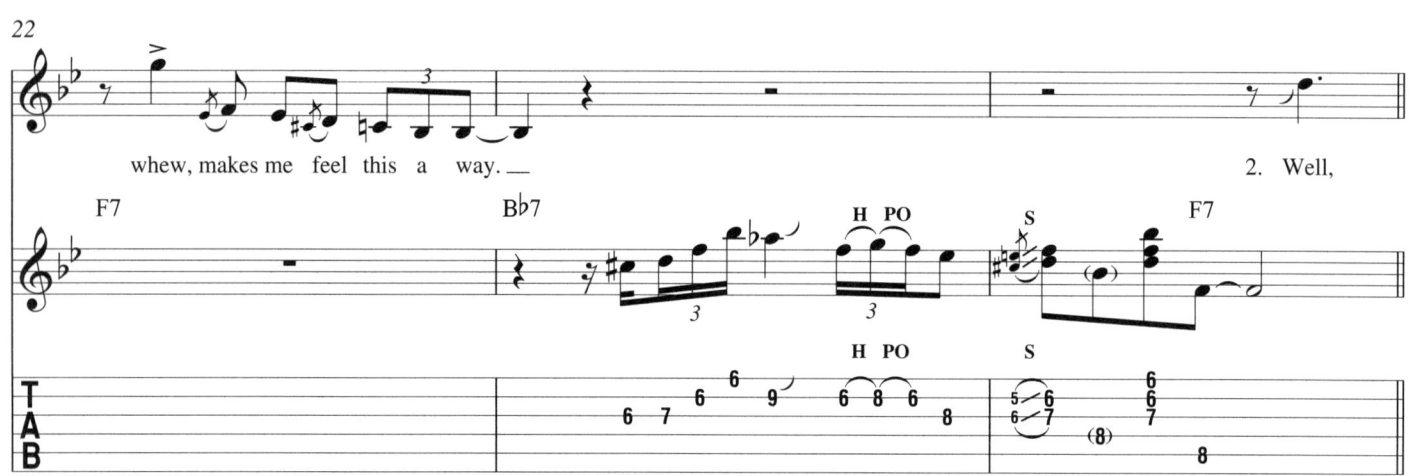

CHAPTER 9 "The Woman I Love" B.B. King

Chorus 3

82 BERKLEE BLUES GUITAR SONGBOOK

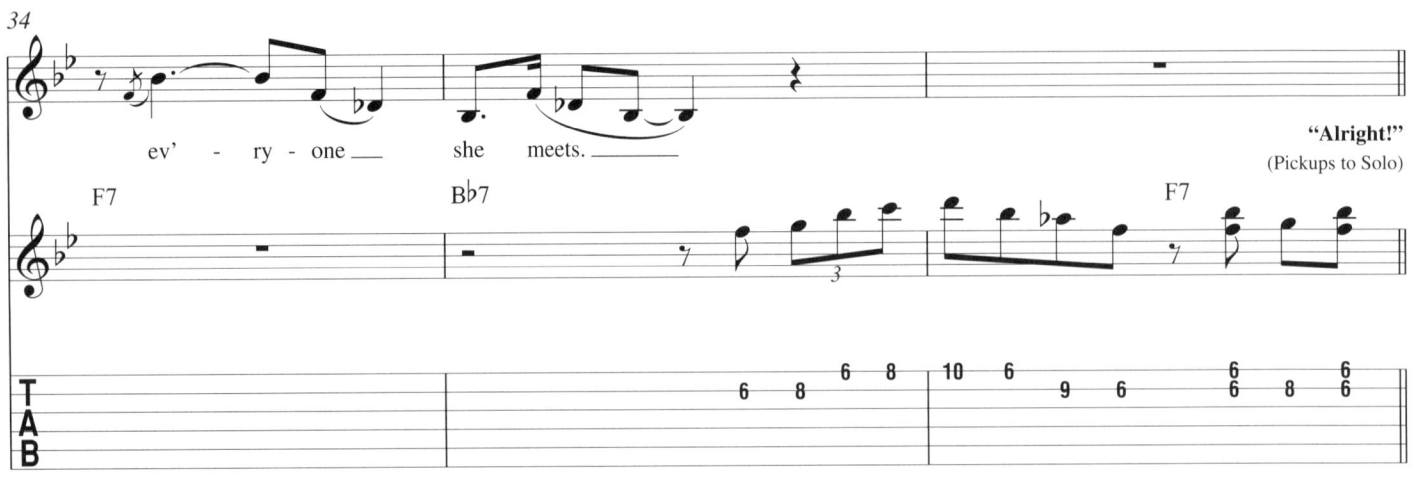

Chorus 4 - Solo

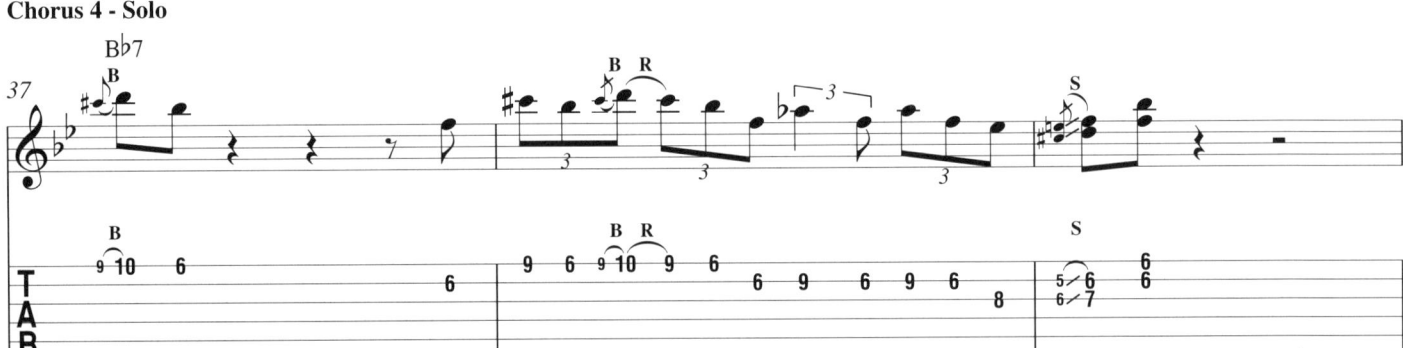

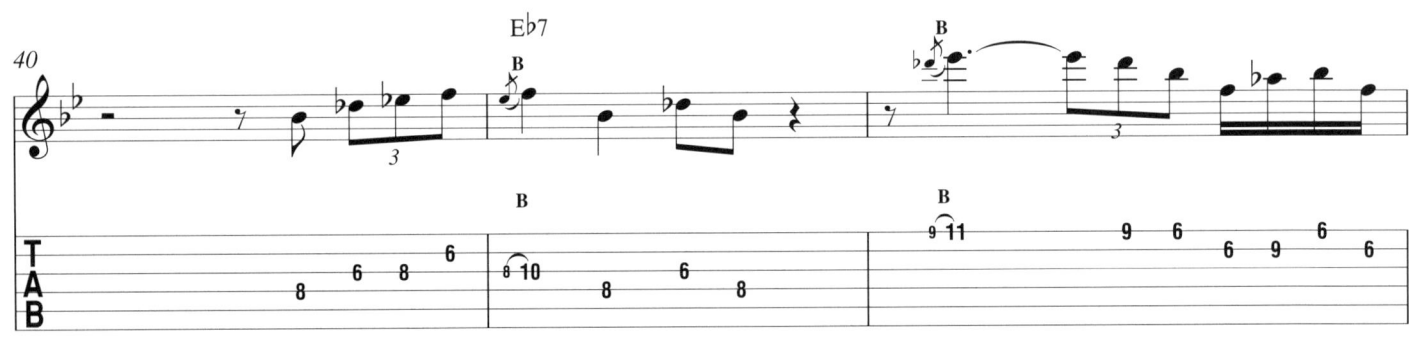

CHAPTER 9 "The Woman I Love" B.B. King

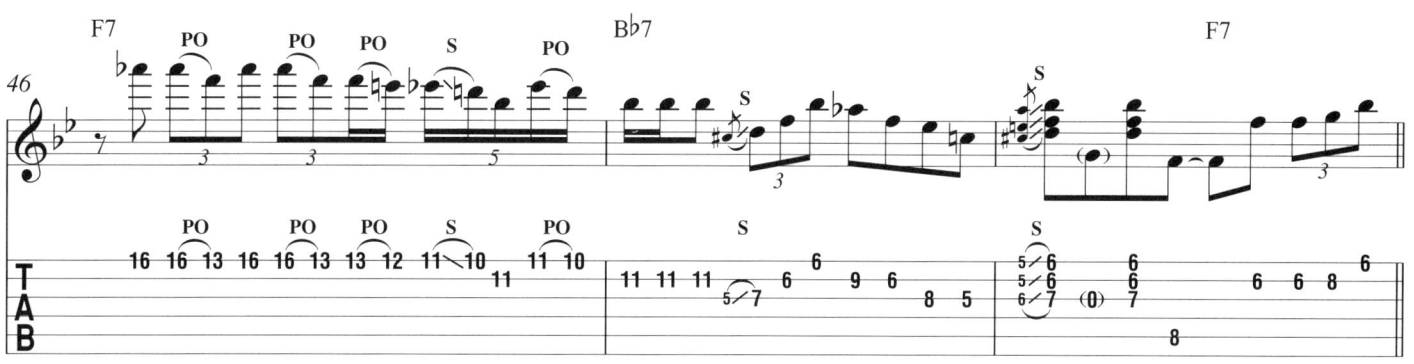

Chorus 5

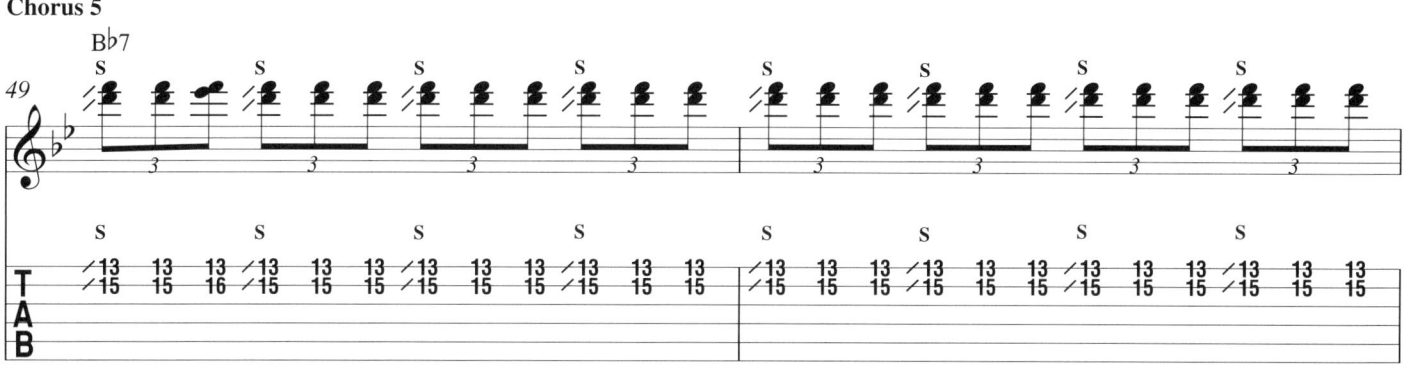

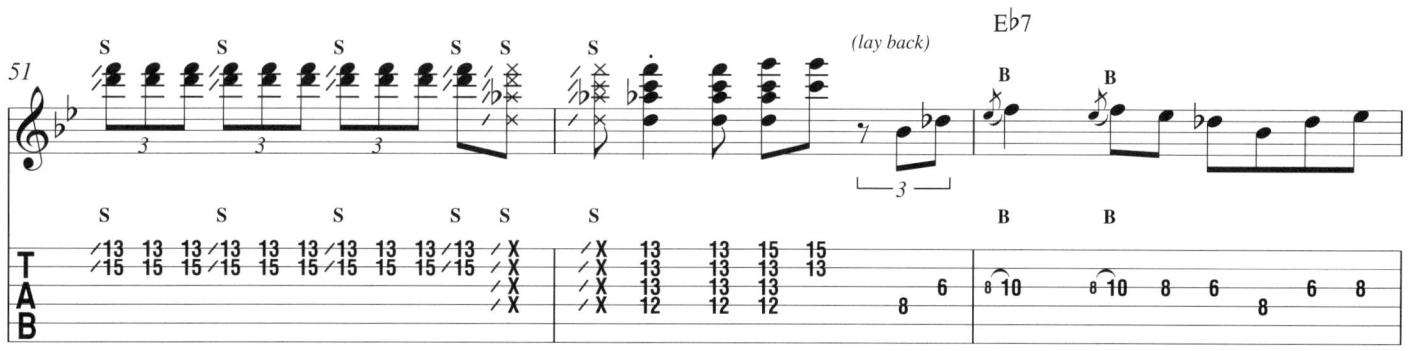

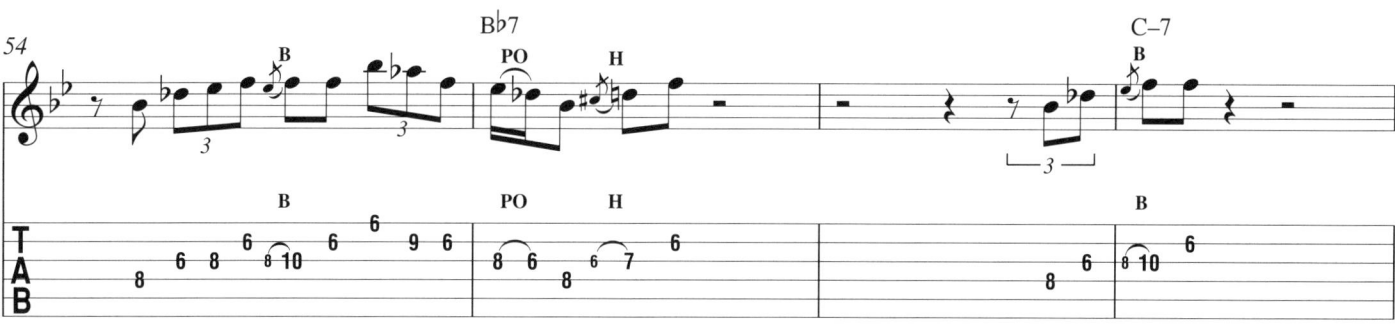

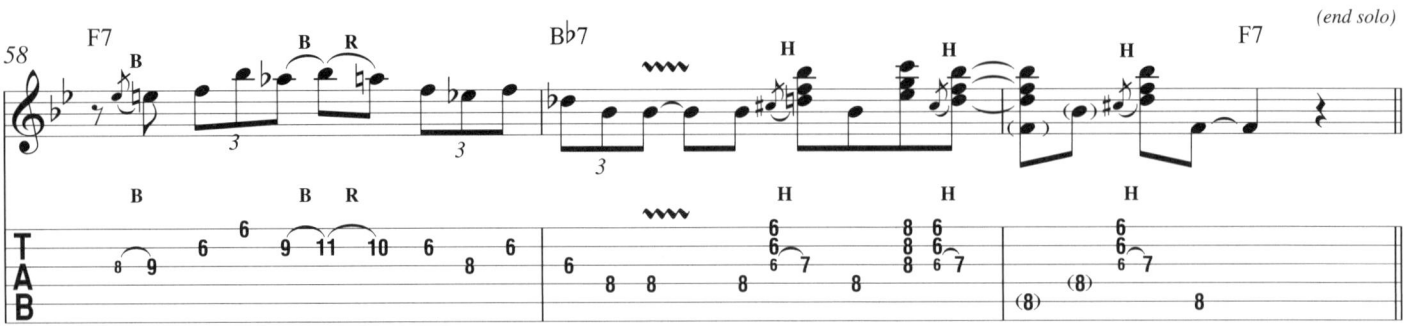

Chorus 6 - Vocals
(see additional lyrics)

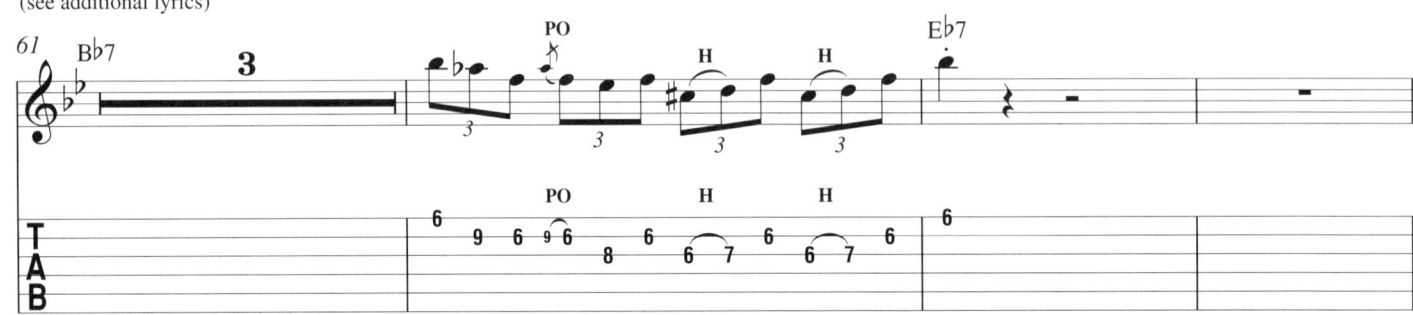

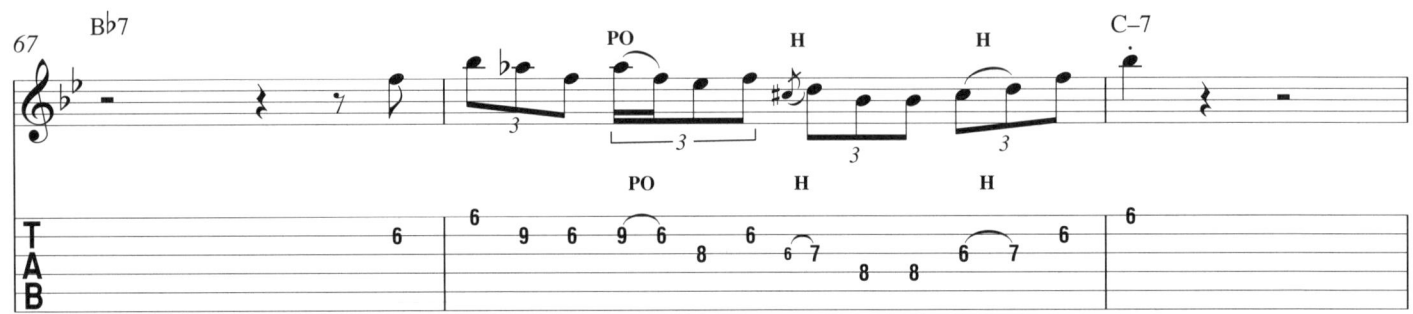

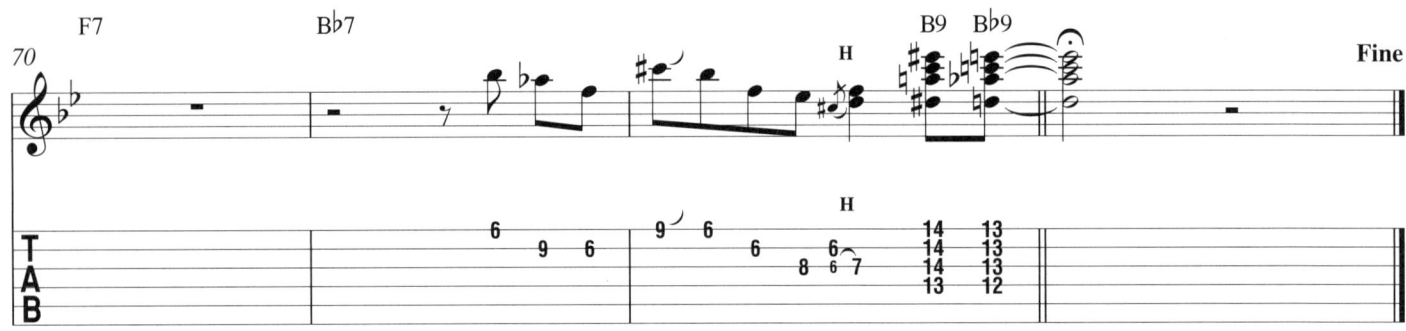

Additional Lyrics

Last Verse
Well, I love ya baby, wow, sweet, like heaven up above
I love ya baby, ooh, sweet like heaven up above
Well, I pray to the Lord, you the only one I love

CHAPTER 10

"Worried Life Blues"
Robert Lockwood Jr.

With his vast vocabulary of chord progressions, inventive turnarounds and fills, and wide command of rhythm guitar styles, Robert Lockwood Jr.'s highly personal and influential guitar playing is instantly recognizable on many landmark recordings in blues.

Robert Lockwood Jr. (1915 to 2006) was born in Turkey Scratch, Arkansas, and he was eleven years old when Robert Johnson came to live with his mother. Lockwood soon began learning the blues from Johnson (who is commonly referred to as his stepfather), and by the age of fifteen, he was traveling and playing parties, juke joints, and street corners with Sonny Boy Williamson, aka Rice Miller. Not content to recreate Johnson's style of delta blues year after year, Lockwood's recordings throughout the decades reflect strong influences and connections to jazz, along with his deep roots from the delta.

In 1941, Robert Lockwood Jr. performed on the very first *King Biscuit Time* radio show on KFFA, out of Helena, Arkansas, along with harmonica player and vocalist Sonny Boy Williamson. The duo performed live on the air for several years, and among their listeners was B.B. King, who cited Lockwood as a major inspiration and influence. During the 1950s, Lockwood settled in Chicago where he performed and recorded with many of the greatest artists in blues including Sonny Boy Williamson, Sunnyland Slim, Little Walter, Muddy Waters, Howlin' Wolf, Otis Spann, and others.

Robert Lockwood moved to Cleveland, Ohio in 1961, and continued to perform in clubs and festivals right up until he passed away in 2006. I witnessed Lockwood's performance at a blues festival in Ohio about a year before he died. At ninety-plus years of age, he walked out on stage dressed head–to–toe in an electric-blue suit, along with his perfectly matching blue 12-string Gretch. Robert Lockwood Jr. put on a stellar performance that afternoon, true to the consummate professional that he was.

Despite a lengthy and distinguished career, Robert Lockwood never became a household name. However, his influences still resound throughout the world of blues. His signature turnarounds, fills, and rhythm parts are still being adopted and played by blues guitarists around the globe.

"Worried Life Blues" (by Otis Spann) was originally released in 1961 on Candid's *Otis Spann is the Blues*. The record features piano, guitar, and vocals only, with no bass and drums, or other instruments. It's considered to be required listening and study for serious blues pianists and guitarists, since Otis Spann and Robert Lockwood were among the very best of Chicago blues pianists and guitarists of the time—and in top form.

PERFORMANCE TIPS

This track is nine choruses in length, and it showcases several of Lockwood's unique jazz-influenced (and challenging) turnarounds. To reap the maximum benefits from this track, memorize each turnaround in the original context of this relaxed 8-bar progression. Then, for a follow-up exercise, reuse Lockwood's turnarounds and phrases in your own way. Change the key, tempo, and context to internalize these phrases as part of your own soloing vocabulary.

Chorus 1 begins in bar 5, after the 4-bar intro. It's a solid place to begin, since Lockwood repeats that chorus nearly note-for-note in chorus 2. In addition, he repeats similar variations of his opening phrase (bars 5–6) for every chorus that follows, with the exception of his solo in chorus 8. For that chorus only, Spann and Lockwood depart from the 8-bar blues form, and play over a 12-bar form instead!

Chorus 1 is played along with Otis Spann's first vocal verse. While Lockwood's chorus serves as a strong counter-line to Spann's vocal part, it sounds great without the vocals as well.

Lockwood begins chorus 1 with repeated eighth notes, as he plays a series of half-step string bends up from the ♭3rd (enharmonically written as D♯), into the major 3rd (E) on beats 1–3. Lockwood takes his time on each string bend, and squeezes every ounce of soul from each note. As with the other solos in this book, the best way to get the feel for Lockwood's string bends and phrases is to play along with his original track repeatedly.

Lockwood plays triplets throughout bars 7 and 8, as he slides up to outline the IV chord (F7), with chord tones A and C (the 3rd and 5th, played as diatonic 3rds on the 2nd and 1st strings). Next, for bars 9–10, Lockwood returns to the C7 (I7) with more string bends from the ♭3, into the major 3rd, as played in the opening phrase (bars 5–6).

To wrap up chorus 1, Lockwood begins one of his signature turnarounds in bar 11 by outlining chord sound on beat 1 with an arpeggio through a C triad (notes E, C, G, played as a triplet on strings 3, 4, and 5). Lockwood repeats the C triad (again as a triplet) in beat 3, and emphasized the note E (the 3rd) throughout much of this first turnaround. The "double–chromatic" approach to

CHAPTER 10 "Worried Life Blues" Robert Lockwood Jr.

the root with notes B♭, B, and C (played as a triplet) on beat 4 creates color and jazz influences. Lockwood filled out the rest of the turnaround, and those that followed, with string bends and notes from the C minor pentatonic scale (C E♭ F G B♭).

Lockwood's turnarounds on choruses 4 and 5 (below) are excellent examples of his innovative and jazz-influenced phrasing. His chorus 4 turnaround begins in bar 35, and it features a sophisticated combination of triplets and sixteenth-note rhythms. Lockwood's turnaround in chorus 5 (bars 43–44) is less complex rhythmically; it's based on triplets, and it emphasizes more harmonic motion and detail, instead. Lockwood begins the turnaround by outlining the I chord with an arpeggio up through a C triad (C E G) on beats 1 and 2. Next, beginning on the 3rd triplet of beat 2, he outlines the IV (F) chord, with an arpeggio up through F6 and FMaj7 chords (F A C D E). Following that, in bar 44, he outlines the I chord again, with an arpeggio though the C triad (on beat 1), and then finishes the turnaround by outlining the V7 chord (G7) with a repeated double-chromatic approach up into the note G on beats 2–4.

Note: The analysis (1 3 5 7 etc.) included below each phrase illustrates its relationship to the chord changes. Notice that both turnarounds consist exclusively of notes from the combined C pentatonic (C D E G A) and C blues (C E♭ F G♭ G B♭) scales.

(Chorus 4 Turnround, Bars 35–36)

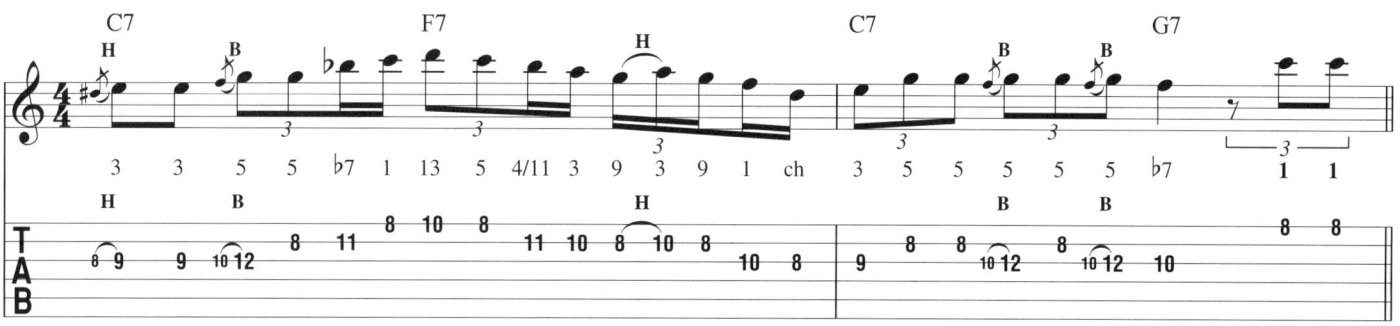

(Chorus 5 Turnround, Bars 43–44)

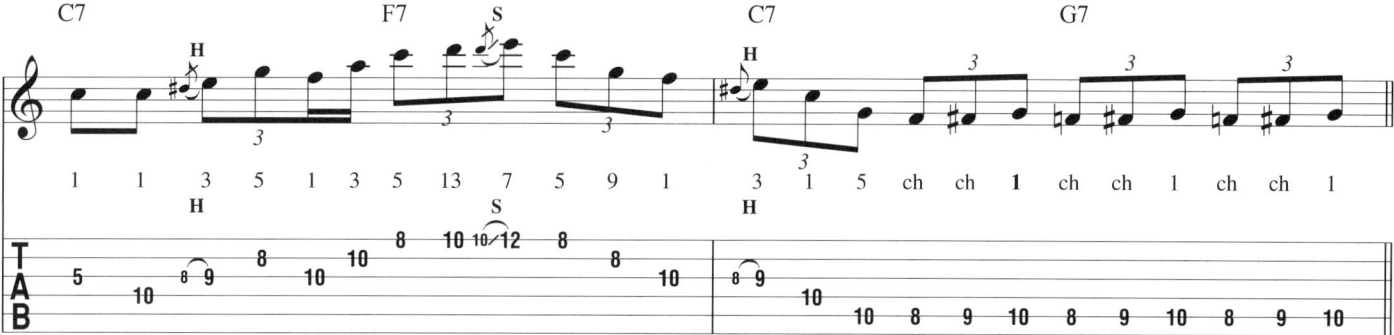

Fig. 10.1. "Worried Life Blues" Excerpts. Bold type indicates anticipations.

Lockwood's solo over the 12-bar form in chorus 8 is by far the most challenging part of this track. Much of that chorus is played at a "double-time" pace. His lines are denser and more complex, and several of the phrases fall rhythmically "between the cracks." (Because of that, Lockwood's phrases in bar 64 and the beginning of bar 65 were quite difficult to transcribe!) Once again, the best way to get the feel for Lockwood's timing and phrases is to listen and play along with his original recording repeatedly.

Good luck with Robert Lockwood's phrases and solo. This is a huge project, so I suggest taking it one chorus at a time!

ABOUT THE CD

 Full Band
TRACK 22

 No Guitar
TRACK 23

Tracks 22 and 23 for "Worried Life Blues" run the entire length of Otis Spann's original track, so they're nine choruses long.

Worried Life Blues
As played by Robert Lockwood Jr.

Words and Music by
Maceo Merriweather

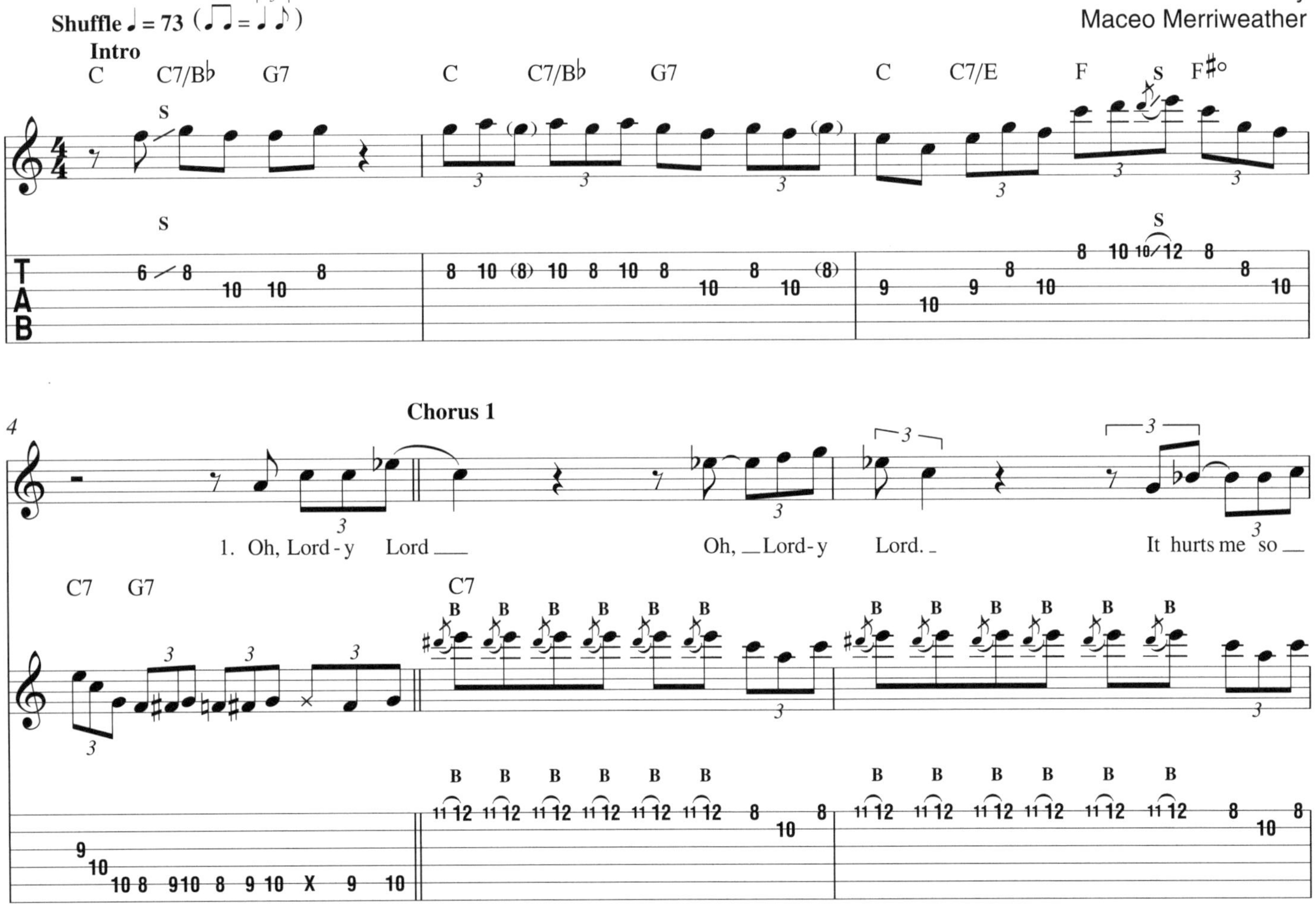

Copyright © 1941, 1947 SONGS OF UNIVERSAL, INC.
Copyright Renewed
All Rights Reserved   Used by Permission

CHAPTER 10 "Worried Life Blues" Robert Lockwood Jr. 89

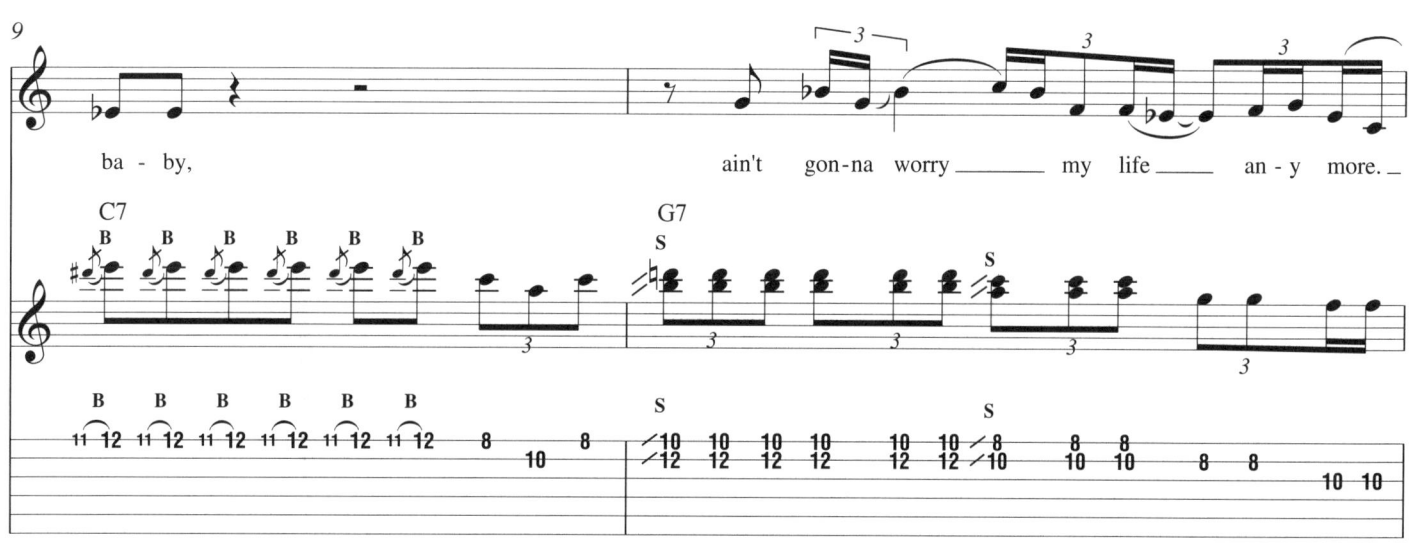
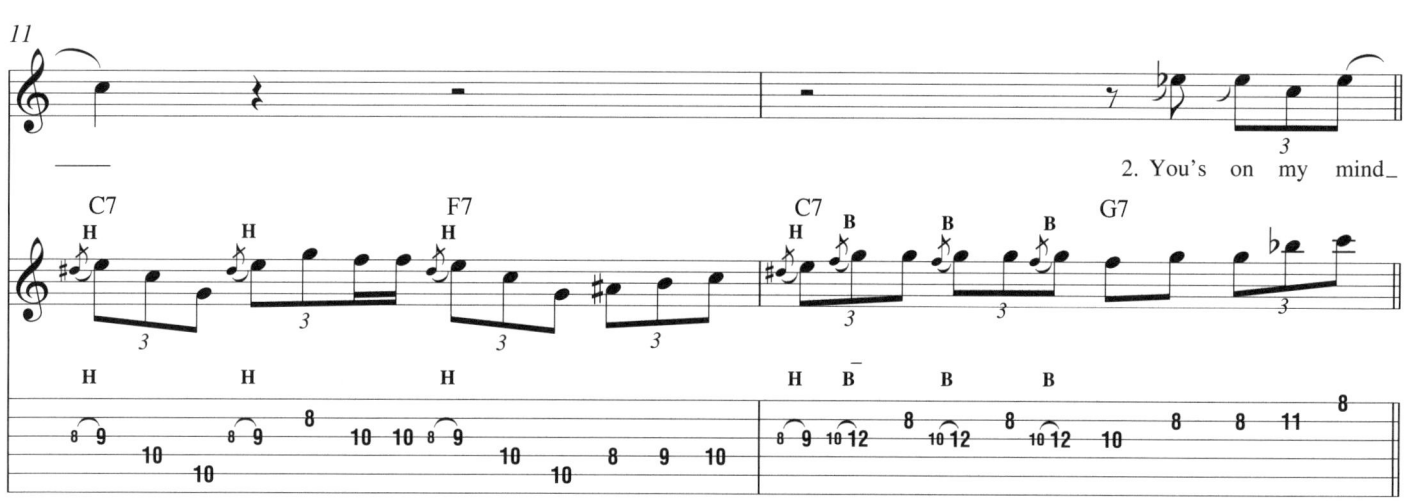

Chorus 2

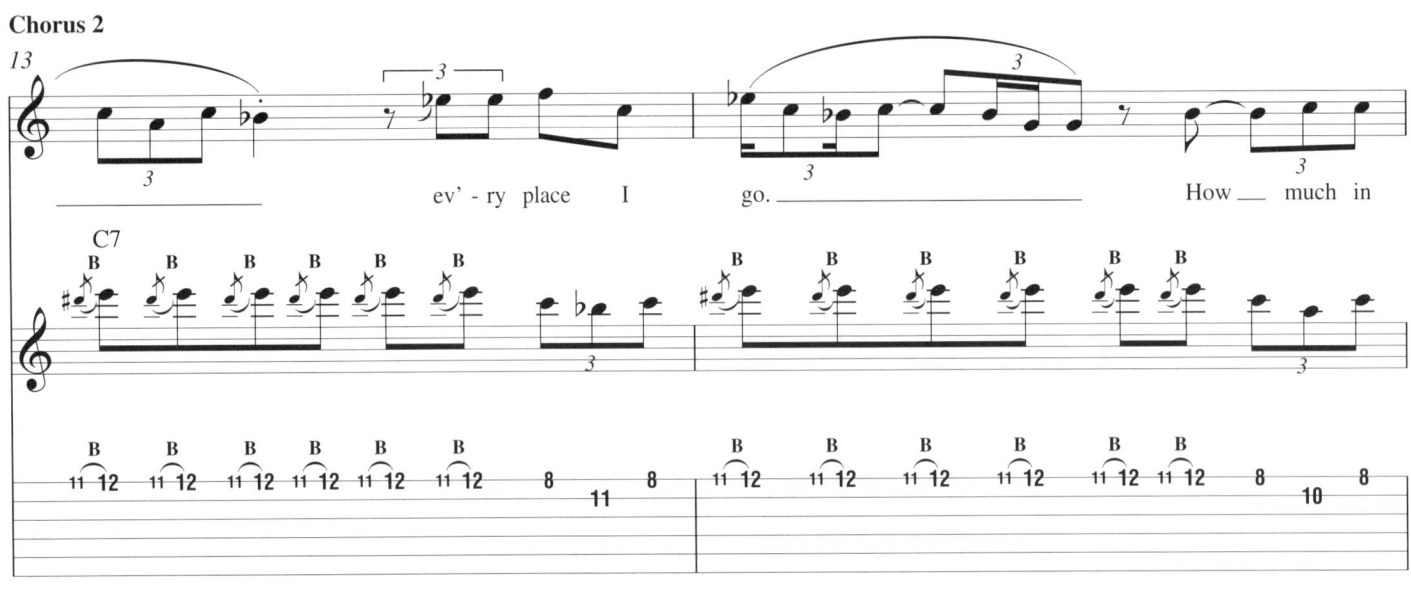

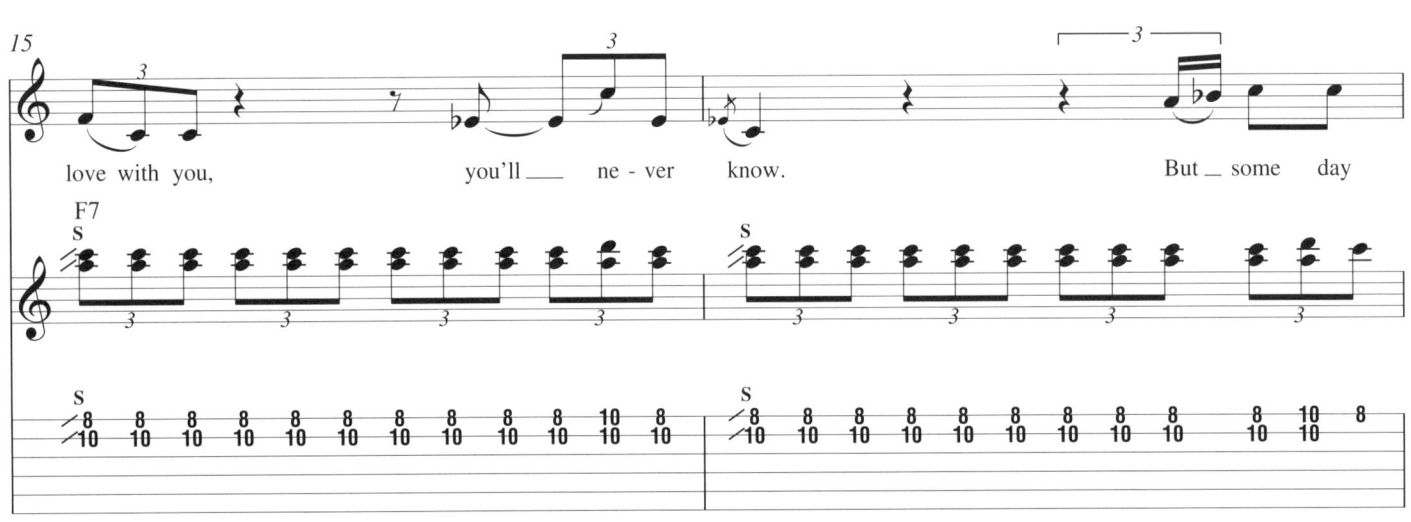

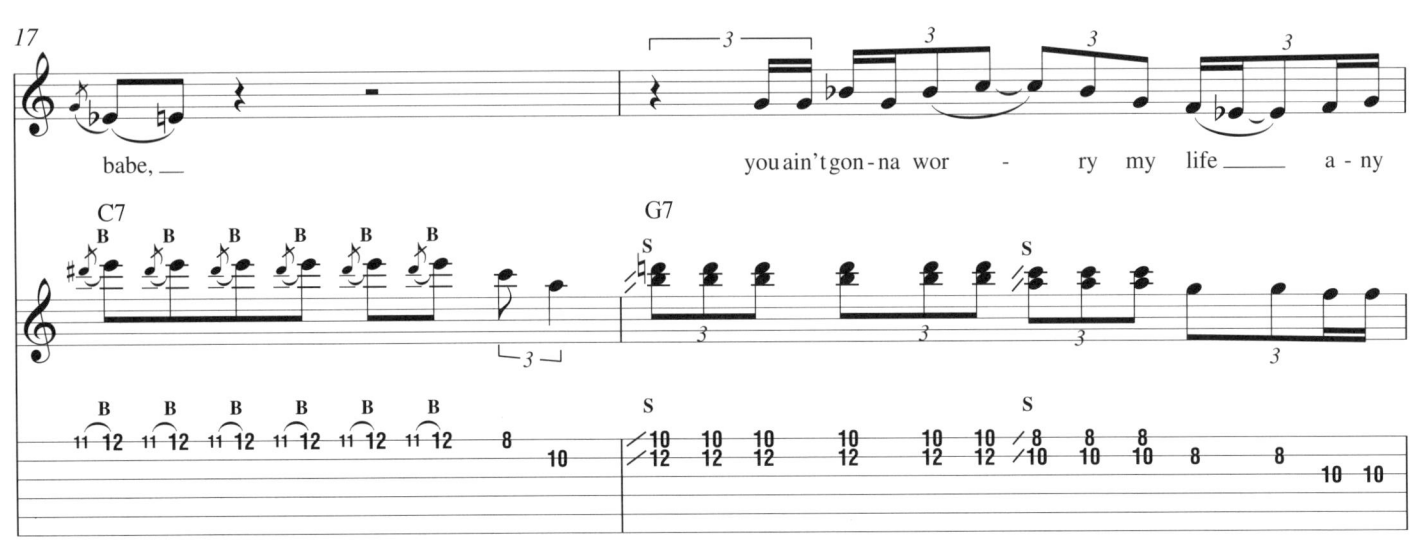

CHAPTER 10 "Worried Life Blues" Robert Lockwood Jr.

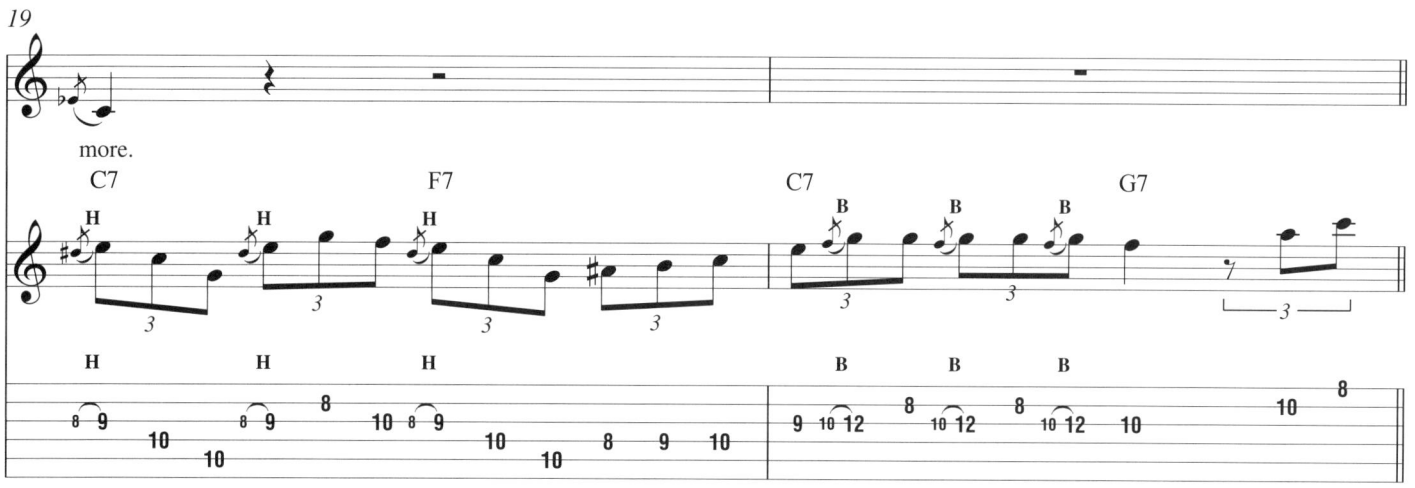

Chorus 3 - Vocals, Verse 3
(see additional lyrics)

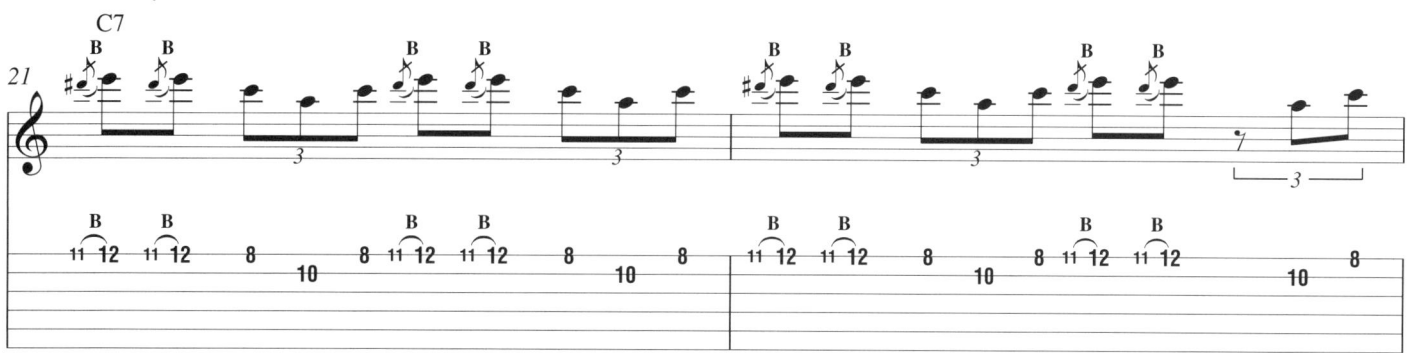

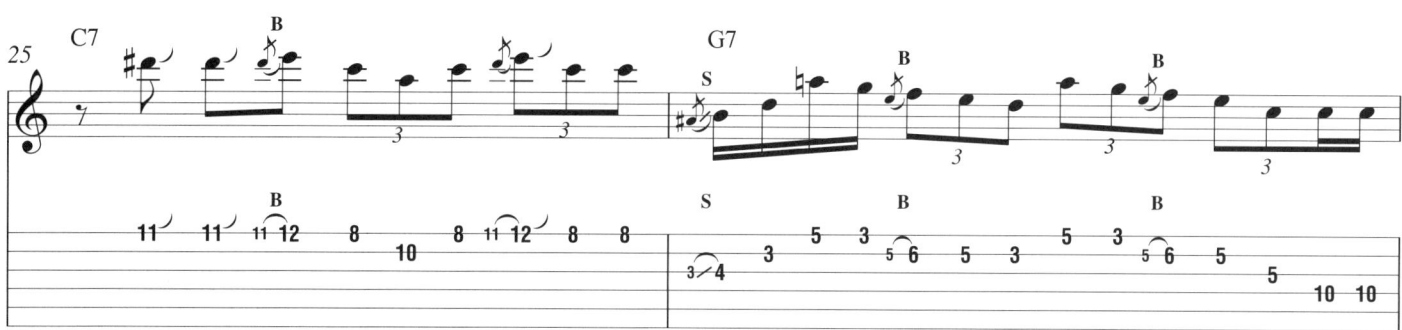

92 BERKLEE BLUES GUITAR SONGBOOK

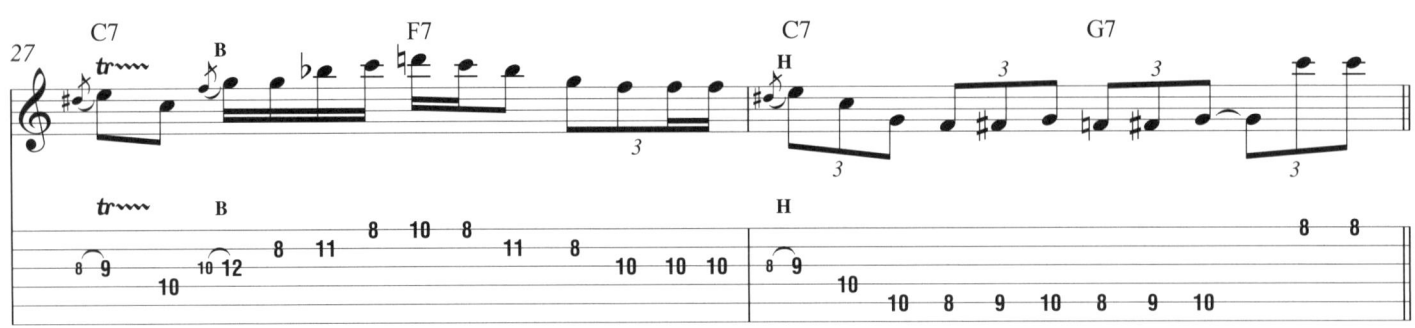

Chorus 4 - Solo

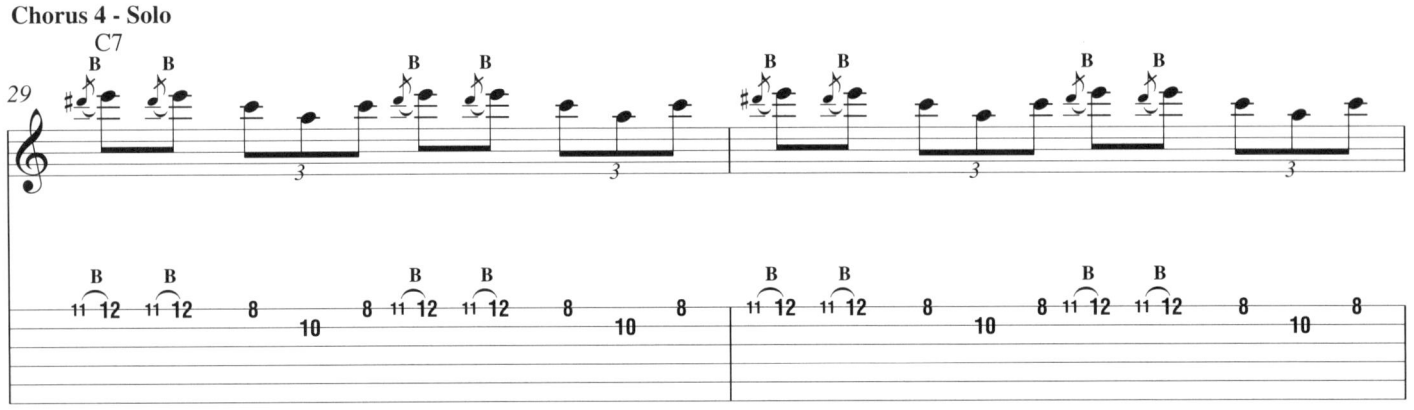

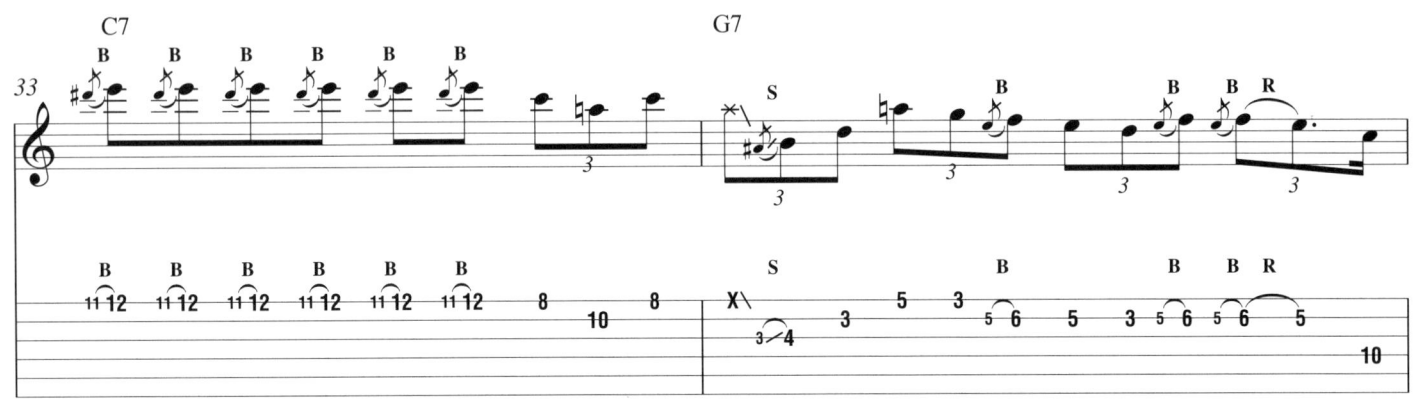

CHAPTER 10 "Worried Life Blues" Robert Lockwood Jr.

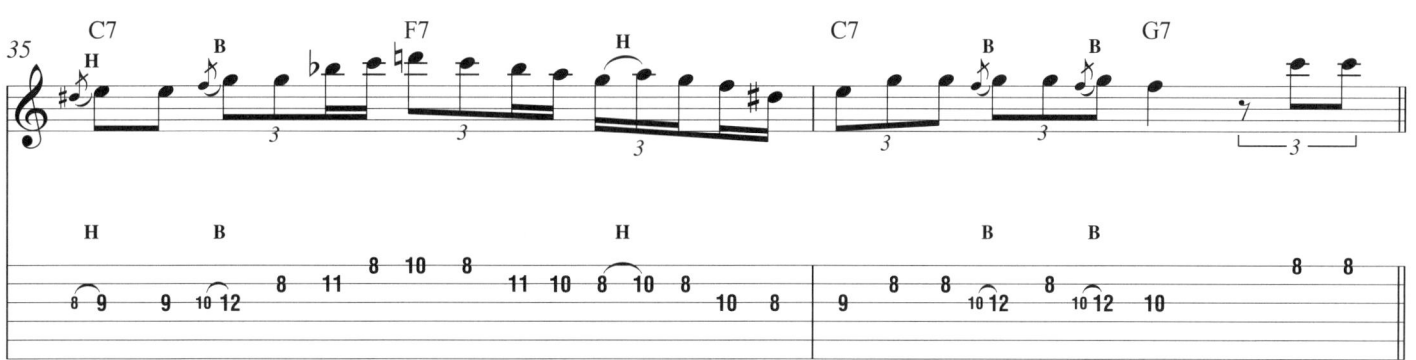

Chorus 5 - Solo

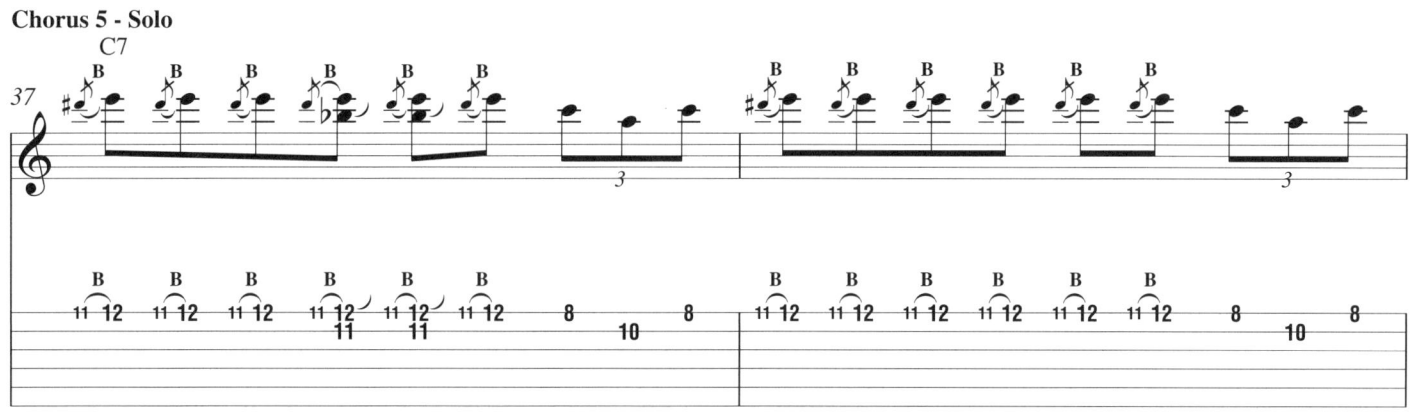

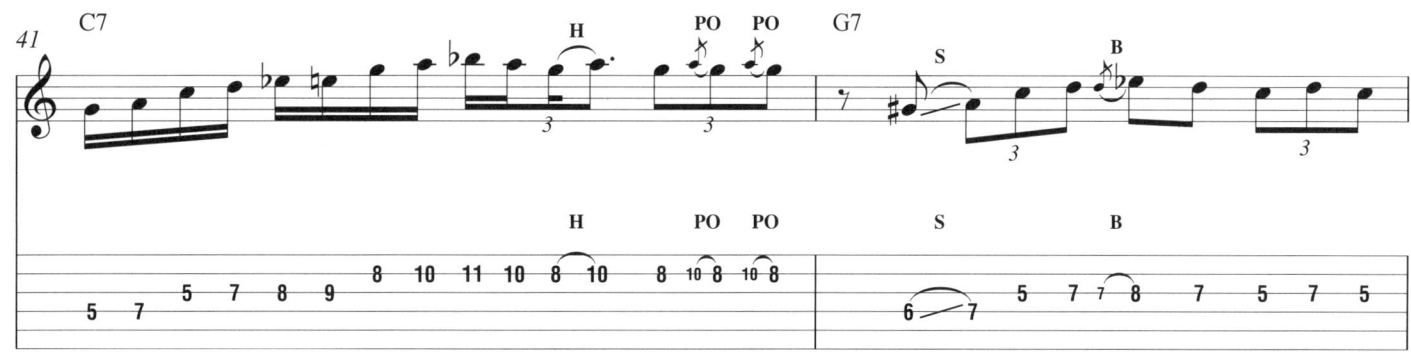

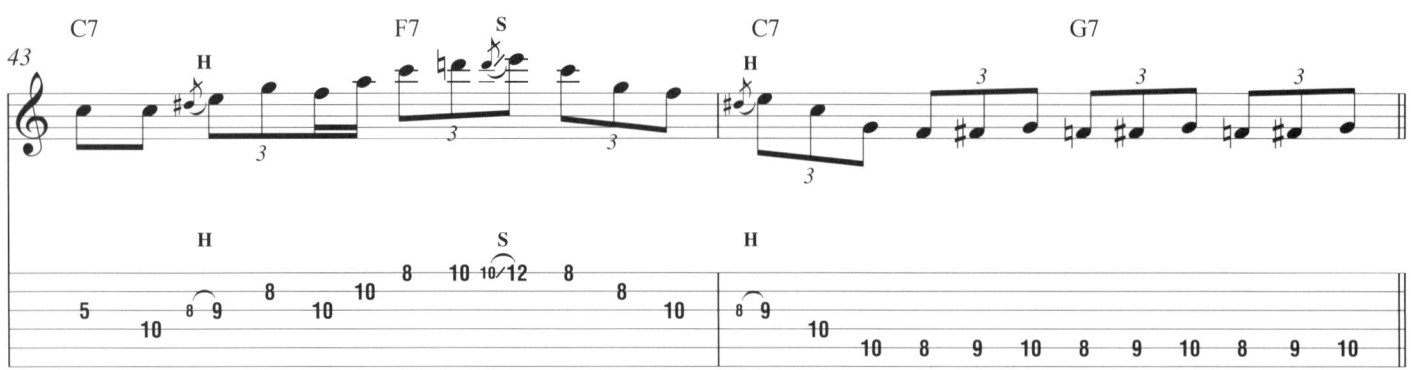

Chorus 6 (vocals, verse 4)

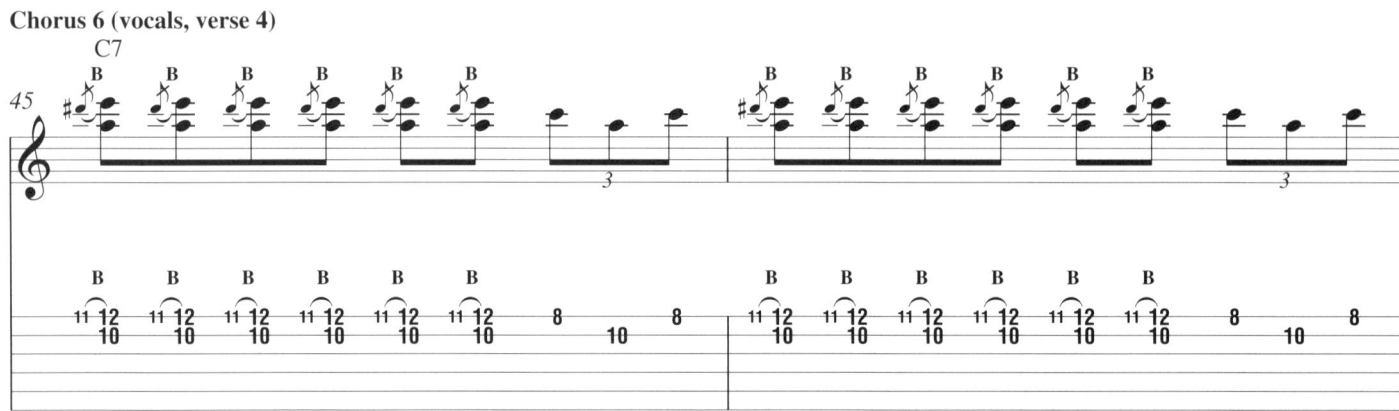

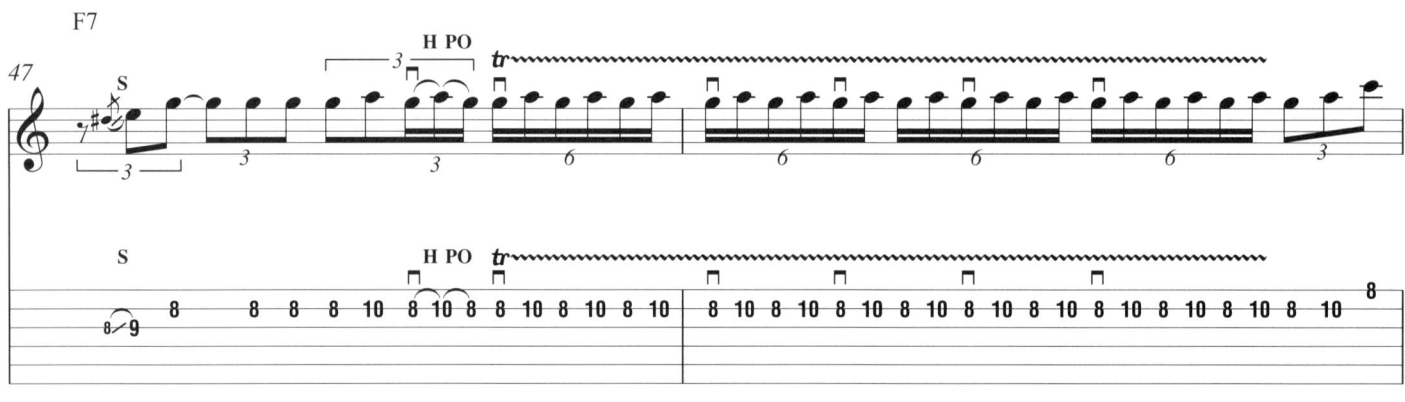

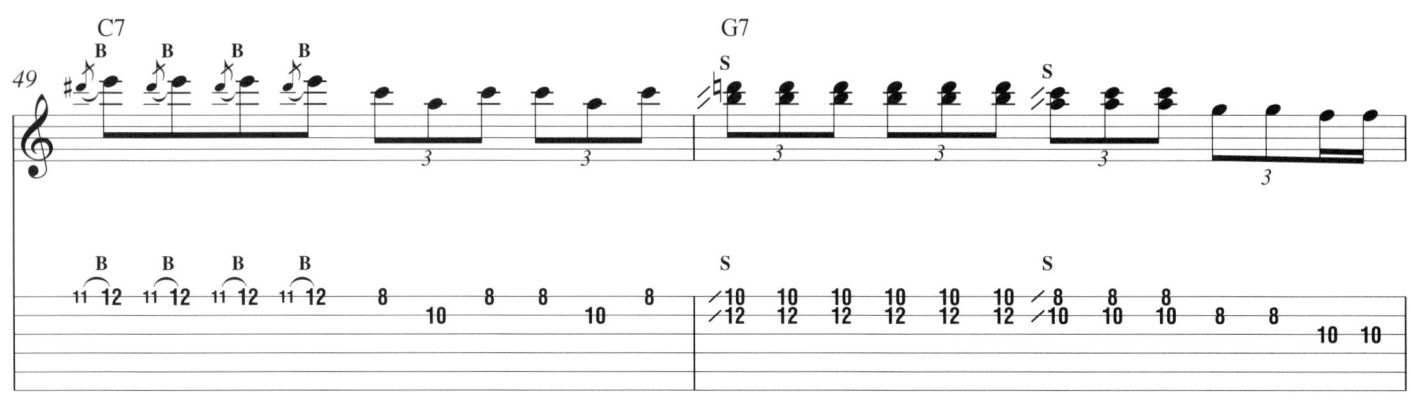

CHAPTER 10 "Worried Life Blues" Robert Lockwood Jr.

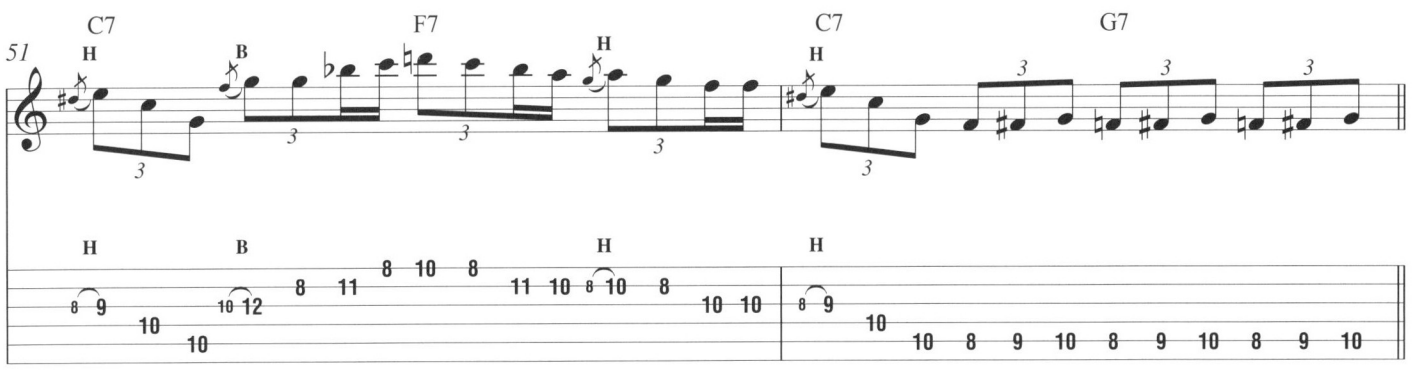

Chorus 7 (vocals, verse 5)

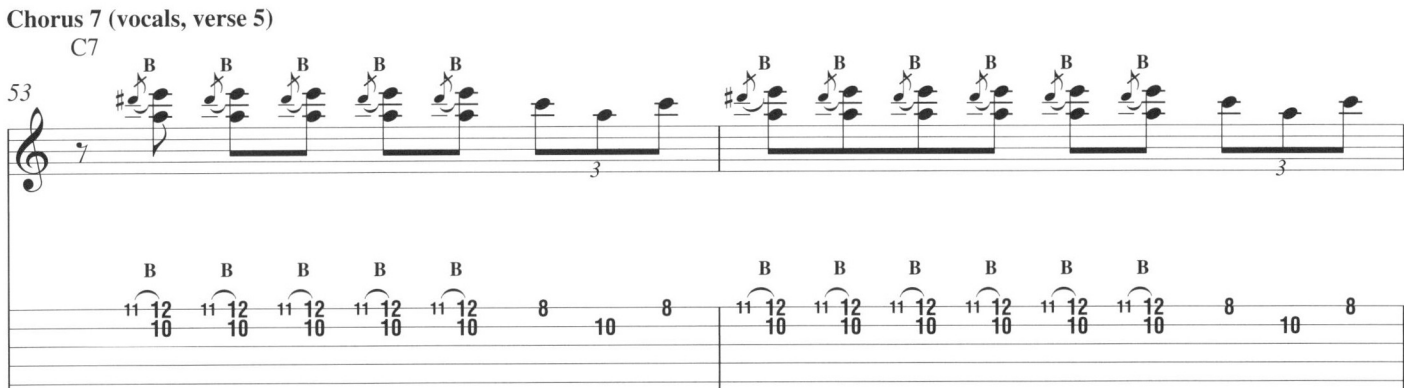

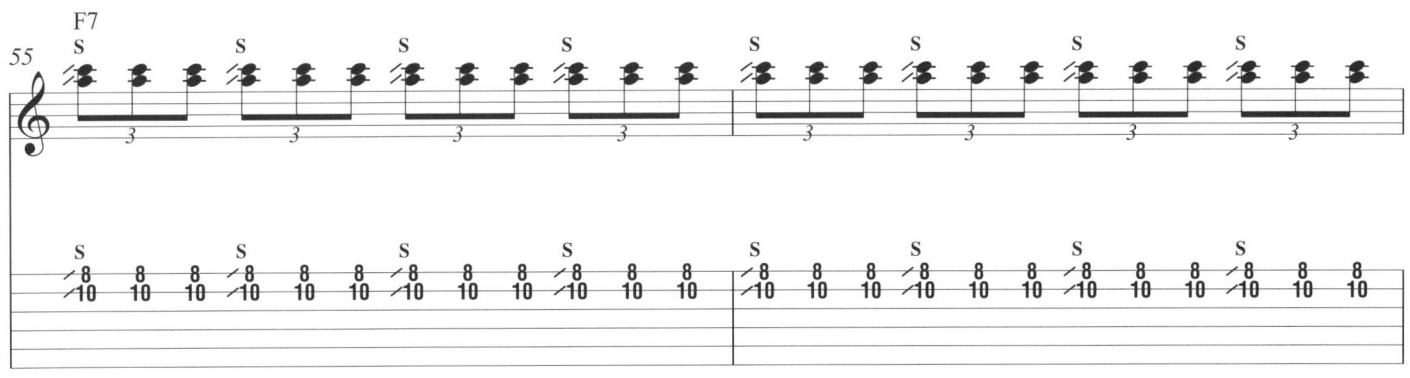

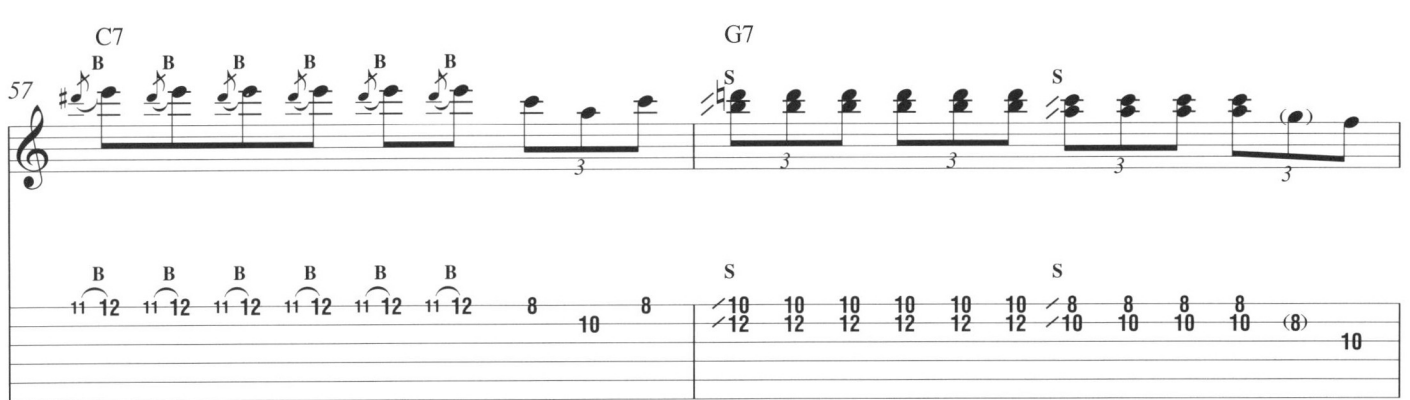

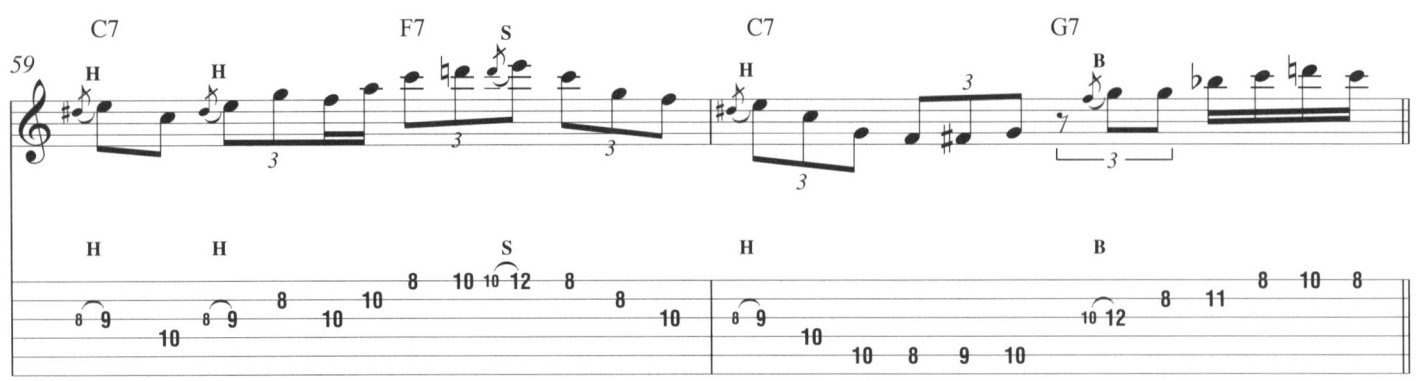

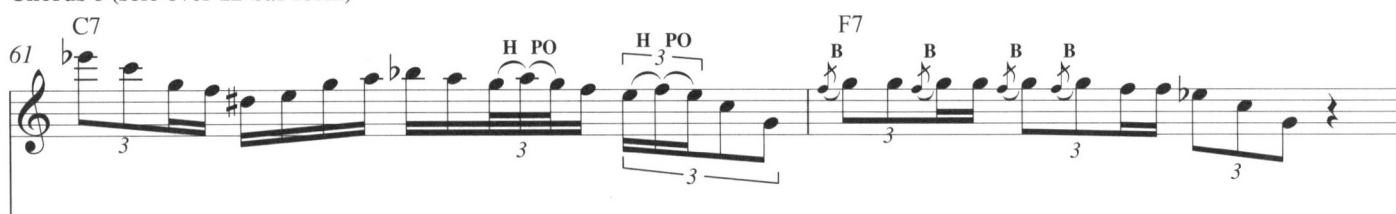

Chorus 8 (solo over 12-bar form)

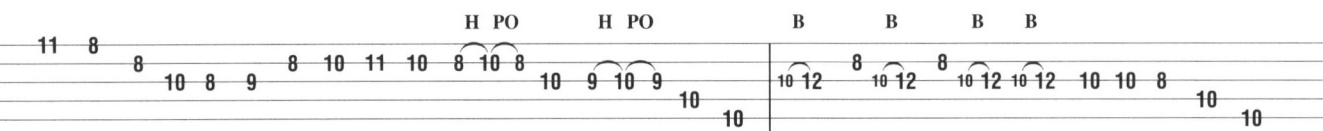

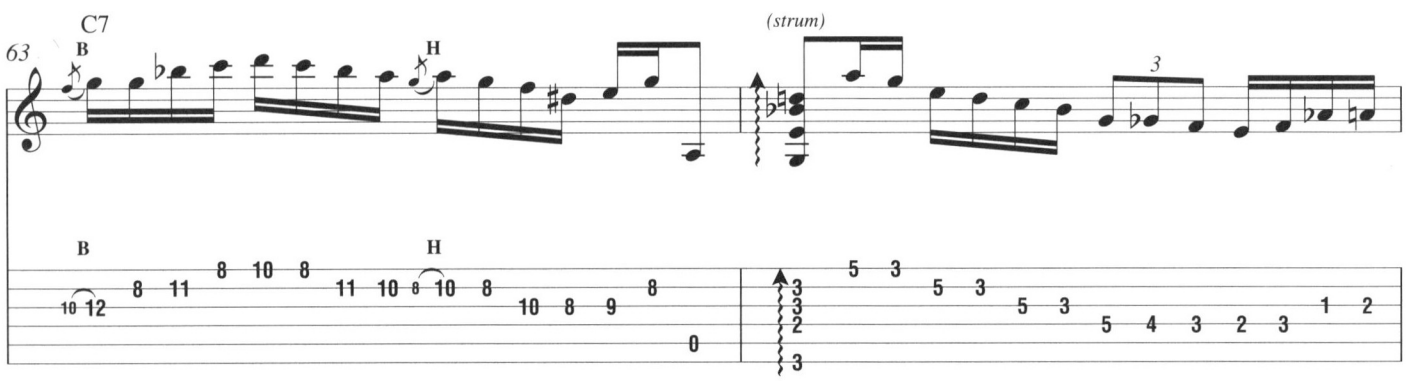

CHAPTER 10 "Worried Life Blues" Robert Lockwood Jr.

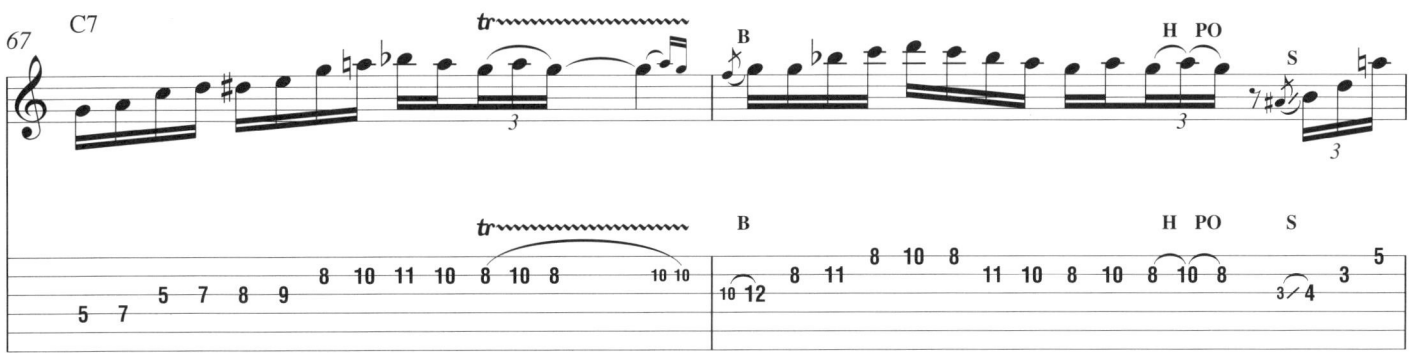

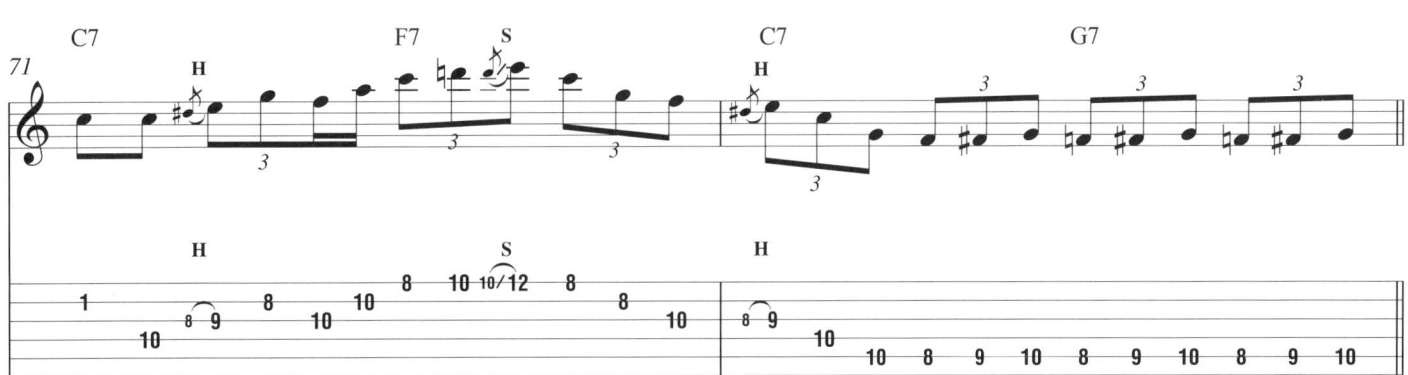

Chorus 9 (vocals, verse 6)

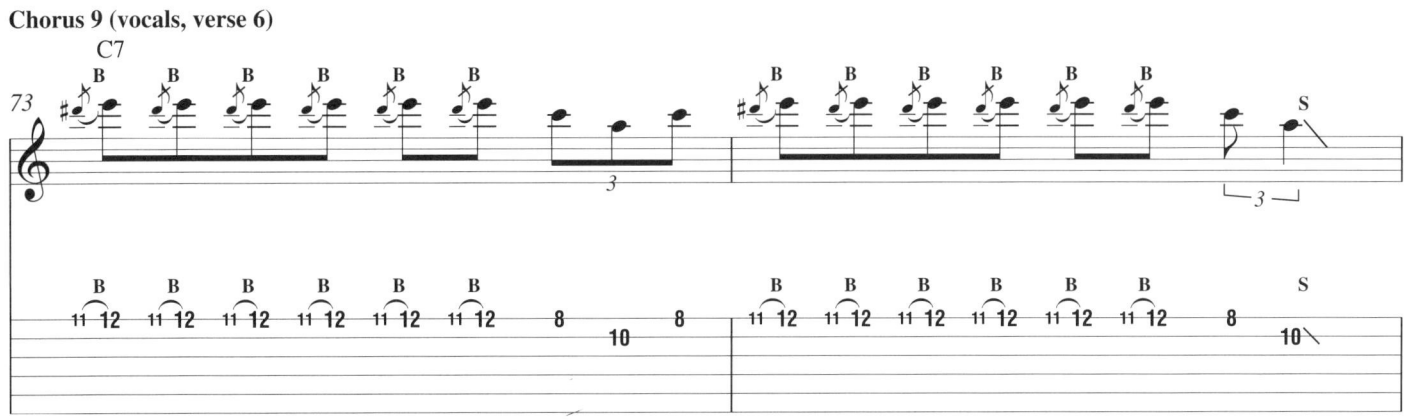

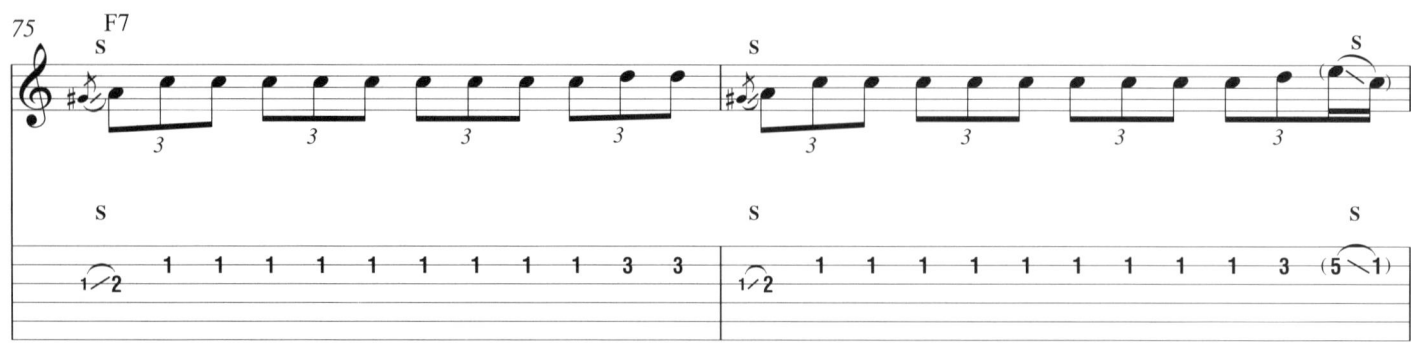
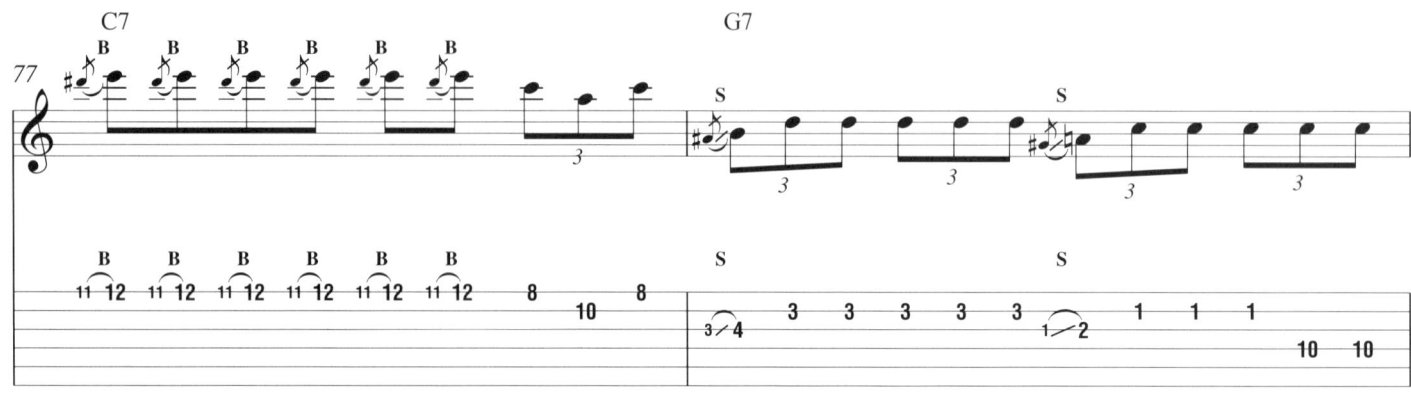
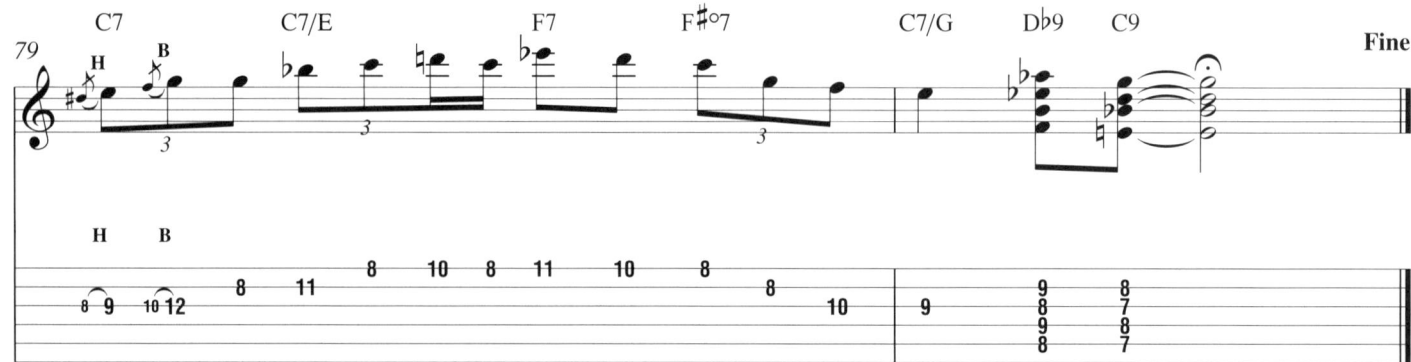

Additional Lyrics

3. So many days, since you've been gone
   I been worryin' and grievin', my life alone
   But someday baby, you ain't gonna worry my life anymore
   (No boy, she don't worry my life no more)

4. Can you remember baby, when you laid across my bed
   Drinkin' that old bad whiskey, talkin' all out your head
   But someday babe, you ain't gonna worry my life anymore

5. Do you remember my love, when you knocked upon my door
   'Member what you told me, you didn't love me no more
   But someday babe, you ain't gonna worry my life anymore

6. So here's my story, all I got to say to you
   So long baby, I don't care what you do
   But someday babe, she ain't gonna worry my life anymore

APPENDIX A

Original Recordings

1. "Frosty" Albert Collins, in *The Cool Sound of Albert Collins*, TCF Hall 8002, 1965. Re-released as *Truckin' with Albert Collins*, Blue Thumb BTS-8, 1969.

2. "I Need You So Bad" Magic Sam, *West Side Soul*, Delmark DD-615, 1967.

3. "The Last Time (I Get Burned Like This)" Robert Cray, *False Accusations*, Hightone HCD-8005, 1985.

4. "Okie Dokie Stomp" Clarence "Gatemouth" Brown, *San Antonio Ballbuster*, Drive 3205, 1948.

5. "Papa Ain't Salty" T-Bone Walker, *T-Bone Blues*, Atlantic 8020, 1959.

6. "The Sad Nite Owl" Freddy King, *Freddy King Gives You a Bonanza of Instrumentals*, King 928, 1965. Re-released on *Just Pickin'*, Modern Records MBXLCD-721.

7. "San-Ho-Zay" Freddy King, *Let's Hide Away and Dance Away with Freddy King*, King 773, 1961. Re-released on *Just Pickin'*, Modern Records MBXLCD-721.

8. "Wait on Time" Fabulous Thunderbirds, *The Fabulous Thunderbirds (Girls Go Wild)*, Chrysalis CHR F2-21250, 1979.

9. "The Woman I Love" B.B. King, Originally released as a single, RPM 408, 1954. Re-released on *B.B. King Original Greatest Hits*, Virgin Records, 2005.

10. "Worried Life Blues" *Otis Spann Is the Blues*, Candid CJM-8001.

APPENDIX B

Blues Guitar Glossary and Articulation Key

Blues Scale	In its standard/textbook form: 1 ♭3 4 ♭5 5 ♭7 (a solo drawing notes from the D blues scale).
Chorus	One time through a song's chord progression (a solo that lasts for two choruses).
Comp (or) Comping	To accompany; to provide rhythmic and harmonic support (chords etc.) behind another instrument (guitar comps behind the vocal head and sax solo).
Fade	Decrease in volume, until silent (repeat the riff and fade).
Fill	Melodic phrase that embellishes a line, or is inserted where there would ordinarily be a rest (a guitar fill for two beats).
Groove	The overall feel/style of a song, such as a slow blues, shuffle, or a calypso groove. Also describes a specific instrument's function/activity in the song. (The guitarist played a great groove on the reggae tune.)
Head	The melody of the song (solo for two choruses, and then play the head).
Hook	A defining and recognizable musical element, unique to a song, and often the song's title or the melody under the song's title (a melodic hook).
In Head	Opening melody to the song (two choruses of in head before the solo).
Intro	Song beginning, before the head begins; it could be an entire chorus or more in length (a guitar intro before the head).
Lick	Short melody or melodic phrase (a guitar lick).
Out Head	Closing melody to the song (after solos, play the out head).
Outro	Song ending. Could be a chorus, tag ending, or a new/different section (fade the outro).

APPENDIX B Blues Guitar Glossary and Articulation Key

Pentatonic Scales	5-note scales (solo drawing notes from the D minor-pentatonic scale). *Minor pentatonic* form: 1 ♭3 4 5 ♭7. *Major pentatonic* form: 1 2 3 5 6.
Relative Major	Major scale with root a minor third above the tonic minor scale. The scales share the same key signature (C major is the relative major of A minor).
Relative Minor	Natural minor scale with root a minor third below the tonic major scale. The scales share the same key signature (A minor is the relative minor of C major).
Riff	A melodic or chord figure that's repeated to form the melody, background, or section of a song ("C Jam Blues" and "Night Train" are classic riff-based heads). Also describes a repeated short melody (a riff-based solo).
Shout Chorus	A section of a song, or an interlude, that often features several instruments playing a (powerful) line or figure, that creates excitement (or a climax) in an arrangement (the horn section followed up with a big band–style shout chorus).
Solo	A melodic interpretation of a song's chord progression, generally improvised (the guitar's turn to solo).
Tag Ending	Repeated chord pattern used to end a song, sometimes followed by a coda or a fade (for the outro, tag the main riff, then take the coda on cue).
Trading	Two or more instruments alternating (taking turns) while soloing over a song form, generally trading on the same number of measures (piano and guitar traded 8's and then 4's with drums).
Turnaround	Chord series, (or a melodic phrase) at the end of a progression, leading back to tonic chord (a II V turnaround).
Upper-Structure Triad	Triad containing a tension (G minor is an upper-structure triad of C7, including 5, ♭7, and 9).

Articulations

Accent (>)	Play note louder.
Bend (B)	Push/bend the string, raising the pitch. Often paired with R (release).
Hammer on (H)	Quickly tap fretting-hand finger on fretboard/string to sound the note.
Marcato (^)	Short and accented.
Pre-bend (PB)	Pre-bend the note before picking/playing it.
Pull-off (PO)	The opposite of a hammer on. Pull-off begins with the finger on the string; finger sounds the note as it slips off the string.
Release (R)	Relax a bent string back to its original (unbent) pitch.
Slide (S)	Glide finger on fretboard to new note while continuing to sound the string.
	Legato slide: pick the note, then slide, without picking again.
	Pick slide: pick the note, slide, and pick the note again at end of slide.
Staccato (.)	Short and unaccented.
Tenuto (–)	Full value, (long), and unaccented.

About the Author

Photo by Wolfie. www.coronium.co.uk

Michael Williams has been active as a blues and jazz guitarist around New England since 1987. He has performed extensively throughout the United States and Canada as a member of Grammy-winner James Cotton's blues band, and with many other artists including David "Fathead" Newman, Mighty Sam McClain, the Bruce Katz Band, Sugar Ray Norcia, Darrell Nulisch, Toni Lynn Washington, Michelle Willson, Jerry Portnoy, the Love Dogs, blues piano virtuoso David Maxwell, and his own band, Michael Williams and Friends.

Williams performed on James Cotton's CD, *35th Anniversary Jam*, which won a W.C. Handy Award, and received a Grammy nomination for the Best Traditional Blues Album in 2003. He performed on Bruce Katz's 2004 release, entitled *A Deeper Blue*, and his playing, songwriting, and arranging are featured on Michelle Willson's CD *So Emotional*, which earned a four-star review in *DownBeat* magazine. Williams has a CD of his own, entitled *Late Night Walk* (Blue Tempo Records), featuring ten original compositions with guest artists David "Fathead" Newman on tenor sax, Sugar Ray Norcia on vocals, and Bruce Katz on Hammond B3 organ and piano.

Williams is a professor at Berklee College of Music in Boston, where he has taught guitar since 1987. He specializes in teaching a mix of blues and jazz styles, and has traveled to Europe and South America on several occasions as a clinician and performer for the college. Williams authored and currently teaches an online course, *Blues Workshop*, for Berklee's online school, Berkleemusic.

"...Williams blends snarl with surprising lyricism."

—Tom Hyslop, *Blues Revue Magazine*

"...Williams' clean, fleet-fingered, yet close-to-the-bone lead lines strike precisely the right moods throughout the jazzy set."

—Bill Dahl, *Living Blues*

"...The shuffles are greasier, and the playing is more primal and cathartic, especially by guitar killer Michael Williams."

—*JazzTimes*

More Great Books & DVDs from

berklee press

A MODERN METHOD FOR GUITAR – VOLUME 1
Book/DVD-ROM
by William Leavitt • featuring Larry Baione
50448065 Book/DVD-ROM Pack $34.99

THE FUTURE OF MUSIC
Manifesto for the Digital Music Revolution
by Dave Kusek & Gerd Leonhard
50448055 $16.95

THE CONTEMPORARY SINGER - 2ND EDITION
Elements of Vocal Technique
by Anne Peckham
50449595 Book/CD Pack $24.99

BERKLEE MUSIC THEORY – BOOK 1
by Paul Schmeling
50448043 Book/CD Pack $24.95

PRODUCING IN THE HOME STUDIO WITH PRO TOOLS – THIRD EDITION
by David Franz
50449544 Book/DVD-ROM Pack $39.95

MELODY IN SONGWRITING
Tools and Techniques for Writing Hit Songs
by Jack Perricone
50449419 $24.95

UNDERSTANDING AUDIO
Getting the Most Out of Your Project or Professional Recording Studio
by Daniel M. Thompson
50449456 $24.95

COMPLETE GUIDE TO FILM SCORING
by Richard Davis
50449417 $24.95

DRUM SET WARM-UPS
Essential Exercises for Improving Technique
by Rod Morgenstein
50449465 $12.95

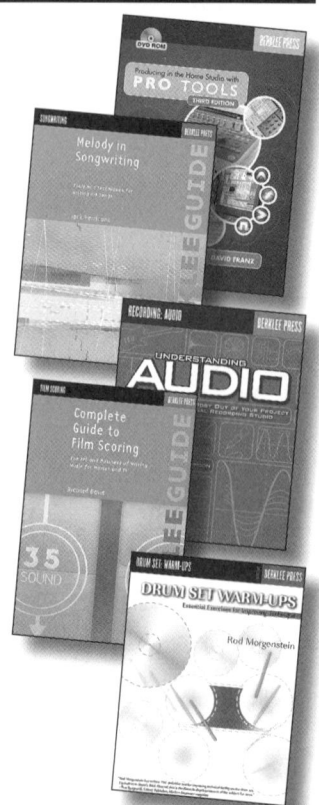

For More Information, See Your Local Music Dealer, Or Write To:

HAL•LEONARD® CORPORATION
7777 W. Bluemound Rd. P.O. Box 13819 Milwaukee, WI 53213

Prices, contents, and availability subject to change without notice. 0510

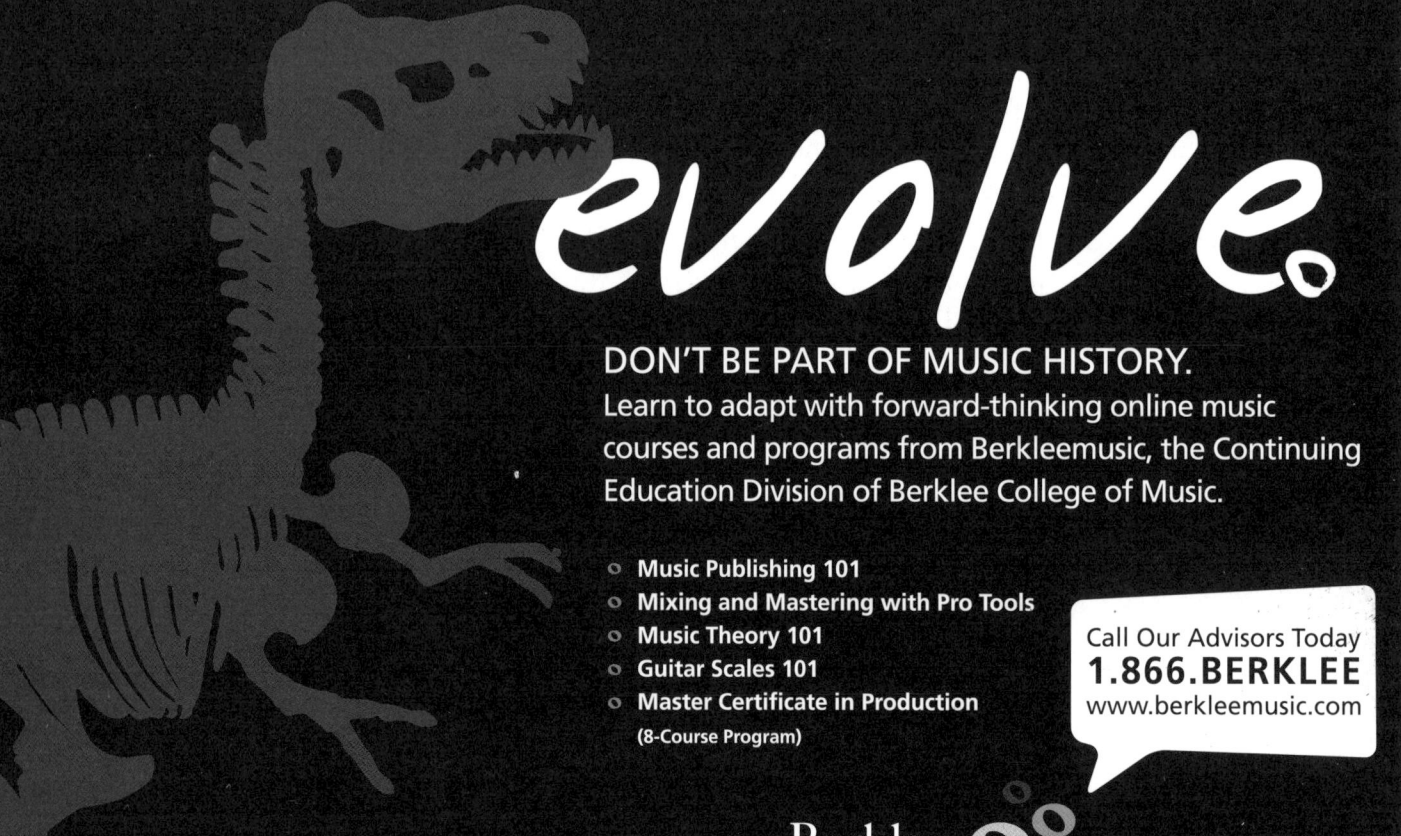

evolve.

DON'T BE PART OF MUSIC HISTORY.
Learn to adapt with forward-thinking online music courses and programs from Berkleemusic, the Continuing Education Division of Berklee College of Music.

- Music Publishing 101
- Mixing and Mastering with Pro Tools
- Music Theory 101
- Guitar Scales 101
- Master Certificate in Production
  (8-Course Program)

Call Our Advisors Today
1.866.BERKLEE
www.berkleemusic.com

Berklee music
learn music online